About Translation

Multilingual Matters

Please contact us for the latest book information:
Multilingual Matters Ltd,
Frankfurt Lodge, Clevedon Hall,
Victoria Road, Clevedon,
Avon BS21 7SJ.

MULTILINGUAL MATTERS 74
Series Editor: Derrick Sharp

About Translation

Peter Newmark

*Centre for Translation and Language Studies,
University of Surrey*

**MULTILINGUAL MATTERS LTD**
Clevedon • Philadelphia • Adelaide

For my daughter Liz

Library of Congress Cataloging in Publication Data

Newmark, Peter
About Translation/Peter Newmark
p. cm. (Multilingual Matters: 74)
Includes bibliographical references and index
Multilingual Matters (Series): 74
P306.N468   1991
418'02   dc20

British Library Cataloguing in Publication Data

A CIP catalogue record for this book is available from the British Library.

ISBN 1-85359-118-1 (hbk)
ISBN 1-85359-117-3 (pbk)

Multilingual Matters Ltd

UK: Frankfurt Lodge, Clevedon Hall, Victoria Road, Clevedon, Avon BS21 7SJ.
USA: 1900 Frost Road, Suite 101, Bristol, PA 19007, USA.
Australia: P.O. Box 6025, 83 Gilles Street, Adelaide, SA 5000, Australia.

Copyright © 1991 Peter Newmark.
Reprinted 1992, 1993.

Index compiled by Meg Davies (Society of Indexers)
Typeset by Wayside Books, Clevedon.
Printed and bound in Great Britain by the Longdunn Press, Bristol.

Contents

Introduction

The 13 chapters that follow are a selection made by Derrick Sharp from the 25–30 papers I have published in the last 23 years. The second is the introductory chapter of the ASLIB *Translator's Handbook* (2nd edn, edited Catherine Picken, 1989); nine originated as papers for translation conferences; three are contributions to *festschriften* (for Michael Halliday, Albrecht Neubert and Wolfram Wilss). Originally I categorised these papers under five heads: overviews; special topics; word and text; teaching translation; translation as a weapon. But the logic of this sequence will become apparent only if and when subsequent volumes are published. These papers stand as independent essays published between 1982 and 1990, and require no connecting links, but the following brief summaries may be useful.

Chapter 1. Translation as Means or End — As Imitation or Creation attempts to unify my dual theory of semantic and communicative methods of translation by proposing a correlation and its corollary; it puts forward a critical and evaluative — as opposed to a descriptive and neutral — approach to translation; it characterises a fruitful method of discussing translation; and it attempts to define the creative and the imitative elements of translation. (Previously unpublished).

Chapter 2. Translation: An Introductory Survey reviews some of the facts about translation and translators throughout the world in 1983. It includes a discussion of the types of meaning that concern the translator. I would today (!) summarise these as: (1) linguistic (explained best through synonymy, paraphrase or translation); (2) referential (denotative, referring to extra-linguistic or imaginative reality, the facts of the matter); (3) pragmatic (the effect on the readers on various occasions, including invariant factors about the writer, the linguistic register used, and evident connotations); (4) phonaesthetic (the significance of the rhythms and sounds in the source language text).

Chapter 3. Translation Today: The Wider Aspects of Translation describes the five purposes of translation, considers translation as a profession, and reviews six recent works on translation.

Chapter 4. Translation for Language Teaching and Professional Purposes summarises the place of translation in language teaching and the qualifications of a professional translator and then focuses on the present importance of German non-literary and literary translation.

Chapter 5. The Use of Systemic Linguistics in Translation is a tribute to M. A. K. Halliday's service in providing both a technique and a vocabulary of translation analysis; it is also a criticism of his perception of the functions of language as applied to translation. Chomsky's insight into personal non-social language is altogether more profound.

Chapter 6. The Virtues of Interference and the Vices of Translationese lists the varieties of interference in translation and demonstrates in each case that if practised out of ignorance or negligence, it is likely to be misleading, senseless and often disastrous. If it is practised deliberately, either because it makes good sense or because it fills a semantic gap in the target language, it may be creative.

Chapter 7. Word and Text: Words and their Degree of Context in Translation examines the degrees of independence/dependence of a word from its context within a text or its translation.

Chapter 8. Translation and Mis-translation: The Review, the Revision and the Appraisal of a Translation points out contrasts between text-linguistics and literal translation in discussing a translation of an extract from Hermann Hesse's *Steppenwolf.*

Chapter 9. Pragmatic Translation and Literalism contrasts the factors of dynamic equivalence and of literal translation for the purpose of verification in assessing an article in *Le Monde* as translated in the *Guardian Weekly.*

Chapter 10. Teaching Translation discusses the qualities of a good translation teacher, describes my own teaching procedure in a typical translation class, and specifies the preferred subjects in the curriculum of a postgraduate translation course.

Chapter 11. Teaching about Translation describes the evolution, the syllabus and the possible translation procedure for a course in 'principles and methods of translation', alias 'translation theory, translation studies, translatology *et al.*'.

Chapter 12. The Translation of Political Language reviews a few of the large number of politico-philosophical concept-words that have a wide range of meanings depending on period and cultural community; they can therefore easily be misunderstood in translation. With the present collapse of Marxist–Leninist ideology and the increasing affirmation of a language based on universal human, animal, and ecological rights, this

confusion may eventually clear a little. *Pravda vitezi* ('truth prevails', Czech
— T. G. Masaryk) — but it takes a long time.

Chapter 13. *Translation as an Instrument of Linguistic, Cultural and Literary Criticism* is an affirmation of close translation as a method of exposing
the weaknesses of a source language text embedded in its familiar culture
and its familiar language, or as an instrument to expose the inaccuracies of
published translations which have long distorted their originals by consciously or unconsciously burdening them with their translators' prejudices.

Acknowledgements

My best thanks to my best informants, Pauline, Elizabeth and Matthew
Newmark.

Sources

Chapter 2
The Translator's Handbook (2nd edn). ed. C. Picken. ASLIB, 1989.
Chapter 3
Translation Studies: State of the Art, Vol. I. ed. G. Anderman and M. A.
Rogers. University of Surrey Centre for Translation and Language Studies,
1988.
Chapter 4
German in the UK. CILT Papers, London, 1986.
Chapter 5
Language Topics (Essays in Honour of Michael Halliday), Vol. I. ed. Ross
Steele and Terry Threadgold. Benjamins, Amsterdam, 1987.
Chapter 6
Festschrift für Albrecht Neubert. KMU, Leipzig, 1990.
Chapter 8
Textlinguistik und Fachsprache. ed. Reiner Arntz. Olms, Hildesheim, 1988.
Chapter 9
Pragmatic Translation. ed. Judy Woodsworth. University of Montreal, 1989.
Chapter 10
Teaching Translation. ed. G. Magnusson and S. Wahlen. Stockholm Uni-
versity, 1988.
Chapter 11
Ubersetzungswissenschaft Ergebnisse und Perspektiven (Festschrift für W.
Wilss). Narr, Tübingen, 1990.
Chapter 12
Discussioni Linguistiche e Distanze Culturali. ed. J. M. Dodds. Trieste, 1986.

1 Translation as Means or End
— As Imitation or Creation

The Process of Translation

Translation is concerned with moral and with factual truth. This truth
can be effectively rendered only if it is grasped by the reader, and that is the
purpose and the end of translation. Should it be grasped readily, or only
after some effort? That is a problem of means and occasions. I begin this
discussion by unifying my dual theory of semantic and communicative translation with three propositions (two correlations and a rider).

(a) The more important the language of a text, the more closely it
should be translated. This is valid at every rank of the text; the text itself; the
chapter; the paragraph; the sentence; the clause; the group (which may
coagulate as an idiom, e.g. 'couldn't help laughing'); the collocation that lexically cuts across the group ('defuse a crisis', 'decisively defeat'); the word;
the morpheme (e.g. 'pro-', 'pre-', 'nephro-', '-junct-', '-less' — all *pace*
M. A. K. Halliday, eminently translatable); the punctuation mark (e.g. that
French colon). Other linguistic units — such as proverbs, metaphors, proper
names, institutional terms, familiar alternatives (*gatos* as Madrilenos,
citizens of Madrid; *hrad* as the Czechoslovak presidency), eponyms
('Ceausescu' as 'tyrant') — may be found at one or more of these ranks.
Sometimes one word (like 'chaos'?) may be more important than the unit at
any other rank of the text. If sound (alliteration) or phonaesthetic effect
(rhythm) is of prime importance, that too has to be rendered, or at least
compensated.

Conversely, (b) the less important the language of a text or any unit of
text at any rank, the less closely that too need be translated, and therefore
it may be replaced by the appropriate normal social language (for example:
*Se algo puede dar un golpe mas fuerte que los que de Gorbachev, solo es
el caos total.* 'Only total chaos could shake the Soviet Union as much as
Gorbachev has done.'). Or again, the less important the nuances of meaning
of the text, the more important the message to be communicated, the more

justification for (smoother) undertranslation, which simplifies or clarifies the place *(Stelle)* in the translation.

But (c), and this is the rider, the better written a unit of the text, the more closely it too should be translated, whatever its degree of importance, provided there is identity of purpose between author and translator, as well as a similar type of readership. If the details and nuances are clearly expressed, they should be translated closely, even though they could just as well be paraphrased. There seems no good reason not to reproduce the truth, even when the truth is not particularly important.

These many references require definitions and illustrations of the terms 'importance' and 'close'. 'Importance' superficially depends on the occasion of the translation and the client's criteria, but it may also be imposed on the translator by the values of the text. 'Importance' may be defined as language that denotes what is exceptionally valuable, significant, necessary or permanent. Further, importance may be conferred on a text or a quotation by the status of whoever is responsible for it — I refer to such a text as authoritative; thus the phrase 'to be or not to be'; *sein oder nicht sein; être ou ne pas être; ser o no ser* (which limits its meaning), or the nouns in the phrase 'Water consists of hydrogen and oxygen', where 'consists of' is not important, since it may be replaced by 'is' *(es de)* or 'is composed of' *(se compone de),* or 'constitutes' *(constitue)* or 'comprises' *(consta de)* or 'is the equivalent of' *(es equivalente a)* etc., in descending order with negligible semantic loss. Similarly, in many contexts it is not important whether one translates *bien* or *buen* as 'good', 'fine', 'OK', 'excellent', *parfait* etc., provided that the message gets across. Note, too, that the important factor in a text may not be restricted to words or other linguistic units, but may be tone (urgency), style (harsh), form (chaotic), metaphor (for its concision), or sound-effect (for emphasis), and they may be imposed by the occasion, e.g. by the requirements of clients or readers. Moreover, if the importance of a text lies merely in its means rather than its end, it is a decorative text, and the translator may change its meaning to suit the sound, as in Jiři Levy's famous Morgenstern example: 'a weasel sat on an easel', 'a parrot swallowed a carrot', 'a cadger was chasing a badger', etc. The important element of a text is the invariant factor that has to be reproduced without compromise in an exercise that often entails many compromises.

Further, the term 'close' has to be defined. The closest translation is transference, where the source language (SL) word *(glasnost)* or idiom ('last but not least' in German) or collocation *(dolce vita)* or cultural *(tagliatelle)* or institutional *(Cortes)* term is already more or less rooted in the target language (TL), provided the term has not yet changed its meaning. The more rooted it is, the more it modifies its pronunciation and its connotations in the direction of the TL, e.g. 'Berlin', 'machismo'. After that, close translation may be grammatical or lexical. Grammatical, first when a group or clause is reproduced ('after his arrival', *nach seiner Ankunft*); secondly, when it is rendered by its standard equivalent ('extremely important', *d'une importance extrême*), where the emphasis is changed, however; thirdly, when it is replaced by a more remote grammatical recasting ('which reaches the height of importance'). Lexical, beginning with word for word translation — 'large garden', *grosser Garten*, although 'garden' may connote a less formal image in English than in other languages; secondly, an average one-to-one up to six-to-six translation — from 'Friday' as *vendredi*, 'measles' as *rougeole*, 'soldier' as *militaire*, 'sailor' as *marin* or *matelot*, up to, say, *la matrone et la mal mariée* as 'the matron and the mismarried woman' — may reach a degree of closeness varying from perfect equivalence through correspondence to adequacy (fruitless to define equivalence — a common academic dead-end pursuit — or to pronounce where equivalence ends and where correspondence, or adequacy, begins). One can, however, state that the longer the passage, the less close the translation may be, but that the dissimilarity between the generics 'bowl' and *bol* may be greater than that between this English 'bowl' and that French *bol*.

Further translation procedures, roughly in order of closeness, are:

- componential analysis ('murky' street as *rue sombre et sale, calle oscura y sucia)*;

- modulation ('no mean city' as *ciudad soberbia)*;

- descriptive equivalent (*escudilla* as 'hollow dish');

- functional equivalent ('knife' as *instrumento cortante)*;

- cultural equivalent (*bachillerato* as 'GCE A-level', *paella* as 'stew') — cultural equivalents are usually inaccurate but they are a shorthand, have emotional force, are useful for immediate effect on the receptor, e.g. in the theatre or cinema (dubbing or sub-titling), and they transport the readership uncritically into the TL culture;

- synonymy, say *dificil problema* for 'awkward-' or 'tricky problem' or *problème épineux,* which is pretty feeble, but all the Larousse (English to Spanish) gives, and which may, in the context, be all that is necessary;

- paraphrase, the loosest translation procedure, which simply irons out the difficulties in any passage by generalising: *por la razon de la sinrazon de un puyazo en el morrillo* ('owing to the injustice of a blow to the back of a bull's neck' as 'why the picador has to do that to the bull's neck').

A general principle of closeness in translation is that normal or natural social usage must be rendered by its normal, equally frequent equivalent in any text; thus for 'cheers', *merci* or *au revoir* or *à la tienne;* in an authoritative text, both innovation or cliché should be reproduced (both to the same degree of deviation from normal usage in TL as in SL); but they should be replaced by normal usage, neat and unobtrusive, in any non-authoritative text. So if Mrs Thatcher proclaims 'The ship of State may founder', or James Joyce writes 'The figure was that of a broadshouldered deepchested strong-limbed frankeyed freely freckled brawnyhanded hero', the first statement has to be rendered by an equally banal phrase, while the second has to be translated virtually word for word, with some attempt to reproduce the alliteration. But if both sentences were the work of hacks, you might trans-late 'The Government may founder' and perhaps 'He was exceptionally attractive and well-built'.

The proposition 'The more important the language of a text, the more closely it should be translated', together with its corollary and its rider, is an attempt to narrow the gap between, on the one hand, translators and trans-lation theorists who are instinctively and intuitively target text oriented — *ciblistes,* as Ladmiral has called them, which I translate as 'targeteers' — and on the other hand their 'adversaries' who like myself are instinctively and intuitively source text oriented (*sourciers* (Ladmiral) or 'sourcerers' (me)). In this or that context, targeteers lean towards ends, sourcerers towards means. Instinctively (a scrap example), a targeteer translates 'Buck House' as 'Buckingham Palace', a sourcerer as 'Buck House, as Buckingham Palace is called by some trendies'. My proposition is a sliding scale which eliminates any dividing line between the two contrasted approaches. I have tried to show that this natural opposition pointed up by key-words such as Beauty versus Truth, Text versus Word, Message versus Meaning, Reader versus Writer, Social versus Personal, Gestalt versus Part, Global versus Particu-lar, are far from irreconcilable, and may overlap or merge. Eugene Nida, the first linguist who took translation seriously and scientifically, pointed this out 35 years ago, and he is the dominant figure amongst the targeteers, who are likely to include most non-literary translators. The dominant sourcerer or literalist was Nabokov, then Benjamin and Stefan George; now perhaps it's Nida's critic Meschonnic. I can only say from my experience in class-rooms that both factions can learn from each other, and bring their versions closer to each other's, although they will never be identical; hence the silli-ness of all fair copies, there are always alternatives leaning the one way or the other, hence communicative and semantic translation (see Appendix).

The Product of Translation

My emphasis up to now has been on the process of translating — on how to translate — the means. If I now discuss the product — the end — either as what we are aiming at or the value of what has been achieved, there are again two views. The first is relative: descriptive, historical, socio-cultural, it sees a translation as a product of its culture and its time, as a component of another — the TL literature — written to meet the requirements of new readers, which it studies. Crudely, it is a package for new customers. It is true that throughout history, and notably in the Roman and the Elizabethan periods, there is little to choose between the styles of many translations and their originals, in particular of poetry and comedy, where the translation is often an adaptation. There are, for instance, few correspondences between Ronsard's *Quand vous serez bien vieille, au soir, à la chandelle,* and Yeats's 'When you are old and grey and full of sleep'. Yeats's poem, which does not claim to be a translation, can be studied as a cultural product of its time (or, more profitably, independently). This attitude, which virtually ignores the source language text, hardly suits serious translations of serious originals, but it is appropriate for adaptations of comedies, ephemeral texts and blockbusters.

The second view of the product is critical and evaluative, and requires a continuous comparison of the translation with the original and a verification of correspondences, grammatical, lexical and often phonaesthetic. It is more concrete and detailed, often more pernickety and pedantic, than the first view, and shows up moral as well as stylistic and linguistic deficiencies. It covers all types of texts — factual as well as imaginative — and exposes a translator's prejudices as well as ignorance. Thus two hundred years ago Tytler exposed Voltaire's preposterous version of Hamlet's 'To be or not to be' where there are no verbal correspondences, and Hamlet is translated into a sceptic and a free-thinker.

The Discussion of Translation

I want now to put forward a view about the discussion of translation. I see this as a continual interplay between generalisations and translation examples. I see no use in uninterrupted theorising, still less in resorting to mathematical models, geometry (diagrams) or algebra (alphabetic symbols), or conjuring up situations miscalled *Beispiele* (examples), unless they are supported by brief SL to TL translation quotations, real or invented, in or out of context. Sometimes a scrap example, if it is typical, is sufficient:

'henceforth' for *désormais* ('in the future'); 'thanks to' for *grâce à* ('owing to'); 'despite' for *malgré* ('in spite of'); 'alter' for *altérer* ('spoil'); 'dilapidation' for *effondrement* ('collapse'); 'now' for *or* ('furthermore') — one has to beware of the slightly old-fashioned now 'literary' words often given in bilingual dictionaries ('sully', 'demur', 'helpmate'), the too personal words in non-literary texts ('strive', 'essay', 'attain'), all of which can also be faulted by the equal frequency translation principle. I feel uneasy if I write more than a dozen lines about translation without producing an example, partly to explain, illustrate and support my 'theory', partly to invite discussion reaction in favour or against, and in the hope of finding a *rapprochement*, a conciliation if not an agreement. I do not pretend that my views are ever other than personal (but they are not subjective) and I have no illusion that when I invoke moral or universal arguments that many of my readers will accept them. The misguided idea that translation is neutral and has nothing to do with human rights or human welfare dies as hard as the view that art or sport have nothing to do with politics. *Die Ubersetzung ist menschlich, la traduccion es humana,* translation is human — that states an end; the means 'translation' and the end 'human' are philosophically 'synthetic', which cannot be perverted or diverted by an odd context or readership or special function.

The central element of translation discussion, whether theoretical or practical, is the typical, whether we discuss principles, examples, structures, occasions, readerships or texts. One can have too much of 'it all depends on what you mean by . . .' or 'give me the context' or 'use decides everything' necessary as these are for non-typical cases. A tree is a tree is a tree in English, though in Spanish and French it may also and quite often be a shaft.

But just as translation, like language, appears to be a rule-governed activity (and you learn most from the rules, the typical), so, as in language, this is not always the case. Language develops mainly by breaking the rules, by innovations — sometimes syntactically ('catch on', 'be on', 'be into'), more often lexically by giving words new senses ('crumbly', 'wrinkly', 'crinkly', 'golden oldy' — all words for 'seniors', 'senior citizens'; note the cultural focus on age). So translation follows language, like a 'royal robe with ample folds', as Benjamin (1979) put it; where the original innovates, the translator is compelled to innovate; where the original uses culture specific language (*glasnost* again, as it breaks with a long cultural tradition), the translator is free to be creative. So rule is violated by play, by circumscribed creativity, by freedom within limits.

The Creative Element of Translation

Ironically, the ludic element cuts right across the balance, the correlation (the more the more; the less the less), the definition of translation method with which I began this piece. Where there is a concise symbol (the flesh as weakness), a weird metaphor (the rocking chair as old age), a deviant structure (the for me intended rebuff), a word that exposes a lexical gap (shin or fair play), the translator may have to improvise or import, both of which are creative acts. So the translator starts denting, distorting the target language, breaking Toury's translation (al) norms, inserting another culture.

The creative element in translation is circumscribed. It hovers when the standard translation procedures fail, when translation is 'impossible'. It is the last resource, but for a challenging text it is not infrequently called on. If it dominates a text — as in Andrew Jenkins's translations in Fritz Paepcke's *Im Ubersetzen Leben,* or in Pound, or in many pre-Romantic translations — it becomes an adaptation, an idiosyncratic interpretation which can hardly be verified (or a bad translation). I think an at least approximate verification, where there are correspondences to be assessed through back-translation, is the scientific element in an appraisal of any translation.

It is not difficult to produce scrap examples of what I mean by creative translation, say in Patrick Creagh's brilliant translation of Claudio Magris's (1986) *Danubio: una vera passione* (a true passion) as 'a downright passion'; *diventando una pure sta straziata rettorica* (becoming a rhetoric, even though tortured) as 'turning into rhetoric, however lacerated that rhetoric might be'; *una mina d'odio* (a mine of hatred) as 'a time-bomb of hatred'; *di neve* (of snow) as 'snow-fresh'; *notte assoluta* (absolute night) as 'night in its most absolute sense'; *la prosa del mondo* (the prose of the world) as 'the humdrum world' — the fitness of these creative translations can be better appreciated in a larger context, but you can see they are a kind of deepening, an *approfondissement,* of literal translation, a for once justified attempt to go below the words to the author's thinking.

The argument for creative translation is the obverse of the argument for the strict impossibility of translation — leaving aside the argument that any kind of translation decision, say translating *Gewalt, force, forza* as 'violence' rather than 'force' (German has only one word anyway) to stress brutality (which is a bottom line argument) could trivially be described as creative. Admittedly or minimally, there is no argument for impossibility in translating routine texts. In informative texts the creative element is limited to fusing the facts with an appropriately elegant and economical style, as often in *The Guardian Weekly*'s translations of *Le Monde* articles. In persuasive texts, creativity often lies in converting source language cultural components (forms of address, evaluative expressions, hypocorisms) neatly into their cultural equivalents, say toning-down Latin hyperbole *egregio, illuminatissimo, carissimo* to British English understatement ('dear').

However, it is in expressive texts — poetry, stories, sagas, that are considered to be untranslatable by a succession of Romantic and post-Romantic literary people (from Humboldt through Croce and Ortega y Gasset to Graves and John Weightman), where words represent images and connotations rather than facts — that creativity comes into play, and the play of words becomes creative. I list the most obvious occasions for the need for creativity:

1. Cultural words — objects or activities with connotations, that are specific to one community (*koa* for 'furniture').
2. Transcultural words with similar referents and different connotations — the 'classical' examples are the staples: bread, rice, wine, etc.
3. Concept words with different emphases in different communities ('liberalism', 'liberty', 'obedience', 'bureaucracy').
4. Peculiar syntactic structures ('Seeing you is good', *Et lui de partir).*
5. Cultural metaphors, idioms, proverbs, puns, neologisms. They may have to be spelt out in the TL — concision, force, nuances of meaning are lost or compensated.
6. Significant phonaesthetic effects ('bauble', 'pullulate').
7. Quality words with no one-to-one equivalent ('downright', 'grand', 'wonky').

This list is not exhaustive, and to a translator it is depressing, but useful. Yet we all know that, more or less anything that is said in one language can be said in another, and often has to be. All the above seven factors are a stumbling block only when their full meaning is functionally important, when it is a component of the actual message rather than a marginal nuance. When they are important, they have to be compensated by overtranslation, which adds further meaning (say, 'grand' translated as *grandiose* or *magnifique*). When they are not, a synonym (*maladroit* or *ungeschickt* for 'gauche'), or a generic term ('jellyfish' for *medusa*), or a recast nominal group (*à te voir* or *Dich zu sehen* for 'seeing you') may do, and the phonaesthetic effect has to be sacrificed (often, it is merely slightly rhetorical — the ragged rascal) — usually it is.

Whilst in principle the meaning of any word in any language is unique, owing to differences in frequency, usage, connotations and lexical gaps in other languages in context, the great majority of non-cultural words have perfectly satisfactory equivalents in other languages. Their number depends mainly on the degree of contact present and past between the languages, and therefore the cultures, in question.

Creativity in translation starts where imitation stops. The imitative procedures — defined 32 years ago by Vinay & Darbelnet (1965) as 'direct translation' — are transference *(emprunt)*, through-translation *(calque)*, and literal translation. The other procedures, four of them defined as 'indirect translation' (but there are rather more than those four) are all in one sense or another creative. The wider and the more numerous the choices, the more (in quality and in quantity) creativity is required. Again, if the translator adopts larger units of translation; seeks dynamic equivalents (say substitutes TL culture for SL culture, 'bits and pieces' for *tapas*); unearths the sub-text, the hidden agenda, the *vouloir-dire*; is pre-eminently target-language oriented, s/he is less circumscribed, more creative — and liberty in translation easily turns to licence. Creativity at its most intense is in translating poetry, where there are so many important additional factors: words as images, metre, rhythm, sounds. Inevitably a good translation of a poem is as much a modest introduction to as a recreation of the original. But again the most successful is the closest, the one that can convincingly transfer the most important components of the source into the target text. The most creative translated poem is one that is most compressed:

Foul yellow mist had filled the whole of space:
Steeling my nerves to play a hero's part,
I coaxed my weary soul with me to pace
The backstreets shaken by each lumbering cart.
(The Seven Old Men, Roy Campbell, 1952)

Un brouillard sale et jaune inondait tout l'espace
Je suivais, roidissant mes nerfs comme un héros
Et discutant avec mon âme déjà lasse,
Le faubourg secoué par les lourds tombereaux.
(Les sept Vieillards, Charles Baudelaire, 1857)

Conclusion

I have attempted to redefine my approach and evaluation of translation, and to show how creativity is called upon in a serious text when strict accuracy combined with economy apparently breaks down. In a shoddily written informative text a different kind of creativity — the ability to turn bad into good writing — is required. In a routine, say economic text, it would be flattering of the translator to refer to the use of the 'indirect' procedures as creative.

I have considered at times both ends and means. Addressing my title, I would say that both ends and means are always important, that the end never justifies inappropriate means (the writing), and that for a serious text its end and means often prescribe those of the translation (it being of greater value) which may require an unaccustomed humility from the translator.

Appendix to Chapter 1

Communicative and semantic translation

(The concepts of communicative and semantic translation represent my main contribution to general translation theory.)

1. In communicative as in semantic translation, provided that equivalent effect is secured, the literal word-for-word translation is not only the best, it is the only valid method of translation. There is no excuse for unnecessary 'synonyms' or elegant variations, let alone paraphrases, in any type of translation.
2. Both semantic and communicative translation comply with the usually accepted syntactic equivalents or correspondences for the two languages in question.
3. Communicative and semantic translation may well coincide — in particular, where the text conveys a general rather than a culturally (temporally and spatially) bound message and where the matter is as important as the manner.
4. There is no one communicative or one semantic method of translating a text — these are in fact widely overlapping bands of methods. A translation can be more, or less, semantic — more, or less, communicative — even a particular section or sentence can be treated more communicatively or less semantically.
5. The vast majority of texts require communicative rather than semantic translation. Most non-literary writing, journalism, informative articles and books, textbooks, reports, scientific and technological writing, non-personal correspondence, propaganda, publicity, public notices, standardised writing, popular fiction — the run-of-the-mill texts which have to be translated today but were not translated and in most cases did not exist a hundred years ago — comprise typical material suitable for

communicative translation. On the other hand, original expression (where the specific language of the speaker or writer is as important as the content), whether it is philosophical, religious, political, scientific, legal, technical or literary, needs to be translated semantically. A communicative translation may well be a useful introduction, a simplified version, to the semantic translation of such texts.

6. There is no reason why a basically semantic translation should not also be strongly communicative.

7. Meaning is complicated, many-levelled, a 'network of relations' as devious as the channels of thought in the brain. The more communication, the more generalisation; the more simplification, the less meaning. (I am writing against the increasing assumption that *all* translating is (nothing but) communicating, where the less effort expected of the reader, the better.)

TABLE 1.1   *Features of semantic and communicative translation*

Semantic translation	Communicative translation
1. Author-centred.	Reader-centred.
2. Pursues author's thought process. Related to thought.	Pursues author's intention. Related to speech.
3. Concerned with author as individual.	Adapts and makes the thought and cultural content of original more accessible to reader.
4. Semantic- and syntactic-oriented. Length of sentences, position and integrity of clauses, word position, etc. preserved whenever possible.	Effect-oriented. Formal features or original sacrificed more readily.
5. Faithful, more literal.	Faithful, freer.
6. Informative.	Effective.
7. Usually more awkward, more detailed, more complex, but briefer.	Easy reading, more natural, smoother, simpler, clearer, more direct, more conventional, conforming to particular register of language, but longer.

TABLE 1.1 *(cont.)*

Semantic translation	*Communicative translation*
8. Personal.	Social.
9. Source language biased.	Target language biased.
10. Over-translated: more concentrated and more specific than original.	Under-translated: use of 'hold-all' terms.
11. More powerful.	Less powerful.
12. Always inferior to the original because of loss of meaning.	May be better than original because of gain in force and clarity, despite loss in semantic content.
13. Out of time and local place — 'eternal'.	Ephemeral and rooted in its context, 'existential'.
14. Wide and universal.	'Tailor-made' or targeted for one category of readership; does one job, fulfils one particular function.
15. Inaccuracy is always wrong.	A certain embroidering, a stylistic synonymy, a discreet modulation is condoned, provided the facts are straight and the reader is suitably impressed.
16. The translator has no right to improve or to correct.	The translator has the right to correct and improve the logic and style of the original, clarify ambiguities, jargons, normalise bizarre personal usage.
17. Mistakes in the original should (and must) be pointed out only in footnote.	The translator can correct mistakes of facts in original.
18. Target: a 'true' version, i.e. an exact statement.	Target: a 'happy' version, i.e. a successful act.

TABLE 1.1 *(cont.)*

Semantic translation	Communicative translation
19. Unit of translating: tends to words, collocations and clauses.	Unit of translating: tends to sentences and paragraph.
20. Applicable to all writings with original expressiveness.	Applicable to impersonal texts.
21. Basically the work of translating is an art.	Basically the work of translating is a craft.
22. Usually the work of one translator.	Sometimes the product of a translation team.
23. Conforms to the 'relativist' position of cultural relativity.	Conforms to the 'universalist' position, assuming that exact translation may be possible.
24. Meaning.	Message.

Related notions

Equivalent effect principle (Koller, 1972), equivalent response principle (Rieu, 1953)
Dynamic equivalence/formal equivalence (Nida, 1964)
Effect-centred text translating (Reiss, 1968)
Cultural translation/linguistic translation (Catford, 1965)
Ethnographic translation/linguistic translation (Mounin, 1963)
Direct procedures/indirect procedures (Vinay & Darbelnet, 1958)
Overt translation/covert translation (House, 1977)
Prospective translation/retrospective translation (Postgate, 1922)
Illusionistic translation (that the translation is the original)/anti-illusionistic translation (that the translation is a translation)
Exporting the TL reader/importing the SL author (Morgan, 1956)
Idiomatic translation
Naturalisation/alienation (Schleiermacher, 1798)
Primary translation/secondary translation (acknowledgements to Simon Chan)

2 Translation: An Introductory Survey

Background

The *Technical Translator's Manual,* edited by J. B. Sykes, was published by Aslib in 1971. The *Translator's Handbook,* launched by a committee led by Catriona Picken, was published by Aslib in 1983 (revised and updated in 1988/9). The change of title is as significant as the change in contents.

The technical translator as such has rarely existed. As a translator, a specialist in one or more technologies is normally additionally concerned with the progress of their products into commerce — packaging, financing, marketing, tendering, wholesaling, retailing, after-service, for instance; further, technical translators are concerned with the various domestic and foreign public and private organisations which directly or indirectly will have some impact on these products. The term 'technical translator' is therefore somewhat narrow, since translators of non-literary material *(Sachbücher)* have to deal with commercial, financial, institutional as well as technological and scientific texts, in fact the area of the social as well as the natural sciences.

The present *Translator's Handbook* also widens the scope of its predecessor by addressing itself to the literary translator, a specialist translator like any others who draw on a common stock of dictionaries, encyclopaedias, gazetteers, etc., as well as their own reference books. It would be parochial to exclude the literary translator from this *Translator's Handbook,* particularly as there is so much common ground in the field of religious and philosophical literature.

Comparing the contents of the present volume with its predecessor, I note the same accurate attention to every detail of the translator's profession — training, working procedure, relation between translator and client, description and enumeration of hardware and reference material. What is new is 'the world view' — the chapters on translation across the world, and national and international professional organisations. Further, greatly more attention is given to machine translation (MT) and to machine assisted translation (MAT).

Translation is a modest but rapidly developing growth industry. The number of translators is not known — there were about 15,000 in West Germany in 1961. (That's the only figure I can find.) A manual such as the *Translator's Handbook* will be in some respects out of date on the day of its publication. Further, like a translation itself, it is never finished, it can always be slightly or radically improved. Ideally it should be revised at least once in two years, and in this respect it will be partly dependent on the assistance and suggestions of its readers.

The translator is continually obsessed with the hunt for reference books, and the hope is that the *Translator's Handbook* (not *manual* — here too there is a progression from instruction (cf. 'car manual') — to education which includes instruction) will become the essential starting point of many such a hunt, a *vade mecum* which is never far from the translator's desk.

There is also a wider background to the appearance of this new edition. In the UK, the number of translators has greatly increased, translation departments of government agencies and large companies have expanded, and translation companies have multiplied. Polytechnic and university postgraduate translation courses have become established as the normal and recognised route to the profession. Even the study of principles and methods of translation has made a modest beginning in this country and is pursued at a few polytechnics and universities.

In this sense translation has an important part in the general information explosion of the last years, which to some extent has led to a reassertion of the written word (Prestel, VDUs, faxes) against the picture but not against the screen. Translation, once considered impossible, an imposture, a poor substitute for bilingualism and knowing the foreign language is acknowledged as an essential world-wide means of communication. It even has an important place as an objective and a technique in foreign language teaching.

In the world 'outside', translation has made greater progress — Congrat-Butlar's *Translation and Translators: An International Directory and Guide,* Deeney & Chau's *ECCE Translator's Manual* and Al-Chalabi's *Bibliography of Translation and Dictionaries* give evidence of an enormous increase in activities, organisations and publications in recent years. The European Translators' College has been established by K. Birkenhauer and E. Tophoven at Straelen in West Germany. There have been a plethora of international conferences, notably in Moscow, Leipzig, Stockholm, Århus, as well as the triennial FIT and the quadrennial AILA (International Association of Applied Linguistics) conferences. In 1987 there were international conferences at Maastricht and Hildesheim. Certain cities have become recognised as centres of translation activity: Moscow (Maurice Thorez Institute), Paris (ESIT), Geneva (ETI), Ottawa (STI), Leipzig (TAS, KMU), Saarbrücken, Mons, Århus, Hong Kong, Tunis, Barcelona, Georgetown, Monterey, Nitra (Bratislava), Amsterdam, Tel Aviv. The fact that English is the most popular world language (just as it has the most popular world music — all the world, especially the East, wants to sing and jive American), that all educated people want to learn English, makes it apparently inevitable although misguided, that there is less serious interest in translation in the UK than in many other countries, and in the USA few — apart from the Bible translators, Marilyn Gaddis Rose at SUNY and G. Vázquez-Ayora at Georgetown University — have even begun to take the subject seriously — certainly the linguists have not (with, of course, the shining exception of Eugene Nida).

What is Translated

A hundred years ago, the majority of translated texts were religious, literary, scientific and philosophical. Apart from the religious texts in Protestant-only areas, translations were mainly read by an educated élite in each country. In this century, translation has become a force and an instrument of democracy — significantly, only about a quarter of *Mein Kampf* was translated into English in the 1930s, and in 1980 a British Council official wanted to learn Bulgarian only in order to berate the natives. The subject-matter translated has extended to the whole range of human knowledge, with particular emphasis on the most important technological innovations and on political and commercial relations between nations as well as on creative literature. Further, the range of languages translated has increased continuously as more countries become independent (in 1945 UNO comprised 50 member countries, in 1978 it had 145) and more languages achieve national status within each country. (Thus at present there is a big demand for Castilian–Catalan and Catalan–Castilian translators in Spain.) The translation budget at Brussels has become notorious.

It is not possible to obtain any figures about the quantity and the areas of the total mass of translations. Unesco publishes figures for the production of original and translated books, from which it transpires that in 1973 out of a world production of 47,000 translated books, literature occupied 49%, followed by social sciences 12%, applied sciences 8.5%, geography 8%, history 7.5%, pure sciences 6%, religion 5.5% and arts and philosophy with a slightly lower percentage. The Federal Republic produced the highest percentage of these translations at 14% followed by Spain at 9.5%, USSR at 9.4% and then a series of countries, Japan, Italy, USA, France, The Netherlands, GDR and Brazil, each at under 5%. The great majority of the translations were from English at 38% followed by 13% from French, 11% from Russian and 9% from German; Spanish, Italian and Swedish each stood at under 3%. It was noticeable that Chinese, Arabic and Hindi appeared incongruously isolated from translation activities.

Compare these figures with 1975, when the number of translations from English had increased by 2% to 40% followed by Russian 13.5% and French had dropped to 10%. There was a sharp rise in translations emanating from the USSR from 9.4% to 13.5% and a fall in West Germany from 14% to 10%. Translations in USA and GDR halved during the period. British translations stood at 3%. In the subject area, literature dipped to 46% while social and applied sciences each increased by 1%.

These figures have to be looked at with some caution, as they are all based only on numbers of books translated. If reports, papers, articles, journals, etc. were included, one could perhaps assume an increase of at least fivefold in the proportion of applied sciences translations and a corresponding decrease in creative literature as well as an enormous additional quantity of non-literary material: publicity, patents, notices, instructions, etc.

There is no sign or likelihood that this translating activity throughout the world will decrease — on the contrary it will increase exponentially with the spread of literacy and education, wider means and channels of communication, the removal of further ethnic groups from a regime of tutelage, and even the spread of foreign language learning, which may eliminate the need for translation for successful learners but will make them into amateur translators themselves and is likely to increase their own appetite for translations from third languages.

As for the languages of translation, international bodies rationalise these by selecting official languages and working languages (UNO has English and French as official languages — 'world languages with the largest range'; Spanish, Russian and Chinese as working languages).

It is unlikely that in the foreseeable future the world language situation will be rationalised by simplifying communication between states. Since the eighteenth century, English has increasingly dominated all international means of communication; it is spoken all over the world, is the language of North America, Australasia and the UK, and is the main language of communication in many Asian and African states. The other world languages:

French, Russian, Spanish, Arabic, Chinese and German, are on the whole regional languages — though Spanish dominates all Latin American countries but Brazil, and French is the language of communication in about 20 African and Asian countries. (Needless to say, the quantity of translations between Quebec and the rest of Canada continues to increase.) In Europe, the use of German with two and two-third states in and between the 'West' and the 'East' is likely to grow at the expense of French, which is well established in the EC. At this level, Esperanto, the only relatively successful world artificial language, is a dead duck.

It should be stated here that in the UK at least, but I suspect in America and much of continental Europe too, German is the most undertaught language, both for translation and for the command of the language. In the UK, German appears to be most in demand for technical and scientific translation (note also that Böll and Grass were in 1984 the most popular non-English living world writers possibly succeeding T. Mann, Kafka, Brecht and Hesse). Any professional translators' course that does not offer an *ab initio* German reading class is severely handicapping its students.

It seems unlikely that the modest advance of Esperanto will reduce the demand for translation from or into other languages; more interesting will be the impact of machine translation and terminology, which should effect economies of scale in labour and financial costs for the translation of important standardised texts with an emphasis on technical and other standardised terms, common syntactic structures and a minimum of figurative language in areas such as finance, trade and meteorology.

To some extent public language, strongly influenced by the EC in the West, Marxism in the East, and the proliferation of bureaucracies everywhere is converging, at any rate in many key-terms, towards an international translationese; one has only to look at a brief list of Russian key terms: *deputat, komitet, partija, Ministr, plakat, plenum, natsija, federatsija, konstitutsija,* or of EC terms: *harmonisation, intervention, collégialité, équipement, concertation, conjoncture, sanction,* to surmise that it is precisely the 'converging' terms, nearly all of which have existed in many European languages since the eighteenth century and are Greco-Latinisms which are most in use, in view and in exchange.

In fact, politicians and diplomats often make speeches with their translated impact in mind as being of more importance to them than their actual words in their own language. Further, much broadcast material as well as the blockbusters of popular literature and TV and the written commentaries of art books and coffee-table books are now written specifically for multilingual translation. Other material, such as secret coded military and government messages, personal letters produced as evidence in a foreign court case and advertisements for new products, sometimes with brand names or trade marks, which if incautiously transferred have an offensive or ridiculous meaning in the foreign language (e.g. 'Pschitt', a French brand of fizzy drink), is later translated and may present cultural difficulties to the translator, given that translation was never in their writers' minds.

I may have given an impression of a world-wide task and necessity for translation that is insuperable. This is far from being the case. Translators, who before World War II hardly existed as a profession (except as a small one in Germany and The Netherlands as *vereidigte Übersetzer* from the nineteenth century), started to organise soon after the War and formed an international organisation, the International Federation of Translators (FIT) with Unesco support in 1953. International organisations, multinationals, large companies and translation companies hired translators; the élite of these, who were normally technical experts first and linguists second, remaining freelance. The mass of translators often began as language graduates and then specialised in a technology on the job. The EC, which was soon to house the largest number of translators ever working under one 'roof' offered high salaries, but translators in many countries remained, as traditionally, undervalued, underpaid and unrecognised. Again, soon after the War some universities (and in the UK, polytechnics) began running postgraduate vocational and sometimes first degree courses for translators; translators' and interpreters' institutes in some countries (notably Federal Republic, GDR, Finland, CSSR) attained academic respectability when they were incorporated into universities.

There is no question that the translation task can be coped with. What has rather to be questioned, in the most general terms, is whether enough material is being translated and whether the standard of translation is high enough. First, are there enough community translators and interpreters for the immigrants, the foreign workers and the refugees in each country? Is enough national and local government material that concerns them being translated? Secondly, are governments and industry translating enough, in particular publicity, correspondence, instructions and after-service material, particularly in relation to exports?

The British Overseas Trade Board Report, *Foreign Languages for Overseas Trade,* issued in 1979 under the chairmanship of the Duke of Kent, implicitly suggests that this is not so, though regrettably the terms 'translation' and 'translator' do not appear in the Report. It is surely time for a CBI report to appear on the translation requirements (a) actual (b) desirable of British public boards and corporations as well as private companies. Such a report, if imaginatively framed, would draw more attention to perceived gaps and needs than to present practice. The last such report, chaired by Anthony Crane, was produced in the old FBI (Federation of British Industry) days in 1964. It is only fair to add that the ten-language Export Centre in the Pick-up Scheme, organised by the Department of Education and Science in 1987, is making up a lot of the leeway. Further, since 1983, Ann Corsellis, under the aegis of the Institute of Linguists, has been running the Community Interpreters project.

Thirdly, is enough translation available for tourists and tourism in the form of notices at public places, brochures and other publicity? In the UK, tourist translation appears to be only at its beginning. (Similarly, multilingual interpretation, live and recorded, is inadequate on British aircraft.) More multilingual guides, brochures and summaries should be available in museums, galleries, country houses, places of entertainment, tourist shops, etc. (Why are foreign record sleeves usually multilingual, English ones apparently monolingual?) Even now there appear to be no standard translations for terms such as 'Citizens Advice Bureau', 'National Trust', 'National Tourist Authority'. It is surely the duty of any government to issue official translations of its important institutional terms in the main languages concerned. Pioneer work in this field is being done by the Europa-Glossaries produced by the Institute for Legal and Administrative Language, Berlin. Fourthly, there is no question that not enough creative literature is being either translated or retranslated. After the War, a tremendous job was done by Penguin Books in having all the nineteenth century Russian classics translated again, since the translations at the turn of the century had given such a false impression of stiffness and gloom, which to some extent still influences the English stereotype of the Russian character.

The Penguin Classics continue to dominate the translation of creative literature and with about 350 volumes, headed by the ancient Greek and Latin classics, followed by French and Russian, they make an impressive list. German literature (Goethe, Heine and the dramatists) has been somewhat neglected. Further, many Russians complain, rightly, that modern Soviet literature is virtually unknown in this country, unlike contemporary British and American literature in theirs; they claim that the British stereotype — that Russians know no English author since Dickens (all fog and slums) — is false; many prefer Murdoch, Drabble, Fowles and Angus Wilson in any event. It is time to translate more non-censored as well as dissident Soviet and GDR literature. In general, while Unesco has done an exceptional job in promoting translation and providing interesting statistics (Lenin was again in 1975 the most translated author, followed at a long distance by Agatha Christie and Walt Disney), not enough is done to promote translation from small countries. It has always been the oddest of suspect coincidences that great writers mainly write in world languages. Would Conrad be known, if he had written in Polish? In fact, Third World countries should promote the translation of their best writers into English; some of their works could become powerful propaganda for aid. (I wave aside the preposterous notion, abetted by many writers, that works of art have no influence on events or behaviour.)

Finally, the number of abstracts written in appropriate foreign languages in technical journals, periodicals and even newspapers, should be increased, in particular in western Europe. All educated Germans, Dutch people and Scandinavians read and speak English (an increasing number of books and articles are published in English in West Germany and The Netherlands), and abstracts in their languages would encourage them to read the complete work in English.

If I now discuss a generally 'low' standard of translation, a meaningless evaluation since it relates to no norm, but which is nevertheless usually agreed for the UK (though translation appears to be worse in France), I would attribute it to translationese (in the course of translating out of one's own language) in commercial texts, particularly publicity; literal translations of technical texts; and inaccurate translation, due to attempts to 'normalise', naturalise and liven up the language with colloquialisms and idioms, in literary texts.

The worst translationese is perpetrated by writers translating out of their language of habitual use. The phrase 'language of habitual use', which was coined by Anthony Crane, is accurate; terms such as 'mother tongue', 'native speaker', 'native language', etc. lead to a suspicion of racialism. Students refused admission to translation courses because they are 'foreign' are apt to protest, since the translator represents the essence of internationalism and the negation of racialism and chauvinism relating to language and culture in particular and of prejudice relating to people in general. Translationese is bad not because it misrepresents the facts — it usually gets them right; not because it exhibits 'incorrect' grammar — on the contrary, its grammar is often copybook, and compared with the horrors of clichés, platitudes, vogue words, weasel words ((Pei) words with meanings changed to manipulate opinion), buzz words (words used for the sake of their sound alone), jargon, insincere phaticisms (a phrase such as 'I hope you're in good health' or 'of course' used to keep the interlocutor happy — invented for this piece), and mindless intensifiers (superlatives and emphasisers, they are often also buzz words), 'incorrect' grammar (and spelling) is a triviality in any event; but because in its reproduction of source language idioms and syntax, translationese is either absurd or heavy and therefore fails to transmit the tone and mood and feeling of the original — its style diverts the reader from its message. Examples abound in the tourist literature of most countries and the translationese is usually made worse when compounded with copious jargon. Since Alan Duff (1981) has written a book about the misuse of this 'third language' (sometimes referred to as 'interlanguage' by applied linguists — it has its uses in language learning), I quote one of his examples.

> The outmoded phrase about the country where the nuts come from has been substituted by objective approaches to realities that were provincial and distant and are now world-wide and importantly close to the life of everybody. (Advertisement for Brazil in *The Guardian*, October 1977)

Alan Duff's 'translation' from this presumably ex-Portuguese English is:

> The old saying that Brazil is the country where the nuts come from is no longer true. The country is rapidly opening up; its problems are no longer local problems, they are shared by people throughout the world. And new approaches to these problems are constantly being found. (Duff, 1981)

Possibly Alan Duff has put too many additional ideas into his version, and if concision is one of the criteria of translation, a more appropriate (and appealing) version might be:

> Brazil is no longer just the country that the nuts come from. It is now a modern country and has important social problems that have world-wide parallels and must be approached objectively.

Bad writing is bad writing in any language, but it is more exposed and therefore apparently even worse writing when it is translated. (Here, as often, translation represents truth or clarification, a weapon against sham, mystification, obscurantism and secretiveness, an argument against mandarin mumbo-jumbo, since at least Luther.)

Often the translationese of a hotel brochure is mildly irritating or amusing: 'we have created a comfortable atmosphere so that you and the further 512 guests may have as pleasant a sojourn as possible' *(Wir haben für Sie und weitere 512 Gäste den Konfort geschaffen, der Ihnen den Aufenthalt so angenehm wie möglich gestalten soll)*. Further, 'our social rooms are at your disposal for the most different occasions' *(für die verschiedensten Anlässe stellen wir Ihnen auch gern unsere Gesellschaftsraüme zur Verfügung)*. (Extracts from the Interhotel Leipzig brochure.) (Note that the translator has handled word order well and rightly treats *auch gern* as a 'modal enclitic', which (cf. *eben, ja, gewiß*) are often left untranslated, but he or she is let down by a few literalisms — i.e. inappropriate translations of words by their primary or most common meanings.) However, such slightly inaccurate translations will sooner or later disturb business customers who pride themselves on their close attention to detail. A more acceptable translation might be: 'We hope that you will find our hotel comfortable, and that your stay will be agreeable. We can accommodate 512 guests and our public rooms are at your disposal for a wide variety of functions.'

Translationese both 'native' and 'foreign often appears in technical texts. 'Foreign' translators have not got the command of the target language; 'native' translators are inexperienced and unaware that interference from the source or a third language may go beyond a few conventional *faux amis* (like *troubler, demander),* to clauses, phrases, technical terms, metaphors, word order and most collocations; they think like many lay people and literary snobs that accurate rendering of the vocabulary of technical terms is all they require — in fact these on an average constitute 12% of the average specialised text — a good bilingual technical dictionary will do the job — neologisms they have to chance their arm with. Such translationese, when read cold, makes one think that (native) translators must have taken leave of their senses, and yet it is often perpetrated, as shown in the following examples:

sa faible viscosité en solution, son bas
translationese   its feeble viscosity in solution, its low
corrected   its low viscosity in solution, its low

poids moléculaire suffisant pour l'empêcher
translationese   molecular weight sufficient to prevent it
corrected   molecular weight, though big enough to prevent it

de franchir à l'état normal les parois
translationese   crossing at the normal state the partitions
corrected   from passing through the capillary walls in

des capillaires, rénaux en particulier
translationese   of the capillaries renal in particular
corrected   the normal state, and particularly in the kidneys

expliquent qu'une de ses grandes fonctions
translationese   explain that one of its great biological
corrected   explain why one of its major biological

biologiques soit représentée par son rôle
translationese   functions is represented by its role
corrected   functions is the

dans le maintien du volume sanguin
translationese   in the maintenance of the sanguineous volume
corrected   maintenance of the blood volume

The interesting thing about the above passage is its large quantity of *amis fidèles* where as always the literal translation (both for technical and descriptive terms) is the only correct one. The fact remains, however, that owing to the translator's blind adherence to the central or primary sense of each word and the French grammatical structures (used, but not so commonly in English), the text is defective.

The last important type of text where standards of translation are deficient is the area of creative literature. Here I think one has to propose certain absolute minimum standards of accuracy, not previously formulated, up to now usually ignored in particular at the world level. I take my example from the first sentence of Kafka's *Die Verwandlung* (which I would translate as *The Transformation* rather than *The Metamorphosis*) translated by Edwin and Willa Muir and Stanley Corngold, but it is too late now to make this change:

Kafka *Als G. S. eines Morgens aus unruhigen*
Muir When G. S. awoke one morning from uneasy
Corngold When G.S. woke up one morning from unsettling

Kafka *Träumen erwachte fand er sich in seinem*
Muir dreams, he found himself transformed in his
Corngold dreams he found himself changed in his

Kafka *Bett zu einem ungeheueren Ungeziefer verwandelt*
Muir bed into a gigantic insect
Corngold bed into a monstrous vermin

It seems to me 'impossible' to translate *unruhig* as 'unsettling' *(beunruhigend), ungeheueren* as 'gigantic' *(riesig), verwandelt* as 'changed' *(verändert)*, and *Ungeziefer* as 'a vermin' since 'vermin' is not a count noun. Similarly, in the same story, *machte ihn ganz melancholisch* cannot be 'completely depressed him'; *üppig* cannot be 'shapely' or 'with a good figure'; *ein schwerer Pelzmuff* cannot be 'a huge fur muff' nor *das trübe Wetter* 'the overcast sky', etc.

I am suggesting that in any type of text, any source language (SL) content word whose meaning is not affected by its linguistic context, has to be translated by its primary most common sense. Thus *unruhig* covers 'unquiet' 'restive' 'uneasy' and even 'restless', though 'restless' is a stronger intensifier than *unruhig* ('-less' and *-los* are stronger than 'un-', *un-); ungeheuer* covers 'huge', 'immense' and 'monstrous' but not 'gigantic'; *verwandelt* covers 'transformed' and 'completely changed'; *ein Ungeziefer* has to revert to the more general 'an insect' or 'a bug'.

Thus in literary translation (as well as in the translation of authoritative statements) content-words (most nouns, adjectives, verbs, adverbs) normally have a certain autonomy as units of translation. They cannot and must not be translated by words which when retranslated into the source language, could not remotely reproduce them. The above seems to me a minimal unassailable principle of accurate translation. It has to be upheld against the translator's wish to translate 'naturally', fluently, colloquially and so on, since one assumes that the degree of unnaturalness of the relevant word in relation to the target language norm will correspond to its equivalent's degree of unnaturalness in relation to the source language.

I am suggesting that more words in a text are either relatively context-free or conventionalised than is often assumed. The word 'home' is often described as untranslatable, but the sentence 'I'm going home' is conventionalised and therefore easily translated into any language *nach Hause, à la maison, domoj,* etc.; 'this is my home' is almost, but not quite, as straightforward; only when we get to 'home means a lot to me' do we find difficulties, and start looking into increasingly wider contexts, and the 'wave' or ripple translation procedure operates. Now my minimal standard of accuracy operates sharply for the first example, approximately for the second, and only generally within limits for the third. I am not denying the existence of words and stretches of text that are bound up in a complex way with levels of meaning covering the whole text.

Naturally, translation does not remain at this simple level; all languages have many 'untranslatable' words whose meaning, if important, has to be spread and manipulated across two or more words or a phrase of the target language. Translation can be described as filling up the gaps between languages. Many words are profoundly affected by their contexts both linguistic, cultural and situational and cannot be translated in isolation. The impact of text linguistics on translation suggests that the whole text should be assumed to be the unit of translation.

However, my argument is in the opposite direction. I am suggesting that on the whole, more words are relatively context-free than relatively context-bound. In the fight against dead perfection, lifeless and pedantic correctness and dry academicism, etc. and for the use of lively modern language, the release of the 'undertext' (in brief, what the author meant, rather than what he or she wrote) referred to by Michael Meyer (1974) as the 'subtext', the spirit rather than the letter, the activity rather than the product, etc., it must, shall we say in the 1990s, in a climate of science and verification (that is the main principle), be on the whole illegitimate to stretch the meaning of a word beyond its hitherto usage, unless one is neologising. It is wrong, and this principle applies to the translation of all texts (unless they are poorly written) to translate for example *caractères généraux* as 'general features' rather than 'general characteristics'. Translators are usually reluctant to use a word so like an SL word, when in fact they should seize the opportunity since it is the one that is nearest to the 'truth' or to accuracy. This is the *rappel à l'ordre,* the call (or recall) to order in translation. In any type of translation, the back translation test is conclusive, one cannot appeal against it, provided no collocations are implicated: 'a rose' is *une rose* is *eine rose,* unless it is an 'English rose', in which case it might be *fraîche comme une rose* or *eine englische Schöne,* or the 'rose', *pomme, Brause,* of a watering can, or is otherwise figurative or technical.

I suggest that this is the minimal 'scientific' principle of translation since the evidence is there, in the words, and translators' loyalty is to them, not to a nebulous readership. Their relation to this language substance is much closer than when the nebulous readership is between them and those words. There is continuous verification. Here, in artistic literary translation, translation is at its most scientific, its most 'rigorous'. So much for the paradox of translation, where art can be transformed by science.

Scientific up to a point, but not dogmatic. There is occasionally a case where instinctively intuitively the translator will use a 'different' word, a word plainly not in the text, but which 'feels' right.

> *Leur haine dès longtemps contre moi déclarée*
> *M'avait à mon malheur depuis longtemps préparée*
> (Racine: *Bérénice,* 1079–80)

> Their hate, long since against me unconcealed
> Had long prepared me for catastrophe.
> (John Cairncross, *Bérénice.* Penguin Classics)

The translator's defence may be that he felt Racine would have used 'catastrophe', if he had been writing in English. But this 'lapse' may be the exception that proves the rule, once in one or two hundred lines.

The arguments that translators should strive for 'equivalent' effect (i.e. their readership should react to the translation just like the SL readership to the original) and that they should write as the SL author would have written if he or she had been a native and had complete command of the target language — both these arguments are eventually nebulous and hypothetical though not equally so. McFarlane (1953) in a too little known article pointed out that Rilke, Julien Green, Albert Schweitzer and Schleiermacher ('portrait of a man as he would have looked if his mother had begotten him by a different father') all produced arguments in favour of 'different' self-translation — Samuel Beckett, on the other hand, kept exceptionally close to his own originals.

However, I return to my subject, which is the inaccuracy of three types of translations, and in particular that the inaccuracies of the first two (publicity and technical reports) are often a mirror-image of the inaccuracies of the third (literature); the first two are too literal, the last is not literal enough.

Finally, I should say that the important factors of a translation (and its text) are its intention, its meaning, its tone, its impact, its 'texture', its function, the text as a unit — but that the evidence for all these factors can only be found in the words in the text — these are the touchstones of a translation. 'Words' — not sentences! — 'are to be interpreted according to their ordinary and natural meaning', says Halsbury. In any challenging text, there is continuous tension between the maximal unit — the text — and the minimal — the word.

What is Translation?

Most people can recognise a translation *grosso modo* — particularly if they find enough corresponding features between the target and source language texts. But asked to define translation, they hesitate, and many dictionaries, which offer synonyms for the verb (render, rephrase, reword, transmit, re-express, transmute, transmogrify, interpret, convert, transform, transpose, express, transfer, turn) and add 'from one language into another' do not state what is being translated; other authorities make use of expressions such as 'equivalent', 'equivalent message', 'equivalent textual material', 'similar', 'like', 'parallel', 'equal', 'identical', 'comparable', 'synonymous', 'analogous'.

If I define the act of translating as transferring the meaning of a stretch or a unit of language, the whole or a part of a text, from one language to another, I am possibly putting the problem where it belongs, viz., the meaning of meaning rather than the meaning of equivalence, identity, similarity, likeness, sameness, correspondence and so on.

By meaning, I am not referring to the whole meaning. *Je suis arrivée* tells us that a woman is speaking and that she arrived either just now or some time ago; *die Sonne geht auf* tells us that the sun is rising now or that it rises regularly, and that it is feminine gender in German. But in the context, it is unlikely that all this information would have to be transferred. We are therefore only talking about functionally relevant meaning being transferred, leaving out all the superfluous features of meaning that can also be found in the text.

Much of the meaning in any stretch of language may have already been conveyed in previous sentences; another meaning is 'potential', e.g. a phonaesthetic meaning, the meaning if any suggested by the sound of the passage, or a philological meaning, for example the etymological meaning of the content words.

Now the main difficulties begin. Is the meaning to transfer the meaning intended by the writer, or to reformulate the meaning intended by the translator? Is it to be modified for the reader, or again is it to be squared with the facts of the matter? There is no straight answer — it depends on the purpose of the translation. Thus in translating the sentence *Crée en 1798, le Conseil d'Etat est une des institutions françaises les plus originales, Conseil d'Etat* may be translated as *Conseil d'Etat,* or *Council of State,* or assigned a cultural equivalent and succinctly defined, and, presumably, the date must be corrected.

Now meaning as such can be summarised as cognitive, communicative and associative and these three varieties of meaning are normally involved in any translation. Thus the meaning of *tu sais* 'you know' may include the cognitive meaning that what has been said is true; the communicative meaning that the writer or speaker is asking for the reader's or listener's assent or mere attention, and the associative meaning that the writer or speaker is on familiar or fairly 'symmetrical' terms with the reader or listener.

Here I should state that every variety of meaning can be transferred, and therefore, unequivocally that *everything can be translated.* This does not mean that every relevant aspect of meaning in a text *is* translated, because this would sometimes be longwinded and cumbersome (a translation should usually be as concise as possible, like good writing) and would require a long explanation. The explanation is then the translation, which is not usually good translation, but the best that can be achieved in the circumstances. The only complete translation of 'the murmur of innumerable bees' into French would entail a literal translation plus an explanation of the English onomatopoeia, which could therefore not be incorporated into a French poem, but would have to be painfully demonstrated in prose. Therefore the translator has to establish priorities in choosing which varieties of meaning to transfer, depending on the intention of the translated text and his or her own intention.

Further, I have to add that the three varieties of meaning I have mentioned each include other varieties of meaning. Thus cognitive meaning includes:

(a) *linguistic meaning;* that is the proposition within the text say *Il était obsédé par l'idée de vendre son journal,* 'He was obsessed by the idea of selling his paper';

(b) *referential meaning:* JJSS was obsessed by the idea of selling *France-Soir* (in Paris in 1970);

(c) *implicit meaning:* the tone of a passage determines the implicit meaning of a sentence. Thus *Vous avez cent fois raison* may mean 'You're quite right' or 'You're quite wrong', or 'You may be making a mistake' or 'No comment';

(d) *thematic meaning,* showing normally the old information as the theme at the beginning of a sentence, and the new information (rheme) at the end of the sentence, with the highest degree of Communicative Dynamism (Firbas, 1972) on the last word (rheme proper). Thematic meaning ensures the maximum 'reasonable' formal equivalence between source and target language text.

Communicative meaning, say in the sentence *Qu'est-ce que c'est, le succès d'un journal?* includes:

(a) *illocutionary meaning,* here requiring a response to the question;

(b) *performative meaning,* e.g. in the sentence *Double faute!* for tennis, signifying the loss of points;

(c) *inferential meaning,* e.g. the sentence *Je regrette mon argent* implies 'I regret the expense, I wish I had my money back', whilst 'He shot the policeman' may mean *Il a tué* or *Il a tiré sur l'agent de police;*

(d) *prognostic meaning, Il se fait tard* may mean 'It's time to go' and *Il y a un taureau dans ce champ* may mean 'Let's get away'.

Finally, associative meaning may be related to the writer's background, the situation, or the sound-effects conveyed by the SL. It covers in particular pragmatic meaning, which identifies the effect which a text is likely to have on a particular readership.

Meaning when relating to the writer's personal background has perhaps been sufficiently analysed and can be conveniently illustrated with single words: the class or sociolect, 'luncheon' rather than 'lunch'; the dialect, *Potschen* (Austrian) for 'slippers', *Schrippe* (Berlin) for 'roll'; the period, for example in the eighteenth century *Er* is 'you'; the age, *Elektrische* for 'tram'; occupation, *Anamnese* for 'case history' and *Gut* (naut.) for 'rigging' — note that single words or sentences may conflate class, regional dialect, occupation and degree of formality, e.g. *Adöpfl* for potatoes, labouring class, Thuringian, agricultural work, colloquialism; sex (distinctions between male and female language are fluid and tend to fade in speech communities where taboos on language are disappearing for social reasons).

Meaning relating to culture may be material or ideological. Words for objects or institutions *(baguette, Institut de France)* may be given a cultural equivalent ('French loaf', 'French equivalent of Royal Society and British Academy') or neutralised by a descriptive term ('long loaf', national institute of arts and sciences). Political and philosphical internationalisms ('democracy', 'socialism', etc.) may have different meanings in the SL and TL, while pejorative (negative) or ameliorative (positive) terms may be used for the same 'objects', conveniently illustrated in the GDR (German Federal Republic) oppositions: *Gewinn/Profit; Wettbewerb/Konkurrenz; Angestellter/Beamter.* Note that some otherwise negative terms may sometimes be used as familiar or informal alternatives: 'Tory'/Conservative; bourgeois/middle class; propaganda/information ('enlightenment').

Familiar alternative terms extend to 'in' words ('squad' rather than 'team') in spite of the difference in meaning; 'flight' rather than 'crossing' of hovercraft; picturesque or catchy words *(l'hexagonal* for 'French' (language); *lo Stivale* for 'Italy'); former names ('Pressburg' for 'Bratislava'); nicknames or abbreviations ('Spurs' for 'Tottenham Hotspur Football Club'); political concepts *(jacobinisme* for 'political centralism'). When used as familiar alternatives, they are intended to have the same cognitive, communicative and associative meaning as the 'correct', terms, though this may be dangerous and must sometimes be avoided ('Ten little nigger boys', etc.).

While metaphors in the form of kennings or metonyms are frequently used as familiar alternatives ('Auld Reekie', the Black Prince, the Iron Lady, etc.), the use of metaphor for the purpose of imprecision, vagueness, insinuation, non-self-committal, shilly-shallying, staying on the fence, halftruths, dissimulation, deceit, etc., and the translator's attitude to this practice, has still to be investigated.

It is difficult for a lover of metaphor to get used to the fact that when people want to be dishonest, to prevaricate, to not commit themselves, they use metaphors — also when they want to be tactful, to mitigate, to soften: 'She may not be ideal, but she has invested a lot in you'. Woman or machine? How to convert this to literal language, to straight talk, to direct honest statement. 'These mentally handicapped people are eroding our beaches' says the mayor of Teignmouth. Translate 'erode' by *minent* or *untergraben,* and the prejudice becomes more explicit.

Meaning relating to culture and ideology may be implicit in a text, and can be expressed either through significant quotation, or through proper names. Thus in a crude propaganda article published by *Die Weltbühne* referring to the anti-Arabic feeling in Munich after the murder of the Israeli athletes at the Olympic Games, and approvingly quoted by S. Bastian in Kade (1979): *Das gesunde Volksempfinden feierte fröhliche Urständ, nur daß es diesmal die Forderung zu formulieren hatte: ARABER sind hier erwünscht!* Suggested translation: 'The healthy popular feeling, of which the Nazis used to be so proud, came to life again, but this time it had to rephrase its demand: Arabs (not Jews) not wanted here'. S. Bastian rather optimistically refers to this type of implicit cultural meaning as the 'pre-information' of a text.

Meaning in relation to situation covers degree of formality (official, formal, informal, colloquial/slang); generality (popular, neutral, technical, etc.); objectivity (impassioned, factual).

Finally meaning in relation to language may be literal (denotative) or figurative (connotative, metaphorical); expressive, expressing the writer's personality; informative, stating the facts of the matter; persuasive or imperative, directed to affect the reader. Further, onomatopoeia, assonance, alliteration, word-play and rhyme may be used directly or indirectly to convey meaning, in non-literary texts as well as in poetry.

The above has been an attempt to enumerate most of the varieties of meaning which may or may not be functionally relevant to the translation of a text. Incidentally, it is evidence, if evidence is required, of how complex and multifarious the translating activity, if not the translated text, can be.

A further illustration of the various factors that impinge semantically on a text can be put diagrammatically, as in Figure 2.1.

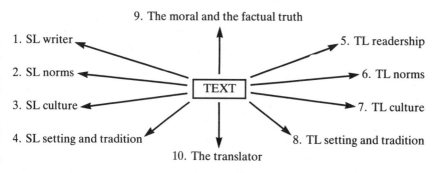

FIGURE 2.1 *The various factors that impinge semantically on a text*

The text may therefore be pulled in ten different directions, as follows:

1. The individual style or idiolect of the SL author. When should it be (a) preserved (b) normalised?
2. The conventional grammatical and lexical usage for this type of text, depending on the topic and the situation.
3. Content items referring specifically to the SL or third language (i.e. not TL) cultures.
4. The typical format of the text in the book, periodical, newspaper, etc., as influenced by the tradition at the time.
5. The expectations of the putative readership bearing in mind their estimated knowledge of the topic and the style of language they use, expressed in terms of the largest common factor, since one should neither translate down (nor up) to the readership.
6, 7 and 8 as for 2, 3 and 4 respectively, but related to the TL.
9. What is being described or reported, ascertained or verified (the referential truth), where possible independently of the SL text and the expectations of the readership.
10. The views and prejudices of the translator, which may be personal and subjective, or may be social and cultural, involving the translator's 'group loyalty factor', which may reflect the national, political, ethnic, religious assumptions, social class, sex, etc. of the translator.

All these ten factors may actually or potentially affect the translation of a text, which may represent a compromise, a balance, a choice from among them. However, the moral and the factual truth must always be made clear when it is concerned.

Now, I have maintained that every variety of meaning in an SL text can be translated directly or indirectly into a TL text, and therefore that everything can be translated. However, any variety of meaning, relating to the SL itself (e.g. puns, alliteration, linguistic terms) can only be translated indirectly, by transferring the SL item, translating, and explaining it, unless there is already a parallel item in the TL or the translation which can produce a compensatory effect within the same paragraph. Such a transfer of SL items is cumbersome, and while the transfer and the definition of the item would be essential in translating a word such as 'supine' or 'optative' to a lay reader in a language that does not possess these phenomena, it is usually not worthwhile to 'translate' cases of say alliteration with this form of metalingual comment. Thus if the sound-effect as well as the meaning of Flaubert's *la poussière des granges, la potasse des lessives et le suint des laines,* 'the dust of the barns, the potash of the washing-water, the grease of the sheep's wool' were considered an essential part of the translation, which would be possible if the passage were being exemplified for its stylistic effect, the words would have to be transferred and the alliterative s's pointed out. The same impact could not be achieved (the target language reader might not know how to pronounce the passage), but the sound effect would be explained: the explanation is the translation.

Normally, however, the translator is continually making choices, weighing up, balancing, comparing the merits of one 'equivalent', or carrier of meaning, against another. Whilst all the varieties of meaning I have listed above may be present in one text, only a proportion of them may be functionally relevant for a translation and some information (e.g. grammatical meaning (gender, number, degree of intimacy, or dialect)) may not need to be repeated as frequently as it is in the TL text, or it may be introduced (e.g. a metaphor) as a compensatory element in a part of the TL text in a place that does not correspond to its place in the SL text.

The subject of the 'invariant' element in translation has been frequently discussed, often with the implication that the cognitive element, the information, is the invariant element which must at all costs be transferred, whilst the communicative and associative elements should be transferred only if possible. No generalisation could be more misleading. The invariant and variant elements will depend entirely on the intention of the text. In the sentence 'fortunately she's ill', the pragmatic element is invariant while the cognitive could be expressed in more general or more specific terms without much loss of meaning. In translating the sentence 'The cat sat on the mat', the invariant element may be the information (approximate as it is), the six monosyllables, the assonance or the representative quality of the sentence. Admittedly, the invariant element in a factual text is the maximum proportion of fact, while in a literary text the invariant element must be some aspect of the associative meaning. The translator makes his or her own decision for each text.

The more 'challenging' (i.e. translationally difficult and interesting) the source language text, the more subtle and delicate will be the new 'mix' of units of meaning, sometimes referred to as 'semes', to be introduced into the translation. Translation equivalence will then not be achieved word for word, collocation for collocation, clause for clause, sentence for sentence, but possibly only paragraph for paragraph, or, rarely, text for text. For this reason, translation equivalence, like the term 'unit of translation', is sometimes a useful operational concept, but it can be only roughly and approximately indicated for a stretch of language, e.g. it is likely to be smaller (in the area of word, collocation, clause) for an 'expressive' text (creative literature and authoritative statements) than for an 'informative' text (e.g. technical

translation, textbooks, etc.) but there will still be plenty of one to one translation in any text.

The translating activity, I hope I have shown, is complex and difficult to
define. A good translation, however, at least of the type that most professional translators are faced with, is not difficult to identify. It is likely to look
surprisingly like the original text to a reader competent in both languages,
unless the original contains errors of fact and deficiencies of style. Provided
one leaves 'creative language' texts and official ex-cathedra statements of
any kind out of account, Nida's (1975) classical definition of translation as
'the reproduction of the closest natural equivalent of the source language
message' could not be bettered. In fact, this type of translation is distinguished by its elegance and concision, its attention to a natural word order,
to the deployment of clauses and phrases more frequently used than their
formal equivalents in the source language, to the occasional unobtrusive dis-
tribution of the meaning of important 'untranslatable' words (e.g. 'privacy',
éclat, sauber, casanier, etc.) over two or three target language words or
a clause: a good translation is deft, neat, closely shadowing its original.
'A misted window-pane that continuously has to be wiped cleaner' (Mary
FitzGerald). (The only merit of such epithets and metaphors is that they are
not yet clichéd.)

Should a translation be 'visible' or 'invisible'? One assumes that a translation devoted to facts and ideas, or persuading people, is mainly invisible,
unless it wants to seize its readership by drawing attention to its curious
syntax ('this hopefully to you not unpleasing postcard') — this is also not
uncommon in advertisements — or by introducing as it explains foreign
words. But a translation, if it is written as I think it should be with syntactic
and semantic structures as arresting and deviant as those of the original
(Villon or Céline, or Thomas Mann), is likely to be visible.

The cultural benefits of translation are obvious. The linguistic benefits
are not uncontested, but eventually they are incontestable. Perhaps 40 years
ago, an American translated *hoffentlich* as 'hopefully', and this neologism
is still shocking some British English purists. In the meantime, other parenthetical adverbs, the equivalents of the German *-erweise*, 'thankfully',
'mercifully', 'sadly' (prominent during the Falklands campaign of 1982)
have appeared with remarkably less fuss, and most have still escaped the
lexicographers. The impact of translation on English has never been strong
enough, mainly due to the insularity — a polite word: Matthew Arnold
translated it (from Heine) as philistinism — of the cultural tradition but also
due to the timidity of tränslators, their reluctance for instance to translate
metaphors literally, what Eric Segal referred to as 'metarophobia' (Robert

Boys, 1979). Many metaphors, images and symbols in classical literature were not translated literally, because the translators thought them too odd, even when they were not culturally determined.

The translation of any original work is bound to some extent to make inroads on, to 'do violence' to (as Karl Kraus said of Stefan George) and in fact to benefit the norms of the target language. Often the self-effacing 'invisible' nature of the translator's activity will emphasise the differences between the source and the target languages, and thus the fact of the translation.

A language such as English would gain by the literal translation of many foreign key-words, idioms and possibly even proverbs, most of them not particularly culture-bound. If translation means filling up the gaps between languages, this is what translators should be doing. A translation is wanted for words such as *aménagement (aménagement du territoire:* 'spatial management' or 'planning'), *Veranstaltung, animateur* (of a club or society) and *naschen, einen Sprung machen,* just as foreign languages need one for 'privacy'. *Lebensraum* should have been turned to 'living space', *détente* to 'relaxation'. Phrases such as 'he's no longer the youngest' and 'the birthday child' (both from German), 'occupational deformation' — more habitual than occupational disease — (French) and particularly 'Good appetite!' ought to be current in English. Words that appear rebarbative at first sight or hearing, particularly to pedants (who often make a deluded objection to the 'sound' of the word — as though the subjunctive *donnassions* 'sounded' worse than *donation*) but also to others with a relish for language old and new, can soon become acceptable (sometimes all too acceptable, as voguewords) on further hearing, when their function is recognised as unique. Here translators have not been bold enough — their primary job is to translate — to import only when there are good reasons for not translating.

On the other hand, translators have to guard against the literal translation of *faux amis* which thrust unnecessary new senses into old words, e.g. 'control' in the sense of 'check' or 'verify', and impose unnecessary new collocations on their own language. Admittedly the French with their manifold instruments of language control and their superb lexicographers have been fighting this losing battle for many years, but translators still have to fight it, till but not after they have lost it.

In general terms, translation is a cover term that comprises any method of transfer, oral and written, from writing to speech, from speech to writing, of a message from one language to another. Professionally, however, the term 'translation' is confined to the written, and the term 'interpretation' to the spoken language. Some years ago Kade introduced the terms *Translation* for the activity, *Translat* for the product, as new German generic terms to cover both translation and interpretation; the first at any rate might profitably spread beyond the GDR and the Federal Republic, where it has been adopted by Wilss, to Romance language countries.

Further, there are two modes of interpreting: simultaneous (from a booth) and consecutive (from notes after each intervention). Inevitably at conferences simultaneous is ousting consecutive interpretation, which is more accurate, since speakers may speak more slowly if they know the interpreters are taking notes and the interpreters have more time; teachers, however, insist on the importance of consecutive as a training technique. In court community interpreting, consecutive is essential, but in police and social work 'whisper' liaison interpreting should be more efficient.

The only generalisation I can make about the difference between translation and interpretation is that other things (i.e. the skills of the 'mediators' and the facilities provided) being equal, but they never are — an interpretation is likely to be more colloquial, less detailed, deprived of the original's metaphors, with more emphasis on the essential point and the gist of a paragraph, a sentence or a phrase.

The translation is likely to be more accurate, more concise, better formulated; the interpretation is likely to be simpler, to include more redundancy, even repetition with more attention to communicative resources, such as phaticisms, e.g. and i.e. words like 'undoubtedly', 'of course', 'assuredly', 'as you know', etc., designed to keep the listener flattered and happy, standardised terms and conventional phrases, since it aims not only to make the participants, delegates, etc. instantly understand the meaning of an intervention, but, more importantly to distinguish its main points from its subsidiary points and the subject of the agenda item. Needless to say, all interpreters have special problems with languages that are more or less inflected than their own. Thus an English interpreter often has to wait too long for the lexical part of a German verb phrase; languages that have no definite or indefinite articles, requiring a linguistically determined rather than a logical or an emphatically determined word order, sometimes slow up communication. Nevertheless experienced interpreters from German, Russian, Arabic, etc. into English develop a special sense and a technique for these linguistic difficulties.

It is often convenient to approximately distinguish three types of translation texts: (a) scientific-technological, which are usually handled by the translation departments of public corporations, multi-nationals and government departments; (b) institutional-cultural texts (culture, social sciences, commerce) handled in particular by international organisations; and (c) literary texts, normally handled by freelance translators (cf. Havranek (1964) who adds 'day to day texts' such as journalism, memoranda, correspondence, press agency items, reports of meetings, etc., the everyday silent translation which goes on all the time, so that to paraphrase the brilliant Marianne Lederer one would think, reading their speeches in quotes in the papers, that M. Mitterrand and Helmut Schmidt *always* spoke in English). The particular difficulties of sci-tech translators lie in the SL neologisms; the lack of an appropriate technical term in the TL, forcing the translator to use a descriptive term in its place; the labyrinth of semi-synonymous technical terms, some archaic, some written, some spoken, some regional, some Americanised, some familiar alternatives, some lay, some professional, some academic, some rarely used, some often used in another sense, in another technology, some just redundant; flowers, insects, thighs, splines, diseases — they all have a mass of alternative terms, and the translator may have to sort them out. (Paepcke (1975) has usefully proposed four varieties of technical language: (a) scientific — e.g. *compartiment réfrigérateur;* (b) workshop — e.g. *compartiment réfrigérateur;* (c) everyday — e.g. *congélateur;* (d) sales/publicity — e.g. *freezer* (French word).) The particular difficulty of institutional-cultural texts lies in relating the various terms that have no linguistic and/or referential equivalents in the TL culture to the readership and the setting of the TL text; the various criteria and procedures have to be related to each other before they are translated. A priori, literary translation has the greatest number of peculiar difficulties, since the source language itself is of cardinal importance and is an integral aspect of meaning, poetry which may use all the resources of language being the most formidable of all translation tasks; it requires a greater empathy with the writer than other text-types. But in this or that case, a discrimination between the value and the difficulties of text types may be meaningless. Literary, cultural and technical translation are equally important; literature in transmitting human values, culture in enriching a way of life and its language, technology in introducing inventions and innovations that improve health and living conditions. Differentiating the value of these three text-types is merely a form of intellectual or anti-intellectual snobbery.

Translation was undervalued when it was left to one person, and when it was anonymous. The King James Version of the Bible (1611) was produced by 54 revisers, consisting of six companies, two each working separately on sections assigned to them. Many of the translations of Marx, Engels, Lenin (and Stalin) were anonymous and their work later had to be officially authorised: the translator was unimportant, the authority was all-important. Literary translators in the nineteenth and twentieth centuries apparently worked on their own, consulting, as did H. T. Lowe-Porter (for

Thomas Mann) for special technical difficulties. Some husband–wife teams (the husband English, the wife foreign) failed to avoid gross errors.

In my view, an important translation of any kind should be reviewed by a second translator whose language of habitual use is the target language. They are the only people who can pick up the almost inevitable slips as well as infelicities and errors of meaning (facts and language) and usage that any translator is likely to make. In addition it is desirable that at an early stage a third translator whose language of habitual use is the SL should check that the text has been understood and a subject-expert be brought in, if appropriate, to check for appropriate register. Finally, the text should be revised bearing the stamp of the translator's idiolect. The translator is responsible for the translation, provided the criticisms of colleagues have been satisfied.

I am aware that these views diverge from much common practice in translation departments of companies and government organisations, where the translator submits work to a reviser and often does not see it again until it is published. One translator complained to me that he could barely recognise his own work. For their part, revisers may complain that translations are so poor that it is 'like hacking through a jungle' before they can reformulate a translation that satisfies them.

The fact that translation has expanded on so many levels (practitioners, languages, subject-matter covered, organisation of the activity, quantity of translations) — further, the fact that it is so various, complex and infuriating in one instance, simple and boring in another — all human life is there — suggests the need for some kind of frame of reference, some checklist guidelines to assist translators by categorising their problems with texts, paragraphs, sentences, clauses, groups, collocations and words (not to mention metaphors, eponyms, proper names, cultural and institutional terms, punctuation marks) by relating criteria to procedures, by recommending solutions. Hence translation theory, a subject and a discipline initiated in the middle 1960s by Nida, Fedorov, Catford, Mounin, Jumpelt, Neubert and Kade in attempts to apply linguistics to translation in a methodical and sensitive manner.

Given the difficulties of defining not only translation as an activity but a good translation as a product, of suggesting a process of translation as well as criteria for translation criticism, the rise of this discipline, which derives from stylistics, literary criticism and cultural studies as well as linguistics, is both natural and inevitable. What is required is a body of agreed principles, some generally applicable, others between one language and another, based always on concrete examples at all levels from the text to the word. This discipline, which is also an unending pursuit of meaning which has its own fascination, may become an instrument to assist the translating activity and finally to establishing translation criticism: the distinction between a good translation and a bad one.

Translation being at once a science and an art, a skill and a taste, an exercise of choices and decisions, is hard enough to define. The definition of a *good* translation is equally problematic. Certainly attributes like 'smooth' 'natural', 'idiomatic', rightly despised by Vladimir Nabokov, are appropriate as criteria for some translations and irrelevant for others. A good translation is accurate and economical — that is the only generalisation I can make. Where it is inaccurate, it is defective, either due to the translator's ignorance or negligence, or because one or more of the ten factors listed above is out of focus in relation to the translator's intention. Further, just as a good translation manifests itself in its words, and only secondarily in its spirit, its tone, its feel, so a poor translation appears in verbal inaccuracy where improper words are put in improper places; that is the touchstone of a poor translation, and if a poor translation is to be 'corrected', it must be by way of a call to order in regard to concrete verbal inaccuracies of plainly one-to-one translatable words. Admittedly, in translation, inaccuracy, wrongness, is easier to demonstrate than accuracy, rightness (aesthetic as well as cognitive), where there may be competing truths to reflect, and where the ultimate taste factor is likely to blur any single choice of a word. But even admitting that translation criteria are never absolute and to some extent follow the social standards of the prevailing hegemony or the countervailing opposition, one can by one's efforts now narrow the degree of variation in the criteria of the future.

The Role of the Translator

Most translators in Europe are women and therefore tend to be underpaid. The image of translators — as underpaid, anonymous parasites, at their best when, like an imaginary window-pane, they are invisible and least noticed, desk-bound, cocooned in a library, a bookworm, obsessed with words, knowing nothing about the culture of the countries whose languages they translate, which they have never visited anyway, ignorant of facts, a remote recluse — is obsolescent but dies hard. It is in sharp contrast with the role of some British naval translators who were translating into Spanish two types of leaflets dropped by Harrier jets on the Argentinians in Port Stanley during the Falklands War: one a letter from the British Task Force commander Admiral Woodward to the Argentinian commander General Menéndez suggesting that his military position was desperate and he should withdraw his troops (not surrender), the other telling the Argentinian soldiers what to do if they wanted to give up fighting and required a safe-conduct pass to return to their home country. The tone of both leaflets was important: to General Menéndez professional and business-like; to the soldiers, friendly and practical. In both cases, an impression of 'solidarity', without threats or domineering. The translator's role was a contribution to the preservation of lives.

Translators' conditions vary widely, and any new image of their job is based on the working conditions of a minority: they have a salary and a career structure comparable with that of other professional people. They work as members of a team in good conditions with a large reference library, continuously updated terminological word-banks, and word processors to hand or they may be operating or post-editing a machine translation system. They informally act as interpreters for foreign visitors, consult experts, visit plant-sites, travel and go on refresher courses in their technology. So much for their material circumstances. More important are their responsibilities: they have a responsibility not only to their employer and the client, but to the 'truth'. They not only have sometimes to make their own independent check of the facts of an SL text, they also have to form a separate opinion of the intentions of the texts they have translated, particularly if they are wrapped up in a degree of overstatement, irony, understatement, hyperbole, bombast which, though accurately translated, may not be apparent to the readership. Above all, they are obliged to indicate any instance of prejudice in the text: sexism, racialism, chauvinism, ageism, prejudice based on class, mental and physical health, colour or religion.

Uncommon ability in writing their own language, shrewdness, perceptiveness, exceptional common sense — these are the qualities translators have to bring to their job. Through the job the translator is a critic, an interpreter and rips up sham; not so much a walking dictionary and a reference book as a person who knows where and how to find the information required.

A hundred years ago, English translators were considered as leisured and literary figures: often a professor of classics or a diplomat who translated in their spare time. Now they are seen in various main roles: in UNO, UNESCO, EC, OECD, Council of Europe and other international organisations, translating working papers, reports, journals, pamphlets, brochures, publicity to facilitate communication between representatives of member countries, as well as publicity for the organisations themselves; in government departments, translating classified or secret material (in UK, Ministry of Defence Joint Technical Language Service, Government Communication Headquarters); in company translation departments (in West

Germany, indicatively, more probably in marketing and sales divisions — information from Adrian Brown), translating correspondence, reports, publicity blurbs, speeches, training films, telexes, faxes, summaries, abstracts, specifications, instructions, manuals to help sell, operate or maintain products and equipment; as freelancers, they may be translating original papers for academic journals to help researchers to keep up with what their foreign colleagues are doing; for publishers, the written texts of art books to be produced simultaneously in various European countries; important books in the field of the sciences, the universities and creative literature for the purpose of disseminating masterpieces and spreading knowledge of their country's culture; a few will be dubbing or sub-titling films and doing literal translations, a regrettable practice or necessity, for better known poets and playwrights who do not know foreign languages to pretend to a translator's role where the essential empathy is lacking; many freelance and spare-time will be translating all kinds of material for the greatly increased number of translation companies — a glance at any *Yellow Pages* is enough to confirm that no licence is required to set one up. Bilingual secretaries being now well paid, some will be working under that guise. The position is improving, but there is a long way to go before a translator has the security and the prestige of an Intertext translator in the late GDR.

Various, difficult to organise, straddled awkwardly across desirably at least four languages and four cultures as well as a specialism, persons who should spend two thirds of their working time at home or a library and one third out and about — the future position of translators is as difficult to define as the term translation itself.

But the future role of translators is less open to question. They must be seen as key figures in promoting better understanding among peoples and nations. They must not be regarded as anonymous. They are responsible for all definitive, therefore written, bilingual and interlingual communications. They have the authority to mediate between parties, and they have their own responsibility to moral as well as factual truth. They are invisible only when a communication is clear and leaves nothing to question. In other cases, where there is doubt or cultural bias — and this includes the translation of political, philosophical and sociological works as well as of creative literature, they should write a separate preface, explaining how they have treated the work, how they have interpreted any controversial key-terms, and, when appropriate, where and why their translation differs from previous ones — a translated novel without a translator's preface ought to be a thing of the past, and therefore the preface as well as the work should draw the reviewer's attention. Thus the translator offers an insight into language and linguistics as well as into another culture.

3 Translation Today: The Wider Aspects of Translation

Introduction

Translation is linked with an awareness of democratic potential; it is a weapon against obscurantism, the realisation that the material, social and cultural inequalities often associated with ethnic and linguisitic groups as well as with gender, race or class, are not God-given or natural, that they have to be at least drastically reduced. And so you have Canada, Spain, Belgium, Romania, Yugoslavia — all countries where social equilibrium is related to free interlinguistic communication, and the publication of their statutes in all their national languages. And so you have the North–South gap, the need for developing countries not only to assert the written expression of their own languages (all countries are more or less multilingual) but also to determine the role of languages of international communication as a means of importing aid (Band Aid, Sport Aid, exam aid — it must multiply). And so you have the problems of Nigeria, Malaysia, India *vis-à-vis* English, particularly when Tamils support English against Hindi and some Catalans even support English against Castilian Spanish. And so you have the formation of world-wide, continental and regional organisations, the official as important as the counter-official, such as Amnesty International, all dependent on translation and interpretation for the conduct of their affairs.

It is a long way — but it is only about 50 years — from the time when translation was largely an activity of literary scholars catering for a cultural and leisured readership remote from the market-place. The millennial discussions about the difficulties of translation — inadequacies, impossibilities, splendours, miseries, treacheries, artificialities, complexities — still persist but they are pathetic, confined to a restricted though important field: authoritative, philosophical, literary texts. The new element now is the why, the function of translation — for what reason, deliberate or involuntary, on what grounds, for what purpose is a translation required? I'm not saying that the 'why' is more important than the 'what' — the function than the substance — the now fashionable view of some translation theorists and clients

42

particularly in West Germany. One doesn't normally translate *Messer, Kölnisch-Wasser, Lufthansa* adequately as a 'cutting-tool', 'a freshener', 'the German airline'; this suppression of the substances leaves the way open for all kinds of ambiguities. What remains true is that in time but not in importance, function comes first, and is always easier to specify than substance or essence, which may be culturally bound.

I have often defined the two purposes of translation as accuracy and economy, begging the obvious question of whether accuracy refers to the content of the source language text or the true facts of the matter, or even the sub-text, the intended effect on the reader. What I now want to propose and re-order are the five wider purposes of translation, and then to relate them to translating.

The first purpose is to contribute to understanding and peace between nations, groups and individuals. Note that this formulation puts more emphasis on the pragmatic than on the referential component of translation — the effect on the readership, the manner, the style, which is scoffed at by many technical translators — the difference between the neutral and the polarised sense: French *régime;* English 'régime', 'potentate', 'ruler', 'raj', 'despot', 'benevolent dictator'. More concretely, it means that however a word such as 'sack' may be disguised as: 'rationalisation', 'redundancy', 'getting rid of the fat', 'early retirement', 'voluntary severance', 'supernumerary', 'supererogatory to requirements' — at the receiving end, the sack is the sack and neither *sacquer* nor *sabrer* nor *rausschmeissen* has the same sickening effect — the unique monosyllabic English deverbal noun.

The second purpose of translation is to transmit knowledge in plain, appropriate and accessible language, in particular in relation to technology transfer — defining technology not in the old sense of applied science, but as all the means and knowledge used to provide objects necessary for human sustenance and comfort. This is the most obvious task of the translator, the dragoman, as the indispensable concomitant of trade, barter, free exchange, gifts — first mentioned separately in the literature by Schleiermacher. This should be seen as the translator's routine occupation, validated in a healthy international community by commercial and co-operative treaties where, since law comes into it, translation problems immediately multiply — and the French barrister who tells you that the French for 'common law' is *common law* (F) is merely displaying his own arrogance as it will not be understood by more than a very small number of French people; a term — perhaps *le droit coutumier britannique* — has to be officially agreed. (Translators should always mention the official or recognised translation, even if they feel impelled to add a comment with their vicious weapons — their disclaiming *sic* or square brackets, which they ought to make more use of.)

The third purpose is to explain and mediate between cultures on the basis of a common humanity, respecting their strengths, implicitly exposing their weaknesses. This does not necessarily mean translating every cultural expression by its cultural or functional equivalent, e.g. *ishmael* by 'paria' or 'kaffir', which is an unspeakable racialist word in South Africa, or by 'giaour' or 'outcast'; or *heart* by 'kissing' or 'feelings'. It means at least an awareness of the irrationality of attributing good or bad human qualities to animals, e.g. dragons, Chinese or European, of the possibility of administering beneficial as well as injurious cultural shock through literal translation, which can expose irrational customs as well as pretentious language; for a Soviet, 'social life' means 'Party work'; in Chinese 'how are you?' is a straight enquiry after a person's health and 'how old are you?', 'what do you do?', 'how much do you earn?', 'are you married?' are all questions which may open up a normal conversation. Language can conceal crimes with generic words/euphemisms such as 'organise', 'nerve agent', 'asymmetric capacity', 'take out', but literal translation can show up the depths of one nation's culture by converting it into words where emotions that have no target language connotations are exposed in their absurdity and grotesqueness. You can see this when you consider the macho and manly language devoted say to boxing or even horse-racing (the 'sport of kings') and bullfighting ('the manly art').

Respecting a people is paramount, but its culture cannot be respected in the same sense; it may be vicious in one particular or another. There can be something sobering and human in translating the excessive cultural expressions of one language into the less besotted language of another through literal translation; take duelling as *une affaire d'honneur,* also *the weaker vessel,* the menacing funeral rites and sacrifices related to some religions, the music, blessing and pageantry once associated with war — these can be deflated like swollen metaphors when they are reduced to a literal sense.

The fourth ancient purpose is to translate the world's great books, the universal works in which the human spirit is enshrined and lives: poetry, drama, fiction, religion, philosophy, history, the seminal works of psychology, sociology and politics, of individual and social behaviour. These are the works which, in principle, should be retranslated for each generation, where the universal outweighs the cultural. Yet here the translator has to resist the temptation to be too explicit, to reduce the metaphor, the symbol, the connotation, to sense; the translation, like the original, is written to delight as well as to instruct.

The fifth purpose is as a general aid or as a skill required in the acquisition of a foreign language.

Needless to say, these five purposes, which may be crudely summarised as the political (or the humanistic — there should be no difference), the technological, the cultural, the artistic and the pedagogical, may overlap, and indeed converge in the translation of this or that text. Further, it would seem peculiarly pointless to rank them in any order; the technological, sometimes the political, may be more urgent, the artistic the more enduring (but it has to be regularly revised) — at one time or another, all may be equally important.

Translation as a Profession

A profession may be defined as a calling requiring specialised knowledge and long and intensive academic preparation; originally it was restricted to divinity, law and medicine. In Romance languages the term usually means an occupation from which one gains one's livelihood (the French equivalent is *profession libérale*). In the twentieth century at least, many occupations have changed their names in keeping with their aspirations to a higher status, often notoriously comically, leading to translation problems: in English not only 'dustman' to 'refuse collector' but 'clerk' or 'secretary' to 'director' or 'chief executive', and there are a number of words related to manual work, intellectual work, and not working at all, such as 'technician', 'mechanic', 'artisan', 'engineer', 'doctor', 'amateur', 'dilettante', 'artist', 'technologist', as in any upwardly mobile world which has left dubious cutural deposits in various languages.

In world terms, the translator's occupation has been transformed since the foundation of FIT (International Federation of Translators) in 1953, the promulgation of the Translator's Charter at Dubrovnik in 1963, and the Unesco Recommendations of 1976 in Nairobi. In brief, this reflects the changing position of the translator from an amateur to a professional status, from private or local to national; from an invisible and anonymous position to a visible and responsible presence; from a person untrained or semi-trained at an institute to one educated at a university. It is stated, in the words of the Translator's Charter, that in spite of the various circumstances under which it is practised, translation must now be recognised as a distinct and autonomous profession. Note that interpretation which is often conflated with translation in this country, unfortunately and misguidedly in the new Institute of Translation and Interpretation, is a separate profession, although the criss-cross of oral translation of written texts and the compromise of consecutive interpretation also have to be practised. Professionalism can be defined in various ways, and I propose now merely to make my own definition of the various attributes of a professional translator.

First a translator must be a member of an autonomous and nationally accepted professional body consisting only of translators — not language teachers, interpreters or *Sprachmittler,* i.e. people working partly in translation or other language activities. Remuneration and conditions of work must be in accordance with the requirements of the professional body and the translator must not be asked to meet unreasonable deadlines. Secondly, the translator is as responsible for any text he or she translates — as its author. The translator has the duty of being 'faithful' to the original text only in as far as it does not conflict with the material and the moral facts as known. If a defective text is likely to mislead the readership (not otherwise) the translator has to correct it or express dissent, within or outside the translation as appropriate. Unless a waiver is plainly issued, the translator is answerable for the translation, to the extent even of appending a 'not found' footnote against a neologism that has to be interpreted. The translator does not have to be expert in the topic of the text, but the text must be understood and translated in the appropriate, peculiar, ordinary or technical language.

I am suggesting the translator has a potential responsibility for 'intervening' if there are the following types of defect in the original:

1. Slips, misprints, miscopying (say *anatomie* for *autonomie)* because the typist misread or misheard. (Any text.)
2. Errors of scientific or material fact.
3. Bad writing, i.e. illogical structure, poor syntax, ambiguity, redundancy, clichés, jargon. (Mainly in informative texts.)
4. Statements infringing accepted human rights.

The manner of the intervention may involve consultation with author, editor, or client and may in practice include corrections, rewriting, deletions and comments outside or within the text (translator's square brackets, '*(sic)*', footnotes or preface, depending on whether the text is authoritative, literary or occasional and anonymous). The translator should refuse to translate a text only if the conditions implied above are not met, or simply if she or he does not feel competent to translate it.

Thirdly, the translator has to be a graduate and to take an appropriate part-time or full-time vocational course at a university-type institution. In my opinion the course curriculum should consist of 60% translation practice according to requirements (in the UK two-thirds technological, one-third institutional (*viz.* economic, political, social, financial) texts) including a course in précis, summary, gist, functional translation (answering specific questions on source language (SL) text) and *ad hoc* or sight translation (written to oral); 10% technical backgrounds, with emphasis on the explanation of concepts (as in Scharf's (1971) *Engineering and its Language*); 10% SL and target language (TL) cultural backgrounds, *(Landeskunde,* area studies) with emphasis on human geography and institutional terms. Further, there should be courses in techniques of machine translation, including practice in the work translators will have to do (the course should be free from jargon, sales-talk and one-upmanship about the latest models), and translation criticism of a variety of texts, which is also an invaluable exercise in revision, and which should include a few literary and philosophical texts. Lastly there should be a course in principles and methods of translation; as a subject-title, I abandon Translation Theory since it gives the impression that theory is one thing and practice is another. The syllabus should include: (a) a theory of the process of translating (approaches, process, revision), a functional theory of language, a broad eclectic theory of translation, and a frame of reference setting out translation problems at all ranks from misprints and punctuation (e.g. the ubiquitous French colon) through metaphors, proper names, neologisms, cultural words, eponyms like 'Thatcherism', words with no clear-cut one-to-one equivalent (no-equivalent words) (e.g. 'jaunty'), acronyms, familiar alternatives (Leipzig's *Weisheitszahn* as the Karl-Marx University), symbols, and grammatical groups and clauses, titles, paragraphs and the general problems of the text, the final court of appeal; (b) the varieties of contextual factors headed by the readership, and the setting; (c) the multiple translation procedures, a different list for each type of problem. But this syllabus should be seen as a tactful setting for the discussions of options and difficulties, in the form of solution-proposals supported by arguments, and references to similar examples. This is the key and core course in the curriculum, the academic discipline that co-ordinates the other subjects. Being essentially a generalisation of translation problems, its purpose is to be useful to the translator.

Depending on national requirements, there could be other courses in the programme or curriculum: subsidiary cognate languages (from scratch), terminology, technical writing (LSPs), and service translation, translating *from* the language of habitual use which has to be done in most countries and most institutions, however much some translators disapprove of it.

The above curriculum is designed for general non-literary translators who would also work on a translation plus commentary of substantial length as a lead in to a specialism. The curriculum would be substantially altered if there were sufficient demand, say for literary or legal translators.

Lastly, translators must have a period of three to five years' work experience as apprentices before they become professionals. The body of professionals are staff translators, including revisers, working in international organisations, multinationals, private companies and translation companies (no longer agencies), as well as teachers of translation and of principles of translation in colleges and universities, who should all be part-time translators. Freelance translators are often specialists in a few technologies; literary translators usually work on contract, and write themselves; in the Soviet Union nearly all poets are translators.

There is a need for a new position of translation consultant, who should have considerable experience as a translator or translation teacher as well as of publications and research. Research in translation is lamentably scarce in this country. A translation consultant should advise governments and ministries, public organisations and companies on their translation requirements and output and, within his or her competence, should give an expert opinion on the interpretation of translated documents and aspects of language planning.

The translator's code of conduct is laid down in the Dubrovnik Translator's Charter, in particular as regards confidentiality and open negotiation of fees depending on the specialised nature of the text and with reference to deadlines which even now are continuously miscalculated or ignored by clients in many countries who think all problems are solved by bilingual dictionaries.

Given a world where everyone wants to learn English, it is not surprising that attitudes to translation are more backward in the USA and the UK than elsewhere, but also in France. Certainly there is improvement: multilingual leaflets in tourist offices, brochures in country houses and churches, notices in terminuses and airports, 'surtitles' (close translations displayed on a screen above or close to the stage) at the Royal Opera House, advertisements for Telecom (now co-written) in the underground. There is an apparently more receptive attitude to translation in British industry. Since the EC, translations abound in every supermarket in the country. Sometimes, when one sees the street notices in Cardiff or even Dublin, they respond to national pride rather than to realities.

All this is in startling contrast to the position of translation say in China and the USSR, where translation as well as translations are eagerly discussed; in Hong Kong, bookshops have substantial sections on translation. In many areas in the world, notably (in my experience) in India, Malaysia and Catalonia, translation is a political and cultural issue in a sense unimaginable here. Take South Africa, the 'bilingual' state, as a Johannesburg professor in translation told me smugly a few years ago; Xhosa and Zulu are each spoken by more than the total number of whites put together, and Sotho by nearly as many. Further, there is a pidgin Fanagolo, formed from Zulu, Afrikaans and English components which is widely spoken. Thus Africa's linguistic problems are enormous, particularly as the Colour Bar state for so long encouraged mother-tongue-only education, thereby preventing the majority's vital access to English, the language of technology. Fortunately in the last 40 years, English has not been so tainted with colour-bar ideology as Afrikaans, the language with a troubled future. According to an ANC representative in London, English is at present the lingua franca. Language planning and renaming of place-names have not yet been discussed. Language planning problems are intimately connected with translation problems, but 'translation' is a kind of taboo word in linguistics textbooks, as semantics once was among linguists. (Thus Trudgill's (1974) excellent *Sociolinguistics* is stuffed with translations but the word is not mentioned.)

I have tried to give you my idea of the professionalism of a translator. Only in one area (perhaps) — poetry — is a translator born not made. Aptitude tests for translators are therefore as irrelevant as they are for language learners and according to John Henderson (1984) even for interpreters.

The specific skills of the translator include first, sensitivity to language; secondly, the ability to write neatly, plainly, nicely (three no-equivalent words) in a variety of registers in the target language as well as having a good knowledge of its cultural background; thirdly, the ability to research often temporarily the topic of the texts being translated, and to master one specialism; lastly, a good reading knowledge of two or more foreign languages with their cultural backgrounds.

The more technical the text, the less important the knowledge of the foreign language; instead, the linguistic skill in the home language comes first. Say you get a specialist medical text peppered with: *nous avons eu l'occasion de . . . nous en profiterons; on note; nous voyons; prenons un exemple; rappelons que; il ne faut pas oublier; il s'agit de; rappelons-le; cela a permis d'attribuer; ainsi est-il possible de soupçonner son intervention; il ne faut pas perdre de vue. . .* The above is an object lesson in discourse analysis, and literal translation goes by the board.

The translator also has to have certain general qualities: (a) common sense, or the ability to detect and expose nonsense; (b) discrimination in weighing one option against another; (c) speed in working against a deadline; (d) the ability to think of several things at the same time; (e) meticulousness, the attention to details — figures, SI units, spellings, omissions, proper names, though this isn't so important if, as it should be, all work is revised; (f) lateral and vertical thinking (the ability to let one's mind *play* around a problem (see Edward de Bono's numerous books).

Translation and Language Teaching

The place of translation in foreign language teaching will always be dependent on the role that the learner and the teacher assign to the native language in the learning process. (I am excluding the case where skill in translation is one of the aims of the learning.) At one extreme you have C. J. Dodson's (1967) Bilingual Method, which maintains that translation combined with pictures is the foundation of good language teaching, that it offers security and eliminates interference. The printed 'word', it is claimed, is best even at primary level, but must be dispensed with in aid of speech as soon as possible and the ostensive method (i.e. pointing) combined only with pictures will always lead to confusion, and so on.

At the other extreme you have the Direct Method, which by excluding the home language automatically excludes translation.

I do not question that both methods, when taught by able teachers who are convinced of their value, are successful — the personality of the teacher transcends methods and materials.

That leaves us with the position of the teacher or learner who wants to use an eclectic method in a climate of communicative language teaching, of variations on notional/functional approaches, role-playing, games, and graded objectives.

There is now fair agreement that psychologically, socially, culturally, and indeed politically, as prestige value, the first aim in non-specialist and general language learning is competence in the spoken language, even though reading the foreign language and translating it for one's colleagues and friends is professionally and personally often more useful. Since language learning (like translation) is beset with opposing forces and arguments, the place of translation in achieving this aim, i.e. understanding and producing speech, is never going to be settled. In the earliest stage it can have only a subsidiary role; translation into the foreign language of any difficult text, the 'prose', is likely to inhibit progressive and graded learning, skipping essential steps, and be time consuming. Translating into the home language will be useful only for purposes of communication whether the texts are easy or difficult. What remains is translation, either of words, sentences or brief texts, from the home to the foreign language as a form of control and to some extent of consolidation, as the quickest and most efficient and objective method of testing the grammar and the vocabulary that should already be known. Since in language nothing is actively known that cannot be produced spontaneously and automatically, such a test, which should be time-limited, is an appropriate complement to a regular oral test.

In universities the purpose of degree-level translation is often not clearly identified. Some teachers use it — L1 to L2 or L2 to L1 — as a means of improving 'style' in the relevant target language, with their own fixed ideas of what a rather literary, refined and old fashioned style should be, without paying all that much attention to the style of the original, thus: 'In these letters D unlocks his heart' *(s'épanche)*; 'here he is in the maturity of his mental vigour' (that's just *pensée*), 'his longing for solitary seclusion' *(son voeu de retraite solitaire)*. Other teachers use it as a means of increasing vocabulary (synonyms, lexical sets and series, antonyms) and flexibility in switching grammatical shifts (they don't call it that). Others see it as an exercise in virtually literal translation, to expose the mechanics of the foreign language.

There are two more uses: (a) as what I call a 'communicative' translation, i.e. a text set in an appropriate social style or register, where the units or stretches that express individual character are normalised for the sake of the readership, therefore converted to natural usage; and (b) as what I call a 'semantic' translation, where unusual collocations, original metaphors, neologisms, words used in a special sense, peculiar sentence-lengths, grammatical constructions, punctuation are all reflected in a corresponding degree of 'deviation' in the translation in a rather literal sense, and the text remains embedded in the source language culture. (Something like these alternatives is suggested in Henry Widdowson (1979).)

I have suggested five types of translation exercises at this advanced but non-professional level; in each case the students should know: (a) precisely what is expected of them; (b) how it is going to be assessed; (c) the title, author, date, etc. of the source language text.

In an exam all translations should be assessed by a second marker as well as the teacher, if not an external examiner as well. Both forms of assessment, viz. the impression mark and the analytical assessment have to be used. I see a marking scheme of pluses and/or minuses, one the mirror image of the other, as necessary; and I think the general impression, the assessment of 'readability' on which both markers must comment with a few words, are equally necessary, provided it is remembered that readability as such bears no relation to accuracy.

Translations should be discussed in class, guided by a teacher who rejects any idea of a 'fair copy' or ideal translation and readily adopts better amendments in his/her own version.

Machine Translation

No chapter with a title as pretentious as mine could omit a passage on machine translation. The reason why this one is so brief is that this subject is not my field. But machine translation, like translation, is not only possible, it exists, and it is developing rapidly. Its *raison d'être* is its cost-effectiveness, and here in some restricted areas, notably weather reports and some fields of scientific translation, it has proved itself. In other areas, notably more general texts such as those in use in the EC, it is not yet cost-effective, and a considerable, some would say excessive amount of pre-editing, interactive editing and/or post-editing are required. There is continuous improvement in pursuing complicated structures and in handling idioms and polysemous words in particular and figurative language in general. In many areas, input has to be restricted to a limited language, and copy is produced raw but sufficiently clear to answer the questions giving simply the information required by clients. Whilst most systems need heavy post-editing, the way that some texts get recast by imperious company revisers suggests that this isn't unique.

Recent Literature

It is somewhat ironical that the main present-day controversies about translation still appear to derive, at various removes, and, as they say, degrees of sophistication, from the conflict between free and literal translation. 'Free' is an umbrella term, and in this broad sense it may be said to cover, on the one hand, the present linguistic preoccupation with discourse analysis, the communicative and social function of language and on the other, translation as ideology, a historical view of translation as shown in the current 'translation norms' prevailing at a period and within a society. 'Literal' represents the look back to the SL text, a meticulous examination of the words, an unfashionable view (it always has been).

In fact in the last seven years a number of more or less important books have appeared in English about translation, perhaps three times as many as in any period of the same duration. B. Bettelheim's (1983) *Freud and Man's Soul* is the only work of the second trend. The others are Albrecht Neubert's (1985) *Text and Translation*; *The Manipulation of Literature* edited by T. Hermans (1985); *Difference in Translation* edited by Joseph Graham (1985); *Translation: Linguistic, Philosophical and Literary Perspectives* edited by W. Frawley (1984); *A High Art. The Art of Translation* (1984) by Kornei Chukovsky. I should also mention *Grundlegung einer allgemeinen*

Translationstheorie by H. J. Vermeer & K. Reiss (1984) and finally Roda
Roberts' forthcoming book on translation theory.

Before I comment on some of these books, I should like to single out a
basic translation contradiction which is sharply illustrated in Tytler's (1907)
classic work on translation originally written in 1790. The translator is seek-
ing to reproduce, in Nabokov's words (1964), the 'exact contextual meaning
of the original'. In Tytler's words, this becomes a 'complete transcript of its
ideas' and a replica of 'its style and manner of writing'. However, as I see it,
this is only true if the original text is authoritative; if it is not, then the translator is trying to reproduce the true facts of the original in a natural and
appropriate manner. All this appears to be scientific, a matter of laws and
principles, rules and precepts, a method based on evidence.

On the other hand, meaning is a matter of interpretation, and interpretation is a matter of choice. As soon as one makes a choice, however
restricted, ideology comes in. Tytler's first two laws of translation concern
the translator and the original, there are no other considerations. But when
he describes a good translation as one in which the merit of the original is so
completely transfused into another language as to be as distinctly
apprehended and as strongly felt by a native of the country to which the language belongs as it is by those who speak the language of the original work,
he brings in a new factor — the reader.

And here, he later abandons science and turns outrageously to ideology. The reader is an eighteenth century gentleman of good taste and judgement and he must be suited. Any vulgarity such as 'you often vomited upon
my bosom and stained my clothes', any slang, any dialect, the style of the
Evening Post, the low cant of the streets or the dialect of the waiters of the
tavern — all this is inappropriate, whether it is in the original or not. When
the original fails or descends to bombast, it is the translator's duty to
improve on it. Later, Tytler in a superb passage criticises Voltaire's distortion of Hamlet's 'To be or not to be' soliloquy, detailing the passages that
Voltaire has omitted, and accuses him of transmuting the 'pious and
superstitious' Hamlet into a thorough sceptic and free thinker.

I have tried to show that one can distinguish a universal from an
ideological side in Tytler's book. The ideological is of interest to the cultural
historian; the universal to the translator.

Hermans's (1985) *The Manipulation of Literature,* some articles in
Poetics Today (Tel Aviv) and the special triple issue of *Dispositio* (1982)
(University of Michigan) tend to discuss translations as ideology within the
target language culture and to analyse their 'norms' without any close refer-

ence to the original. (Thus there is an article on 'Translated Literature in France 1800–50' without a single quotation, let alone a translation example.) 'The new approach tries to account in functional terms for the textual strategies that determine the way a given translation looks, and more broadly for the way translations function in the target literature' *(Dispositio,* Vol. 8, nos 19–21). The approach is descriptive and target-language oriented. There is particular emphasis at one end on the types of patronage that induce the translations and at the other, on the receptions and reactions of audiences and readers at the time and subsequently. The approach is interesting, but what is missing is naïvely betrayed by Hermans. 'The old essentialist questions about the prototypical essence of translation are simply dissolved, and the way is open for a functional view'. How simple, how simplistic. I think this means that the importance of accuracy and truth in translation is a question to be ignored, or 'simply dissolved' and all that matters is the function of the translation in its 'new' setting. In spite of its abstractions, this is the crudest statement I know of the view that once one knows the why (purpose), both the what (content) and the how (form) become irrelevant.

Hermans's group is not interested in value judgements, in the retrospective comparison of translations with originals (after all, the group is merely TL oriented), in the setting-up of criteria relating referential to pragmatic accuracy in a way that might be helpful to translators today. All studies are relativised to a consideration of the functions of a translation at a given period. Any idea that functions might be universal and not entirely bound to a literary coterie or social class at a particular period, that translation may have an essence if not necessarily a prototype, is seen as beside the point. In the language of these writers, function becomes its own self-justification.

I take Neubert's (1985) *Text and Translation* as at once the most *durchdacht* (thought through) and *untererläutert* (under illustrated) work on the application of discourse analysis to translation that I know. Some of the few translation examples he does give are disconcerting: thus Goethe's celebrated *'das Übersetzen ist eines der wichtigsten und würdigsten Geschäfte in dem gesamten Weltwesen',* 'translation' (not 'translating') is quoted as 'one of the most important and most "honoured" *professions* in the world'; *'das spezifische Leipziger Fluidum'* becomes 'what adds up to' or 'what comprises the sense and character of Leipzig'. *Fluidum* where the nearest translation 'atmosphere' is not available, is arguable enough, though I think 'sense and effect' or 'influence' is nearer to the version offered.

What worries me is that although *spezifisch* has two quite satisfactory one-to-one translations available, viz. 'specific' or 'particular', two paraphrases, one idiomatic ('adds up to') one formal ('what comprises') should be preferred. If there is no valid argument *against* what someone writes, why translate with something else? Is it to make it flow better? That is the danger of discourse analysis.

Neubert runs through the gamut of most of what has been written on discourse: Grice's co-operative maxims, Fillmore's frames, all the world's scenarios, Beaugrande's coherence, Halliday's cohesion, Van Dijk's macro-structures, Beaugrande & Dressler's intertextuality, Marx & Engels, no less — they all get roped in, and there are some, though all too few, lively pages on cricket headlines, meal differences and newspaper reports. Beaugrande's jargon — textuality, situationality, intentionality, not to mention various '-icities' and '-ibilities' is heavily drawn on, but Beaugrande's precise 'prototypes' (e.g. 'the man on the Clapham bus') which derive from Rosch are mysteriously transformed into prototypical texts, superstructures and encounters of which no instances are given.

The weakness of such overdetermination of discourse, this oversociali-sation of language is demonstrated in Neubert's (1985: 116) declaration: 'Deviations from the expected, i.e. intertextually accustomed texture, ranging from the whole format to individual words and structures in L1 texts may be attributed to mainly subjective incompetence'. This suggests to me (clearly it's not deliberate) that any original writing (any unexpected for-mats, words, constructions) is an instance of sheer incompetence — there-fore studying Joyce or Shakespeare means studying incompetent, deviant, unsocialised (a sin) discourse. When Neubert says that in translated texts, deviations from the expected are the result of an objective divergence between the textual conventions of the two communicative communities he implies that all texts should run on tramlines. He can't imagine that one may want to translate for oneself sometimes or just for one person rather than a ghastly or ghostly communicative community.

In this atmosphere, it is refreshing to return to Chomsky who in spite of his view that the growth of language is predetermined by genetic factors, that linguistic competence is rule-governed, continuously asserts a creative view of language that appears to escape preconceived ideas and social con-straints — and denies an exclusively communicative role to language — what a paradox.

There is a dreadful dogmatic tyranny about such remarks as 'Equiva-lence holds between texts only'. In fact, there is normally much closer equivalence between corresponding words or collocations in original and translation than in their texts, and such equivalence is more objectively measurable. 'In translating', writes Irona Sorvali (1986) 'one is transferring texts, not words nor meanings'. I would say one is transferring all three, it depends on how you prefer to look at the process — at least all words in the SL text have to be accounted for. You may not translate the *or* in *or, il était déjà 8 heures,* or the *ja* in *das ist ja unmöglich,* but that would be a deliberate choice if you think *or* or *ja* is better implied than overtranslated.

Text or discourse is the ultimate court of appeal, but in the majority of cases, the collocation or the frame or semantic field are enough to anchor the words — thus *auge* will be 'knot', if *Holz* is around, or *arbre* will be 'shaft' if *puits* is around. The more structured the text, the more important and useful the findings of text linguistics to the translator. Twenty-five years ago Halliday rightly wrote that all grammatical units of language: sentence, clause, group, word, morpheme had equal value (that was before text had been discovered). I'd add text and paragraph to this series of five equals, though I suspect that Halliday would regard 'text' as superior now.

An important aspect of text linguistics' application to translation is the prosodic analysis of discourse, which gives it a third dimension of 'relief', showing what elements in a sentence are new, give an answer to an implicit question or an obscure remark, or are to be emphasised. This is realised through the word order, or the particular emphatic words or structures *(c'est lui qui,* 'there arose a quarrel') of each language. Functional sentence perspective incorporates this technique, where emphasis is shown by the degree of communicative dynamism.

Jacques Derrida is one of the few surviving gurus in French culture, and his interest in translation, culminating perhaps in the essay *Des Tours de Babel* (1980), has always been significant. When he discusses the multiplicity of meanings in key words, his work has translation applications.

Thus he warns that proper names like 'Babel', far from being, as Mill said, outside language, contain a multiple layer of historical meanings: not only the proper name but, also 'God', 'confusion of languages', 'confusion of a situation'. Again, when one is translating philosophical texts, if one meets *pharmakon* in old Greek, or *Aufhebung* or *Gift* in German, one has, in a full new translation, on the level of an educated readership, to transfer these key words as well as giving one or two of their contextual and relevant senses. Thus *pharmakon* may be 'remedy', 'recipe', 'poison', 'drug', 'philter', thus bizarrely akin to the German *Gift* or 'poison' which was once a 'gift' as in *Mitgift,* a 'dowry' and is a concomitant gloss on the view of gifts as obligatory not free, the basis of social exchange, in Marcel Mauss's *Essai sur le Don* (1925). Lastly take Hegel's notorious *Aufhebung,* the synthesis that thesis and antithesis lead up to, Derrida's *La Relève,* 'the relief', the 'supersession', which includes the contradictory activities 'take up' and 'put away', a continuous process of simultaneous inclusion and exclusion — again, if this word is used in a translation in the Hegelian sense, it has to be transferred and relevantly 'pin-pointed' in English not disguised as 'sublation' (the fashionable term given in Flew's *Dictionary of Philosophy*).

Thus it is not surprising that for Derrida the translation does not depend on any theory of reception nor does translation have any form of communciation as its essential mission. Here he is following Benjamin (1955) who as I see it always sees a translation neither as a copy nor as an interpretation but as the complement or the completion of the original. It is the skin on the fruit, the shell on the kernel, the cape enclosing the body. Benjamin's implication is that this is best demonstrated in interlinear translation, where the literal translation of the words, though impeded by grammar will lead to a pure universal language which is truth, where the dualities and varieties between languages will appear side by side in a new language, a strange prophecy coming from the analyst of the varieties of reproduction, who might have realised that the ultimate effect of this incest or intertranslation is the grey uniformity of Common Market language. It will not lead to the richness of meaning of the pure universal language which absorbs and ingests the half-cultural half-universal meanings contained presumably in the 4,000 languages of the world. So what can the translator learn from Derrida and his adepts? Mainly I think a kind of sensitisation, an awareness of the slipperiness of meaning, the continual displacement, difference, dissemination, disuse, deposition, deconstruction, which, according to Derrida, calls all translation into question if it affects subtle texts.

Chukovsky (1984) is a delight to read. He opens a world which I have found in India and China, but not in Europe, where translations, translation criticism and even translation theory, are passionately discussed. While he frequently condemns literal or mechanistic translation ('translation is concerned not with words nor sense, but with impressions' — equivalent effect again), his most damning criticism, directed as much against Soviet ('party hacks' he implies) as against English translations, is that a writer has strayed from the original. When he quotes scathingly, he is normally concerned with some lexical inaccuracy and I assume that his condemnation of literal translation is directed mainly at quaint Victorian syntax, of the type 'were he to come', 'may we not now consider'. Chukovsky is so keen on faithful translation ('it is easier to do more than to do the same'), documentary fidelity, precision, authenticity, it is hard to see him as an anti-literalist.

On one page he says he wants 'precision' above everything else. The next three pages he is condemning 'precision' at every turn.

If one defines an idiom as a current and frequently used group of collocated words whose meaning is not clear from the common meanings of its constituent words, then any literal translation of such idioms into another language is more often than not a nonsense. Take the German *das hat mir noch gerade gefehlt,* inadequately translated in Collins as 'that was what was missing', 'that was the last straw', 'that caps it all'. 'That was all that was missing' comes closer in various contexts. If the mistranslation of idioms was all that Chukovsky was campaigning against, no one could quarrel with him, but his wholesale outcry against literal translation is misleading.

William Frawley (1984) has produced a new theory of translation in suggesting that an SL text is drawn from a matrix code which supplies phonological, syntactic, semantic and 'literary pragmatic' information; in principle, it should translate into a 'target code' which represents the corresponding norms of the target language. However, the translator creates a 'new code' which has its own life, where fidelity to the original is a 'dubious criterion' — such a notion has to be abandoned. All translations are either 'moderate' (viz. faithful or free) or 'radical', where they follow the new (third) code. In support of his theory, Frawley analyses a translation of just three lines of a Neruda poem by Nathaniel Tarn, where interestingly he gives reasons at every level for Tarn's deviations from the literal truth. As a model for poetry translation criticism, Frawley's theory is so general that it can be summoned to prove anything or nothing. (The rest of the book includes a brilliant and debatable analysis of eight stages of poetry translating by Robert Nye and much reworking of old themes, such as a distinction between 'tree-men' (literalists) and 'forest-men' (freemen).)

The translation issues I have been reviewing have all reflected variations that are *grosso modo,* in their rough outlines, on the side of free translation. In my view, on the side of literal translation, as successor to Valéry, Benjamin, Nabokov, there is only the psychologist Bettelheim. However, Bettelheim's (1983) great work of translation criticism, *Freud and Man's Soul,* is not as arcane as Benjamin's, nor as crude as Nabokov's translation of Pushkin (1964). He clears the ground on the basis of plain truth, using linguistic and contextual evidence. He demonstrates and corrects not only several critical technical terms, written by Freud in German ordinary language but translated by James Strachey as Greco-Latinisms: e.g. *Fehlleistung* as 'faulty achievement' or 'failure to achieve', not 'parapraxis' (it's now 'Freudian slip'); *Trieb* as 'drive' not 'instinct'; *Schaulust* as 'sexual pleasure in looking' not 'scopophilia' (but note the neatness of the Greek and 'voyeurism' is also available). Bettelheim also points to the plain inaccuracy of the translation of ordinary words: *grausam* ('terrible') as 'shocking', *Unheil* ('disaster', 'evil', 'harm') as 'trouble', *Gruppe* ('group') as 'mass', *Elend* ('penury', 'misery') as 'poverty'.

These are typical translator's undertranslations — 'understatement' Bettelheim calls it — the meanings of the German words are stretched beyond their contextual limits by Strachey. Undertranslation is the translators' occupational disease, their *déformation professionnelle*, a tendency to water down words and metaphors, a fear of the truth in the source language.

But Bettelheim's merit is not simply to point out a few mistakes. He interprets and contrasts the 'ideologies' of the original and the translation. Freud, Bettelheim explains, saw psychoanalysis as a subtle gentle layman's art or skill, as one of the *Geisteswissenschaften*, the humanities. Freud's English translators, however, wanted to assimilate psychoanalysis to the *Naturwissenschaften*, the natural or physical sciences. Thus they deliberately coined a latinised jargon to translate mainly simple commonly used words, culminating in the three main concepts, the *id*, the *ego* and the *superego* in place of the 'it' *(das Es)*, the 'I' *(das Ich)* and the 'over-I' *(das Über-Ich)*, as well as the 'psyche' in place of the 'soul' *(die Seele)* a word said to be as embarrassing to the Anglo-Saxons as a reference to God. (It is unlikely, however, that either of the translators, Strachey or Brill, leaned toward behaviourism.)

Bettelheim identifies the two ideologies (humanism and behaviourism) and interprets them against their different backgrounds in time (50 years) and place: the first's broadly educated Hapsburg readership contrasted with the second's narrowly educated Anglo-American readership. Here Bettelheim shows an objective sociological grasp; but he goes beyond neutrality when he insists on the translator's respect for the original, on values beyond culturally and socially-bound translation norms, on a respect for the 'literal truth'. (The punning collocation demonstrates the deceptive, imaginative nature of figurative language.) Freud's terms were used in German in unusual, even bizarre, collocations and contexts, but they have to be translated literally, however odd they may sound, since it is a principle of translation that when a word is used in isolation (e.g. in an inventory, in a nonsense or surrealist poem) and so is relatively context-free, it returns to its primary most common meaning. Further, the more frequently such original terms are used, the less odd they become, the sooner one gets used to them (cf. the so un-Mozartian first 22 bars of the Dissonance Quartet K 465, where oddity soon deepens into profundity).

Bettelheim is a good person to stop at, since his analysis offers a kind of synthesis: on the one hand, a faithful rendering of an important, authoritative text; on the other, the translator's obligation to translate 'not only the words but what is implicit in the words' (in this case, the Greek mythology of Oedipus, Narcissus and others) when the putative readership is unlikely to understand them. Essentially, this can only be done in the form of a preface linked to brief footnotes. This is an integral part of the translation — this is the translator's responsibility.

4 Translation for Language Teaching and Professional Purposes (With Particular Reference to German)

Translation from L1 to L2 in the initial stages of language teaching is mainly useful as a brief time-saver. Assuming the class is conducted in L2 and ostensive definition fails or is not possible, occasional recourse to L1 is helpful to ensure that the pupils are not guessing the wrong meaning. For English pupils this practice may not be as frequent in German or Dutch teaching as in non-Germanic languages, as the latter have fewer basic words in common with English.

In the elementary stages, translation from L1 to L2 may be useful as a form of control and consolidation of basic grammar and vocabulary, particularly where L2 is a synthetic language such as German or Russian, whose words are less context-bound than those of more analytical languages. This form of control should be regular but sparing, should not usually introduce new L2 items and must not dominate the teaching, which is aimed at L2 production of a freer kind. Literal translation of occasional L2 idioms may also be useful as a pathway to comprehension and memorisation. The distinction between word-for-word and global meanings of idioms and standard collocations has to be made clear.

In the middle stages, translation from L2 to L1 of words and clauses may be useful in dealing with errors; therefore interference, interlanguage or unconscious translationese can be illuminated by back-translation, as an aid in the production of creative discourse or texts. I am assuming that texts as such will not be translated. Occasionally, translation from L2 to L1 is useful for the expansion of SL vocabulary, particularly for items within one semantic field or topic; this becomes an exercise in synonymy.

In the advanced or final stage of language teaching, translation from L1 to L2 and L2 to L1 is recognised as the fifth skill and the most important social skill since it promotes communication and understanding between strangers. Translation from L1 to L2 is usually imperfect, approximate and essential in many situations. Usually, the L1 text or discourse should be modern, topical, natural and common. Translation from L2 to L1 covering fiction, newspapers, periodicals as well as notices and advertisements, is a means of expanding language knowledge as well as consolidation. A distinction must be made between, on the one hand, the natural language of communicative translation and, on the other hand, translation used to clarify the mechanics of L2 or the particular use made of it by the L2 writer, possibly without heed to communication. Translation at this stage encompasses dictionary and encyclopaedia, 'universal' communication and national culture, words and proper names, both geographical, personal and institutional — all are important.

Translation is important as an exercise in accuracy, economy and elegance in manipulating a variety of L2 registers in a first degree.

Translation is a relatively new professional, sometimes dated from the Nuremberg trials, or the recruiting of staff translators in the 1950s — new, due to the great increase in the varieties of translation texts and the number of texts and languages translated. There is a changed emphasis from literary to linguistic, from art to skill, from proposition to communication.

The first qualification of the translator is the ability to write neatly, naturally and deftly in his language of habitual use, in a variety of registers appropriate to the topic and situation: to write 'plain' language. ('Plain' — honest, direct, clear, unadorned, sincere, smooth, simple — can hardly be translated one-to-one into any other language.) The translator uses fresh language, with the stress not on outdated grammar rules but on avoiding the vogue for jargon words like 'interface', 'parameter', 'perception', 'expertise', 'interaction', 'crucial', 'communicative', 'input', 'grassroots', 'end of the day', 'coal-face', 'strategies', 'precipitation', 'presentation', and so on, and still knowing when to use them.

Secondly, the translator has to be conversant with and responsible for the topic, the referential meaning of the text: he or she has to check figures, facts, places, proper names. The translator's first responsibility is to the truth, to the facts of the matter, and in informative texts this responsibility precedes his or her responsibility both to the author and the readers of the text. Further the translator has a responsibility to the principles of human rights — in this sense, the translator is neither objective nor anonymous.

Thirdly, the professional translator has to have an appropriate knowledge of at least two, and normally more than two, foreign languages.

Translators are trained in vocational courses, normally at a university. At least half of the curriculum should consist of translation practice, and over a quarter of background subjects — viz. area studies *(Landeskunde, national culture)* and the relevant technical subjects, centred on the understanding of their concepts and terms. There should also be a place for translation theory and methods, viz. the body of knowledge about methods of translating texts, syntactic strutures, metaphors, neologisms, proper names, institutional and cultural terms, etc. within the context of the setting and the readership that have won some acceptance. Translation theory and methods, which is always nourished by and calls upon translation examples, is the nucleus of the discipline of translation and should occupy about 10% of a full-time course. Translation criticism should not be neglected either; it will assist students to improve and look critically at their own work.

Lastly, in the UK, a vocational course should normally include optional instruction in translating additional languages cognate with the main languages.

German, in spite of the recent improvements in numbers taking examinations some years after comprehensive reorganisation in the maintained schools, is the most undertaught foreign language in the UK and apparently the language most in demand in the translation profession. It should have a privileged position in vocational translation courses. There are particular opportunities available for translators with English as their language of habitual usage in the four mainly German-speaking countries, where translators are more respected and better paid than in the UK, as well as in most international organisations.

German is a significant contemporary language of world thought and world literature (*Geistesgeschichte* (Dilthey) and *Weltliteratur* (Goethe) are both German coinages — I cite the work of Goethe, Nietzsche, Freud, Marx, Weber, Engels, Lukacs, the Mann brothers, Kafka, Brecht, Böll, Luxemburg, Celan, Husserl, Einstein, Hahn, Heisenberg, Grass, Heidegger, Hesse, Schnitzler, Kraus) where translation and retranslation are necessary. It is also the language of the heart of Europe, the meeting-point between East and West, the language of *détente*.

Among the particular problems of German-English translation are:

- German's lack of an informal language register corresponding to the English use of the impersonal 'you' and English phrasal verbs and

nouns — a German text is therefore often more formal than its
English translation;
- German has longer sentences which sometimes have to be divided;
- the English translation may be 30% longer;
- German's use of modal connectives such as *ja, eben, also,* etc. which
are omitted or overtranslated in the English version;
- German's often specialised use of Greco-Latin words;
- German's syntactic structures (e.g. participal, premodifying groups,
das plus adjective as a nominal group) which offer choices;
- the contrast between FRG and GDR institutional and politically
coloured terms;
- Swiss and Austrian political and legal terms;
- differences in nominalisations, where British English is rivalling
German through American English;
- German's more flexible use of word order.

Translation is a valuable means of promoting understanding between
individuals, groups, organisations and nations as well as a medium of cultural transmission and information and technology transfer. In the 'age of
translation', it now has a certain vogue. It has its own fascination, is a source
of personal pleasure, is continually a puzzle and a mystery, and is a source
of access to new words and facts.

5 The Use of Systemic Linguistics in Translation

Introduction

Since the translator is concerned exclusively and continuously with meaning, it is not surprising that Hallidayan linguistics which sees language primarily as a meaning potential should offer itself as a serviceable tool for determining the constituent parts of a source language text and its network of relations with its translation. In fact, ever since the appearance of 'Categories of the theory of grammar' in 1961, followed by Catford's (1965) *A Linguistic Theory of Translation* (which acknowledges its debt to Halliday and to Firth) Halliday's approach to linguistic phenomena that are at once formal and functional appears to me as a translation analyst (rather than theorist) to be more *useful* than Chomsky's TG or the behaviourist Bloomfield's immediate constituent analysis (who ever uses ICA now?) or any of the variants of artificial language or logic propounded, for example, by the Montague Grammarians, in spite of the latter's not infrequent references to translation.

Already in 1960, when he wrote 'General linguistics and its application to language teaching', Halliday (1967) was stating that 'the theory of translation is an important, if somewhat neglected, aspect of general linguistics' and suggesting that translating proceeds by three stages: (a) item for item equivalence; (b) reconsideration in the light of the linguistic environment and beyond this (it is almost an afterthought) 'to a consideration of the situation'; (c) reconsideration in the light of the grammatical and lexical features of the target language (TL); where language no longer provides any information.

Writing in 1960, Halliday omitted the indispensable 'cohesive' stage, which he and Hasan (Halliday & Hasan, 1976) were virtually to introduce into linguistics in 1976. As I see it, these are *levels* rather than *stages*. It is part of the artificiality of translating, that the translator has to be thinking of and working on the four levels ((1) textual, (2) referential, (3) cohesive, (4) naturalness — that is, the correspondence to or deviation from normal social usage) at the same time, whilst admittedly all translation problems are ultimately those of the TL, even at the fourth level of translating, the source language (Language 1) continues to provide information, since the translator may be wrestling to adjust his or her version to various formal and semantic aspects of, say, the SL sentence. (I should qualify this by stating that many translators and translation analysts such as the ESIT–Paris school would support Halliday's view when they state that *les mots* (of the SL text) *disparaissent.*)

Halliday stresses the need to have a set of descriptive terms based on a theory of language to compare any two languages, whether for the purpose of teaching or translation. From a translator's point of view, I think the main descriptive units (an extension of Halliday) are a hierarchy: text, paragraph, sentence, clause, group, word, morpheme. In abstract terms, none of these are more important than another (as Halliday states) though in practice, the text is the ultimate court of appeal, the sentence is the basic unit of *translating* (not of translation), and most of the cruxes are centred in the lexical units, if not the words.

On the basis of this terminology, it is possible to show that, say, an SL nominal group may translate into a TL nominal group or a TL adverbial group or be shifted upward to a clause or sentence or downward to a word: thus the semantic equivalence between on the one hand *la science linguistique* and, on the other, 'linguistic science', 'in linguistic science', 'the science devoted to linguistics', 'the science which is concerned with linguistics', 'the science is linguistics', and 'linguistics', much as it varies in stress is closer than the lexical synonymy of 'linguistics' and 'philology'. Systemic grammar demonstrates the flexibility and multiplicity of grammatical variations, which, however, within a text have always to be adjusted to factors of emphasis.

An SL group can often be 'rank-shifted' into a TL word or clause: crudely thus

> Es gab *einen guten Grund* für ihre Tat
> Il y avait *une bonne raison* pour leur action
> There was *a good reason* for their action
> They acted for *a good reason*
> They acted *because they had reason to*
> They acted *justifiably*

(On the surface, the literal translation appears the most appropriate, but there could be contextual reasons for preferring one of the others.) As I see it, most 'linguistic' shifts (or 'transpositions' as Vinay & Darbelnet call them) can be described in this way, and Catford, by usefully introducing 'level' shifts (grammar to lexis, and vice versa e.g. *il ne tarda pas à arriver,* 'he soon came') is introducing another dimension of grammatical change.

For the translator and the translation critic, Halliday's terminology is invaluable for the pin-pointing of problems at varying grammatical levels, which are lexically criss-crossed by collocations such as *inaugurer une exposition* (open an exhibition) including almost nonce-collocations *(not* 'clichés') such as *zeste de citron, d'orange)* and metaphors expanding from 'one word metaphor' through 'extended metaphor', 'proverb', 'parable' to 'allegory'.

Halliday states that

the equivalence of units and of items is lost as soon as we go below the sentence; the further down the rank scale we go, the less is left of the equivalence. Once we reach the morpheme, most vestiges of equivalence disappears. The morpheme is untranslatable; the word a little less so, but it is nevertheless very rarely that we can say that a particular word in language 1 must always be translated by one and the same word in language 2.

This calls for some comment. In general terms it has a truth, and it is a warning against translationese. However, there are thousands of Greek and Latin morphemes in hundreds of thousands of words in many world languages (say 'trans-', 'histo-', 'junct-' '-ism') which are usually perfectly translatable, either as TL morphemes (i.e. one-to-one translations) or as words, groups or clauses. Further, most, but far from all, specific technical terms in a language must always be translated by one and the same word in L2. As for common words for common objects, events and qualities within an analogous pragmatic and referential situation, all I can say is that it's a pity they are not more often translated by 'one and the same word in language 2' (rather than by some egregious 'synonym'), since this would assist truth and mutual understanding, the two things that translation is all about. Whilst it is true in principle that a particular SL word is very rarely translated by one and the same word in every context, most lexical units have a core (most frequent) meaning, which should not be stretched beyond certain limits, and it is perverse to avoid using its TL equivalent because it is too obvious, or because its TL form is similar to its SL form. Denotatively, 'music' and 'theatre' are similar in most European languages except Czech — except where a theatre is an hospital theatre! (Figuratively, the translations vary.)

Halliday's article on 'Linguistics and machine translation' (1967) is not particularly enlightening about the nature of translation but *Introduction to*

Functional Grammar (Halliday, 1985) includes at least two chapters that demand attention.

'Beyond the clause: metaphorical modes of expression' in particular draws attention to grammatical metaphors, and is centred on the non-physical figurative use of verbs. In metaphor, translators always have a choice, and whilst they have no need to distinguish between ideational and interpersonal metaphors, or metaphors of transitivity and modality, (Halliday's definition of metaphor is wide) the numerous examples of metaphorical forms and 'congruent' (or 'literal') rewordings could sensitise a translator to the need for frequent recasting. Thus Halliday's (1985: 331) rewording of: 'The argument to the contrary is basically an appeal to the lack of synonymy in mental language' as 'In order to argue that this is not so (we) simply point out that there are no synonyms in mental language' could be a normal translation of this sentence in French or German. The removal of verb-nouns ('argument', 'contrary', 'appeal' and 'lack') is a common 'shift' (Catford's word) or transposition in translating informative texts, often for the purpose of elimination of jargon. Halliday (1985: 328) gives eight further examples of such translations to 'congruent versions', or of the dejargonising of language.

In another example:

In bridging river valleys, the early engineers built many notable masonry viaducts of numerous arches (Halliday, 1985: 330)

the congruent 'natural spoken' (?) version seems to me to be unnecessarily explicit or explicated:

In the early days, when engineers had to make a bridge across a valley, and the valley had a river flowing through it, they often built viaducts which were constructed of masonry and had numerous arches in them; and many of these viaducts became notable.

French and German could, I think, do this more succinctly:

En faisant des ponts qui traversaient les vallées, les premiers ingénieurs construisaient beaucoup de notables viaducs à arches nombreuses.

As I see it, this chapter could form a useful part of any translator's training course where English is the source or target language. Halliday's advice to a linguist: 'unscramble as far as is needed' (cf. Hass (1962) 'The unit of translation should be as short as possible and as long as is necessary') is even more pertinent for a translator faced with such sentences as 'The fifth day saw them at the summit' (C'est au cinquième jour qu'ils sont arrivés au sommet) or 'The guests' supper of ice-cream was followed by a gentle swim',

(Zum Abendessen haben die Gäste ein Eis gegessen und nachher ein gemütliches Bad genommen). The emphasis (FSP) in the German has, however, been sacrificed to naturalness.

Note that though the German is a little clumsy, both translations are less scrambled than Halliday's English versions ('In the evening the guests ate ice-cream and then swam gently'), which demonstrates (a) that meaning is better explained by interlingual translation than by so-called 'intralingual translation', and (b) that the qualitative difference between 'interlingual' and 'intralingual' translation is so great, that it makes a nonsense of the concept of translation; however there is a fuzzy area of adaptation in between (e.g. Coghill's version of *The Canterbury Tales*).

Cohesion and Connectives in Translation

The topic of cohesion, which may have first appeared in Hasan (1968), was expanded in Halliday & Hasan (1975), and revised in Halliday (1985), has always appeared to me the most useful constituent of discourse analysis or text linguistics applicable to translation. In brief, it is a matter of looking carefully at the connectives or missing (cf. case and translation) connectives between sentences, both notionally and in their linguistic substance, and, in the case of an 'informative' or 'social' (vocative) text (as opposed to an expressive or authoritative text) deciding how far to intervene, thus:

> *On sait, depuis le début du siècle, que le sérum sanguin est, per se un mauvais milieu de culture. Mieux même, dans un nombre appréciable de cas, on a pu démontrer qu'il était d'un certain pouvoir bactéricide. (L'immunologie. Que sais je Series.* PUF)

Linguistically and logically, but not referentially, this extract would appear to be nonsense: the first sentence (with its 'mauvais') appears to be negative, the second positive. Is the translator to leave it as it is or to 'explicate it'?

> Since the beginning of the century it has been known that blood serum is in itself a poor culture medium (for bacteria). An even greater advantage is that in a substantial number of cases it has been shown to have a certain bactericidal capability

— or to produce a compromise translation that implies rather than spells out the further advantage of the second statement?

Examining connectives is an essential part of revision, and Halliday's (1985) chapter 'Around the clause: cohesion and discourse' offers a comprehensive treatment.

Many connectives may belong to more than one of the notional categories. The main translator's problem with 'grammatical' or functional words in any language — connectives and prepositions in particular — is that being within a closed system, each has such a large number of meanings often shading between 'additive' and 'adversative' in a way that may make a considerable difference in the semantic relation beween the sentences.

Social Translation

Even though man is a social animal whose psychical life is primarily concerned with his relations with his objects, each individual is also a separate psychobiological entity with a continuous and independent awareness of self. (Rycroft, 1956)

Through the interpersonal function of language, social groups are delimited, and the individual is identified and reinforced, since by enabling him to interact with others, language also serves in the expression and development of his own personality. (Halliday, 1970: 143)

Halliday (1974) believes that Bühler's expressive and conative functions of language are not distinguished in the linguistic system and for this reason he has collapsed the two functions into the interpersonal function. Perhaps there is a danger that as in the second epigraph, the individual may tend to get lost rather than 'identified and reinforced' among all those social groups.

This is a philosophical argument, with which I am not concerned. But if the translation of some texts takes place more or less at the author's level, and that of other texts at the readership's level — a sometimes amorphous readership which I have to postulate as a translator and at some risk to mentally characterise, then operationally I have to insist on the distinction between on the one hand, expressive (individual, subjective, idiolectal) language, language that primarily reflects the thought processes of one person's mind, and on the other, conative (vocative, social, phatic, informative) language, language used for purposes of communication, of social exchange, that mediates an aspect of reality or social goodwill. As I see it, this is reflected in the difference between a sentence such as *Je suis un arbre* which normally has to translate as 'I am a tree', and a sentence such as *Veuillez agréer l'expression de mes sentiments les plus distingués* which is normally 'yours faithfully'. Consciously I am making no value-distinctions. (Implicitly I am.) I merely indicate that I, like everyone else, use language for much longer periods, and more intensively for the purpose of talking to myself or for thinking and dreaming than for the purpose of speaking or writing to other people.

As I see it, there is a basic distinction between the individual and the social use of language that reflects the two different functions. The individual or expressive use of language is that of thinking, of personal writing, of reflection. It may be realised in serious imaginative literature, in autobiography, in personal correspondence, in innovative writing. The social (Lyons' term) or 'vocative' (Holmes) or 'operative' (K. Reiss) use, is that of phatic language such as 'Take care' or 'Have a nice day' to 'How long did the flight take?' or 'Did you stop over at Delhi, or Bombay?'); the normal forms of conversation, that are required for immediate comprehension; the formulas and the informal language used in notices, instructions, propaganda and advertising; the more or less predictable language of persuasion and direction. In a period of limitless and ubiquitous reproduction, photo-copying, faxes, prints, walkmen as well as records, videos and cassettes, the link between the TV and the fat paperback, everything tends to encourage the social use of language, which, in translation terms, is addressed to a readership rather than one reader. With all that the social use of language is not necessarily contaminated by repro, retro and jargon; I am not suggesting that there is a correlation between good and bad writing on the one hand and individual and social language on the other. Further, individual and social language merge (the 'cline') — here, as so often in language, there are fuzzy fluid furry edges.

I have made in terms of *notion,* a distinction between types of text and thinking that broadly represent social communication and individual expression. In terms of *substance,* social communication is expressed in phaticisms, standard idioms, standard metaphors, standard collocations, jargon, clichés, colloquial language, normal unsurprising language use.

Individual expression is shown in unusual language such as unconventional punctuation and sentences with innovative grammar, original metaphors, unusual collocations and neologisms (old words with new meanings as well as new coinages).

Since the substance and the forms of one language are most cleanly exposed in translation, I propose to take two instances from writers whose work is a continuous example of 'deviant discourse' (a hideous expression, referring to 'odd' poetry and the like, apparently used in contrast with communicative discourse). Take Butor's (1957: 208):

Rose, ma Perséphone, ma Phèdre, ma Rose qui s'est ouverte dans ce marais de paralysie et de gaz lourds, depuis le temps des grands

brouillards, hélas non point ma Rose, mais seulement Rose, l'interdite
Rose, la dérobée, la réservée, la vive, la simple, la tendre, la cruelle
Rose.

Rose, my Persephone, my Phèdre, my Rose who has opened in this
marsh of paralysis and heavy gasses, since the time of the great fogs,
alas not at all my Rose, but only Rose, the banned Rose, the concealed,
the reserved, the live, the simple, the tender, the cruel Rose.

The expressive elements here are the long apostrophe without a verb, the
repetitions, the enumerations, the three unusual adjective-noun collocations *(interdite, dérobée, réservée)*, the unusual placing of *paralysie*. Most
of these can be reproduced in the translation, although the rendering of
interdite, dérobée and *réservée* is inadequate in relation to the original. The
two proper names are hesitantly transferred for the purpose of retaining the
original sound effects (lost in *grands brouillards)* and the powerful connotations of the word *Phèdre* for at least some anglophone readers.

Note that I have distinguished the expressive features, but that they
merge with the normal conative and 'neutral' (semantic, informative) features in the passage. A passage consisting only of expressive features would
be unintelligible; they are always in contrast to the 'normal' features of
natural usage.

Secondly, take a passage from Joyce's (1969) *Ulysses,* interlined with
the published French (Joyce, 1975) and German (Joyce, 1976) translations:

E: White horses with white frontlet
G: Weiße Pferde mit weißen Federn am
F: Des chevaux blancs, avec un frontail

E: plumes came round the Rotunda
G: Stirngeschirr kamen bei der Rotunde um
F: de plumes blanches tournaient le coin de

E: corner, galloping. A tiny coffin flashed by
G: die Ecke, galoppierend. Ein winziger Sarg blitzte vorbei
F: la Rotonde au galop. On entrevit un tout petit cercueil

E: In a hurry to bury. A mourning coach
G: Im Trab zum Grab. Eine Trauerkutsche
F: En trombe vers la tombe. Une voiture de deuil.

E: Unmarried. Black for the married
G: Unverheiratet. Schwarz für die Verheirateten
F: Non marié. Noir pour les gens mariés

E: Piebald for bachelors. Dun for a nun
G: Scheckig für Junggesellen. Dunkelbraun für Klosterfrauen
F: Pie pour les vieux garçons. Bai pour les curés

The main expressive features here are the sound effects: the shortening staccato rhythms, stichomythic phrases, the two rhymes, the vivid onomatopoeic sounds.

Note that the German brilliantly reproduces virtually all the expressive features, with a semantic weakening only at *Trab* ('trot') for 'hurry'. The French has to sacrifice many features; but *on entrevit un tout petit cercueil* is a strange dull normalising transfer from expressive (semantic) to social (communicative) language, and I find *bai pour les curés* ('bay for the priests') inexplicable, unless it is translated from a variant, or intended as a poor rhyme.

As I see it, *Ulysses* is the exemplar of a work where the expressive function of language operates at all levels — sound, word order, sentence length, metaphor, register-break (period, dialect) (cf. *Stimmungsbruch),* collocation, neologism, archaism, allegory, and given the exceptional richness of this multi-contracted English, it is a translator's nightmare to produce congruent deviations not deviances from the communicative norms of their target languages. A glance at the opening lines of the novel ('bearing', 'bowl of lather', 'ungirdled', 'aloft', 'halted', 'faced about', 'thrice') is evidence enough; continuous undertranslation appears to be inevitable.

I have tried to show by argument, category, linguistic analysis and instances that when language renews itself, the expressive and the conative function are continuously distinguished. The expressive is the agent of renewal, of the individual, of creation both in thought and substance; the conative, the function that ensures that an appeal is readily understood, usually relies on accepted social forms of language — with the exception of startling advertisements (and commercials), where expressive forms break the linguistic conventions.

Cultural Translation

Language is a substantial but partial reflection of a culture, culture being defined here as the total range of activities and ideas and their material expression in objects and processes peculiar to a group of people, as well as their particular environment — thus 'pampas', 'tandoori' and 'curculio' are cultural words. Language is also universal and individual: thus 'sea', 'head' and 'earth' are universal words. Translation is always more or less possible because of the universal and the culturally overlapping constituents of language.

Culture is an aspect of the social in language. There is hardly a book on intercultural or interlinguistic relations between Chinese and English that does not state that 'dragons' are kindly and protective in Chinese, baleful in English; 'red' is ceremonial and happy in Chinese but 'cruel' or 'frightening' ('Red' China) in English; mourning is black in English but white in Chinese; the sun is as oppressive in Arabic countries as it is lovely in England; thus demonstrating the 'impossibility' of translation. But this is not so. Many cultural beliefs and connotations are brittle — in particular, the superstitions that associate animals with human qualities in the various languages and countries. They are always a translation problem, but not in the sense of the strong Whorf-Sapir thesis, which suggests that different languages represent separated thought-worlds. In fact, the only problem is the degree to which the cultural expression is to be explained in the translation, which may range from not at all (leaving the readers to calculate the meaning from a combination of the linguistic context and from their own reading in the SL culture), through a few hints to a full explanation in terms of functional (neutral) or even TL cultural equivalents. Cultural items demonstrate or conceal universal values. The fact that in Chinese, many conversations start with 'How old are you?' 'Are you married?' 'What's your job?' 'How much do you earn?' may disconcert a Western reader, may cause temporary cultural shock but it is salutary and productive of more interesting conversation than the customary nauseating Western phaticisms. Through translation, this may break through to non-Chinese readerships.

If the translator's first task is to contribute to understanding (and peace) between individual groups and nations, and the second is to transmit knowledge (technology transfer), then the third is to mediate cultural features not so much in terms of target language cultural features ('cultural equivalents') which are pragmatically vivid but usually inaccurate (e.g. 'A level' as *baccalaureat*, 'cricket' as *pétanque*, 'sun' as 'oasis' or 'shade' etc.), but in terms of universal experience and ultimately common humanity. Thus the 'dragon' or the 'sun' or the Egyptian or ancient Greek 'serpent' may be glossed as 'mild' or 'kindly' rather than replaced. In this or that context translators are hampered by the house-style or the tacit censorship of their employers or clients, but their function is to enlighten, their loyalty is to material, visible truth as well as the moral truth of the ever expanding human rights documents. No longer concealed figures, to be put as so often even now in tiny letters on the back of a title page (see e.g. van Razzori, 1985) they should make more use of their two most powerful weapons: the distancing square brackets in the middle of but marked off from the text —

[. . . . . — TR] — as opposed to the round brackets that are a parenthesis as a part of the translation; and the introduction that puts the translated work into perspective rather than the ignored footnote.

Culture may be tenacious or brittle; its vestiges are deposited in languages in the form of animate objects *('die* Sonne'), ways of looking at time and weather *(il fait du soleil)* and a host of dead and standard metaphors ('kick the bucket') which no one notices until the unfortunate linguist or philologist draws them to your attention.

Culture is often mindlessly accepted within the SL and may cause cultural shock in the TL readership through a stroke of devastating literal translation, since culture is expressed in 'universal' as well as in 'local' words. (Thus 'democracy' in one country may be in universal terms, a travesty of the word.) In this sense, a translator's job may be to smash culture; the most interesting translation of *Mein Kampf* I ever saw had a preface, square brackets and notes three times as long as the translated text.

'Modernising' Translations

It has often been noted that a literary masterpiece is not usually rewritten (in the theatre it is sometimes adapted), but it should be retranslated perhaps once in a generation, normally into the modern language; this gives the TL readership a certain compensating advantage *vis-à-vis* the SL readership, who are more familiar with the culture but less so with the language of previous generations, hence *unser* (1797–1810) Shakespeare; all the translations reflect not only the literary interpretation but the translation fashions of the time. The translators are said to be the victims of their ideology as inevitably as the literary critic. They follow or occasionally challenge the 'translation norms' (Toury, 1980) of the time, by which they are in any event measured.

These statements have a certain truth, but they need to be qualified. The great Tytler (1790) in insisting on a 'just taste' and the elimination of coarseness, vulgarity and impropriety in translation, was certainly following the Augustan models of his time. Translators of novels of the First World War sometimes followed the prejudices or 'group loyalty factors' of their own country rather than the authors' (see Ivars Alksnis, 1981). One could go on subsuming or labelling one translation after another, in the manner of José Lambert (1985) and others according to various genres and ideologies. When one comes to the translation of Scott Moncrieff, Andreas Mayor, Leyris, Stefan George (there is a vast qualitative difference), I don't know what is gained thereby.

After the First World War, science began to have an impact on language (and then literature) for the first time through lingusitics, which itself was often proclaimed to be a science. If scientific method can be said to be centred in the process of verification (through evidence rather than proof), then it was inevitable that concomitantly with the enormous expansion of types of texts to be translated, translators would begin to talk about and to set up principles for the science of translation (Tytler had mentioned laws, rules and precepts, but for him translation was an art). Note, however, that Nida (1964) was concerned only with the 'science of translating', not of translation as a material for scientific description. Whilst Wilss (1982) rashly calls his translating book *The Science of Translation,* he does not define the science, apart from telling us that it is 'neither a nomologically nor nomothetically sealed but rather a cognitive/hermeneutic/associative one'.

However illusory it may be to suggest that translation is a science on the analogy that it is concerned with a 'substance' (the spoken or printed word) conterminous with if not a part of the physical and material universe, I am suggesting that with the introduction of scientific method, in particular through the important discipline of translation criticism (which was initiated not by the polysystemists, but by Bettelheim (1983), a new fact comes into translation. It does not exclude but it qualitatively restricts both the area of ideology and the free play of translation norms.

The new factor is summed up in the principle of accuracy. Given varieties of meaning and the conflict of loyalties between the author, the readership and the objective facts of the matter, accuracy is not an easy principle to define. But it has a weapon in the back-translation test, where it can at least often demonstrate when a translation is obviously (referentially, linguistically, stylistically) wrong. It rests on the assumption that there is a limit to the areas of meaning of words as well as sentences. Setting aside tasks of adaptation and partial translation (summaries, enquiries, functional translations) as cases apart, every word of the original has to be accounted for though not necessarily translated. Corresponding features and units of language have to have equal status and frequency in the two texts. Every deviation from literal translation has to be justified by citation and evidence if challenged. While allowing an area of taste in translation (the more linguistically challenging and difficult the text, the wider the area), one assumes that the scientific element in translation is vastly more important than the artistic element, that, when the crunch comes, truth will win out on beauty. The opposite was often previously the case.

Given this principle, the fact remains that translation like any other literary product more or less reflects an ideology, the less when it is concerned with facts, the more when it is concerned with feelings. Possibly it is not useful to be continuously reminded of the ideological nature of translation when one is trying to use it as an instrument for disclosing the universal behind the cultural as well as for respecting observable facts. A personal view of translation is like a personal interpretation of a literary work. If it includes a lot of other views, it is going to be blurred and ineffective rather than objective.

Conclusion

In this rather discursive paper, I have attempted to show that Halliday's functional approach to language produces many valuable insights into the process and purpose of translation. (I have not here referred to his stimulating interpretation of case, which I have attempted to make use of in another paper (Newmark, 1985).) In the examples cited, attention is rightly given to the substance as well as to the function of utterance, which some 'functionalist' translation theorists tend to play down.

In contrasting the social with the individual, the cultural with the universal, and in regarding Saussure's view that 'language is merely (?) a social fact' as a dangerous simplification which entails a semantic loss to translation, I implicitly question Halliday's view of 'social man' (his expression). None of this affects or detracts from my admiration for his work on categorising varieties of language, that is the concept of register (field, mode and tenor of discourse), familiarity with which is invaluable both in analysing a text, in criticising a translation, and in training translators.

6 The Virtues of Interference and the Vices of Translationese

In the narrow definition, interference in translation takes place when, apparently inappropriately, any feature of the source or a third language — notably a syntactic structure, a lexical item, an idiom, a metaphor, or word-order — is carried over or literally translated as the case may be into the target language (TL) text.

In a wider definition, interference includes cases when sentence length, punctuation, proper names, neologisms, or cultural words are evidently transferred in the translation, in fact all cases where the language of the translation is manifestly affected whether appropriately or not by the language of the original. In this sense interference is an intrinsic factor in any translation.

I take translationese to be the area of interference where a literal translation of a stretch of the source language text (a) plainly falsifies (or ambiguates) its meaning, or (b) violates usage for no apparent reason.

Translationese is an error due to ignorance or carelessness which is common when the TL is not the translator's language of habitual use, and not uncommon when it is.

Translationese should not be confused with interference which is sometimes indiscriminately regarded as an error, as it was till this decade in foreign language learning, where interference merges with interlanguage. 'Interlanguage' has only been treated creatively in recent years — learners often speak a foreign language with such an imaginative fusion of some features of their own and the foreign language that it would be mistaken to correct them except in formal situations.

In translation, there are various degrees of interference, and its appropriacy depends partly on the type of text that is translated; in a literary work, both idiolectal and cultural interference often enriches the translation.

Interference in translation has another characteristic: it confuses or brings together two meanings, and therefore resembles a pun. Its first impact is often hilarious: 'Venetian blinds' becomes 'blind Venetians'. Translationese jokes are usually instances of interference — they are a perennial and sometimes tiresome form of humour (as with puns, the people subjected to them have to laugh (or groan) to prove that they have understood the double sense/mistake). This applies particularly to *faux amis,* false friends, false cognates, where the form of the source language (SL) word is still transparent in the translation, e.g. from French in 'in *scabrous* conditions', 'a *petulant* speaker'; from German 'a *scrurrilous* incident', 'a *genial* idea'; from Italian 'a *trivial* expression'. This type of mistake is humiliating (and usually not repeated because never forgotten) since words have been taken at their face value, with the idea that they exist in the foreign language with the same meaning as in the language of habitual use.

Interference in translation, like the pun, may suddenly open up two senses both in the SL and the TL. A crude example is the description of Mitterand and Chirac as a *couple infernal,* an 'infernal couple', where the French has the sense of 'insupportable' and the idea of 'strange bedfellows' is introduced. 'Professional deformation' suggests 'conditioning' 'deformation' and work habits carried over into social custom.

The positive aspect of interference comes into play when the translator decides to introduce into the TL some specific universal, cultural, personal or linguistic values in the source text. As well as this, the translator may unconsciously devise a kind of interlanguage which, in the following extract is neither English nor French, but has its own charm:

> The past of Liège is the warrant of its future. Its old neighbourhoods invite you to lounging. The bluish atmosphere gives the 'Ardent City' its own complexion. Liège offers you some more quiet gardens where the 18th Century plays the shepherd. (Tourist brochure)

In general, interference can have positive effects on a second language when idioms (or words that have developed a special sense) that are not culture-specific, are literally translated, and become comments on universal human behaviour.

'Best Matt' (letter addressed to a friend)

'He's no longer the youngest'

'I wish you a lucky hand, as we Germans say'

'She's a natural animator *(animatrice)*'

'I'm the birthday child'

Strange as they may sound at first, I suggest these are a better way of enriching the language than the wholesale importation of foreign words, which is appropriate when they denote foreign natural products, particularly foods, and sometimes manufactured products, but not when they denote qualities like *perestroika* (restructuring?) or *glasnost* ('transparency' rather than 'openness' or 'publicity') which are imposed by the media too early for translators to deal intelligently with them.

Translation is simulation (pretending to be what one isn't) and in interference, the disguise shines through. The routine of both language and translation is relieved when one triumphantly comes down on the 'howler' (dreadful public school word, but there is no other), the *Schnitzer,* the *bourde.* Miles Kington has earned his living from franglais or fractured French.

The computer has classically rendered 'The liqueur is ready but the meat is thin'. Through literal translation, puns, so often pronounced as untranslatable, can be rendered effectively. Thus SI, a West German sewer cleaning firm, issues its slogan *SIcher ist sicher* which comes out neatly as 'SI-cure is secure'. Puns, on the margin of translation but with their own fascination, often go hand in hand with deliberate interference.

Interference in the language of large international organisations is positive where it improves communication by standardising terms for constitutions and procedures, but negative when it produces a loose lowest common denominator kind of jargon, stigmatised by Kenneth Hudson (1980) as 'diseased English': ('optimise', 'orientated', 'economisation'), 'activist' (anything from a 'terrorist' to an 'exemplary hero of socialist labour'). Many of these words register an indiscriminate invasion of English by Romance words.

In literary translation, disagreement is inevitable about the nature of interference. What some call translationese is accurate or close translation in the minds of others. What some dismiss as a violation of usage, may appear more imaginative and have a deeper truth than the smoother clichéd version — even though the first is mere literal translation or *transcodage,* whilst the second requires some clever, not exactly creative effort. Thus from Pompidou's eulogy for de Gaulle (10th November 1970) *Mesurons le devoir que nous impose la reconnaissance,* the easy, fluent official translation: 'We are conscious of our duty to express our gratitude' may be contrasted with the 'closer' translation: 'Let us measure (weigh) the duty that gratitude imposes on us'. Note that the second translation is more forceful, and more individual and that the collocation *mesurer notre devoir* is not much more usual than the English 'measure our duty', although the semantic range of *mesurer* is wider. Again, Pascal's *le coeur a ses raisons que la raison ne connaît pas* can be wrapped up in many ways, e.g. *Die Gründe des Herzens sind fur die Vernunft völlig unergründlich* (Paepcke, 1986), where the two senses of *raison* are brilliantly compensated by the wordplay on *Gründ* but the version is debilitated by the Germanic (not German) *völlig* and the change of emphasis and sentence perspective. The English translation is, I think: 'The heart has its reasons which Reason knows nothing of' (I have modernised the eighteenth century 'knows not of'). The stress on *connaît* is paralleled by that on 'nothing' whilst the German could be *Das Herz hat seine Gründe, die für die Vernunft unergründlich sind* which takes advantage of Paepcke's compensatory word-play but retains Pascal's stresses and is closer to the sentence perspective of the original.

Many literary translators are so afraid of interference that they would not even dream of translating a title literally. Thus Primo Levi's *Se questo è un uomo (If this is a man)* is translated as *Survivor from Auschwitz;* Malraux's *L'Espoir* as *Days of Hope;* Svevo's *La coscienza di Zeno* (Zeno's conscience or 'awareness') as *Confessions of Zeno,* his *Senilità* as *As a man grows older!* There is no justification for such distortions. Scott Moncrieff's *Remembrance of things past* is a beautiful quotation, but it should have been *In search of lost* (rather than 'wasted'?) *time* — it is too late to change it now.

Interference verges on the mandatory, on direct translation in the case of a title such as Malraux's *La Condition humaine; The Human Condition, Der Zustand der Menschen* (Extant translation titles: *Man's Estate, Storm in Shanghai!*). When a word-group is as autonomous as this one, one translates what the author actually wrote, what he would have written in the TL, not what he meant to write. Flaubert's *L'Education sentimentale,* which means 'The education of the feelings', is known always as *Sentimental Education* and though this is now somewhat misleading, virtually a mistranslation, it is too late to change it.

What I have written so far shows a general sympathy with interference. In fact, interference is the spectre of most professional translators, the fear that haunts the translation student; the ever-present trap. The term *cervicotomie* sounds English enough, but if expert assistance isn't available and if the translator resists the mesmerising effect of the SL text and realises that it appears to mean 'excision of the neck or the cervix' he may play safe by writing 'incision of the neck' since the passage deals with the carotid artery, not the cervix. Judging from the medical dictionaries, 'cervicotomy' doesn't exist in French any more than in British or American English.

Lexical interference traps are common enough, but more insidious are innocent looking collocations which appear to make sense until one asks oneself what they mean in the particular context. *Frandev (France*

Developpement) intronisée au second marché au début du mois where 'the
second market' is meaningless and the reference is to the 'secondary stock
market' or the USM, where unlisted and unquoted securities are dealt with
by private placings and dealings. *Coupes sombres dans les bois* might well be
'sinister, dismal sound of wood cutting', but *coupes sombres* is a technical
term for 'thinning out' the wood (removing the shadow, *s-ombre*?). Again,
in an economic text, a reference, in a list, to *revenu économique* may sound
insidiously innocent, and I think many translators, English or French, might
write 'economic income' vaguely identifying it with 'real income' or 'income
one can live on'. However, such meanings cannot be foisted on to *économique* and as a technical term, *revenu économique* does not exist. In fact,
in this case, only the context *(les variations des différentes composantes du
revenu disponibles des ménages: prestations sociales et revenu économique,
revenus salariaux et revenu d'entreprises* identifies *revenu économique* with
'income from self-employment' (usually *emploi indépendant)* because there
is nothing else left for the term to mean. (I call this 'default translation'.)

My last example: it appears to be irresistible to translate *fracture unituberositaire* as 'a (single?) fracture of the (tibial) tuberosity'. The tibia
(shin-bone) has a tuberosity (or tubercle) and such 'tubercular' (*not* tuber-
culous!) fractures are not unknown. But the two tibial condyles are more
important than the tubercle, and they are *also* tuberosities. And so, in that
context, *fracture unituberositaire* becomes 'fracture of a single condyle'.

There are even cases, as Paul Schmitt (1986) has shown in a brilliant
article, where standard scientific terms (e.g. 'alloy steels', *legierte Stahle)*
have different values in English and German, and therefore a transference
procedure will produce an incorrect translation.

I have given a few examples of cases where the temptation to let lexical
interference slip through is understandable, but where lexical interference is
uncreative as well as wrong. This is the other side of the coin. It may be the
mark of a bad translator to endeavour to avoid translating literally (particularly in literary works; see Newmark, 1988) but much more often, it is the
mark of a bad translator to translate literally, to look at the words without
regard to the sense, to remain on the surface of the text. The translator is at
the 'interface' (used in the technical, not the grisly jargon sense) between
two texts, and as soon as there is a translation problem, the translator at once
becomes concerned with its span — can it be solved at the word rank, can it
be compensated at another word position, or will it bring in larger stretches
at the rank of group, clause, sentence, paragraph, text?

When interference is a mistake, a 'false friend', a sign of the translator's
ignorance or inadvertence, a mark of the mesmerising effect of the SL or the
SL culture, it can be categorised as follows:

Syntactical

Many structures become ungrammatical, but perfectly comprehensible 'nonsense' when translated by a tyro, e.g. 'the by architect Wiesner built house' which could only be 'justified' if the translator were deliberately promoting it as a valuable contribution to the grammar of the target language, or as a new *Time–Newsweek* premodification gimmick.

More significant is the SL structure which exists but is less common in the target than the source language, such as French 'grammatical metaphors' (Halliday, 1985): *Une étude rétrospective nous a permis de préciser . . .*, which could be more appropriately translated as: 'After making a retrospective study, we were able to clarify . . .', or *Les malformations congénitales: de l'épidemiologie à la syndromologie,* as 'Congenital malformations: their epidemiology and their syndromes'.

The commonest syntactical mistake is when the translator neglects the peculiar properties of his or her own language's grammar, and translates *après l'avoir fait* as 'after having done it' rather than 'after doing it'.

Note that some syntactic structures could be described as phrases: *On dirait un gant,* 'It looks like a glove', but these are usually impervious to interference. In other cases, where the SL (written) construction seems so logical and to be shared by any foreign language one meets *(mon livre et celui de mon ami),* it takes some time to detach such a mainly written language form from 'my book and that of my friend' and bring it down to 'my book and my friend's'.

Lexical

Lexical interference is more dangerous than grammatical interference. Whilst the latter is usually stylistic, lexical interference can distort the meaning of a sentence. Its most obvious form is the *faux ami,* where both source and target language include thousands of Greco-Latinisms which have developed a second sense in another language (for a brief list, see Newmark, 1986: 162).

Due to the influence of international organisations, the media and other regulated language contacts, many of the senses have converged or are converging again (e.g. control, actual, *ignorer, réaliser,* global) but others, not only those denoting objects, keep the Greco-Latin sense, and translate accordingly. There are more *vrais amis* than *faux amis.*

Another type of interference mistake is when a word is translated by its usual meaning *(métier* as 'occupation') instead of by an appropriate other meaning (technical: 'loom').

Many tourist brochures are a (treasure!) trove of lexical and grammatical interference: 'A *rich* network of *internal* canals *allows* to sail up the river Piave and to enjoy the *magic show* of the lagoon valleys, where *the* nature is still the same as long ago'. Whilst 'rich', 'allows to' and 'the' are examples of interference, 'show' could be instanced as 'counter-interference', wrongly used in place of 'spectacle' to translate *spettacolo*. (In the *Sansoni* dictionary, *spettacolo* as head-word is given *ten* English translations in 13 lines, but not 'spectacle', which shows how lexicographers can connive in inaccurate translations because of their fear of interference — at least the *Collins French–English* (*spectacle*) does not go in for such silliness.)

Figurative (Metaphor)

Here interference can take many forms. If we take dead and universal metaphors (conduit metaphors) like 'space' (e.g. of 'six years'), 'foot', 'bottom', 'field' (from the human body or the universe), these appear to pervade all language but there are always differences of application, where a literal translation is of more interest in contrastive linguistics than in the rendering of precise contextual meaning.

In the case of standard, semi-proverbial metaphors (say 'between the devil and the deep blue sea', *entre Charybde et Scylla, sich in einer Zwickmuhle befinden*) there are a number of possible translation procedures which have to be weighed against contextual factors such as status, frequency, modernity, register, naturalness, and appropriacy of a metaphor in the TL. We have to bear in mind that *anything* that has a material meaning can in principle be intended or interpreted figuratively, and the translator decides whether the metaphor or the sense is to be made more explicit than it is in the original.

Word Order

Word order may have the following functions or part-functions:

(a) to indicate time sequence in reality or in the mind
(b) to indicate a statement, a wish, a question or a command
(c) to designate topic and comment
(d) to show the progression from old to new information
(e) to designate purpose, agent, action, object, indirect object and instrument
(f) to indicate time, place and manner (e.g. in German adverbials)

(g) to indicate (absolute) emphasis
(h) to indicate parenthesis or parenthetical comment
(i) to indicate that one person (or thing or action or quality) is in question, rather than another (relative emphasis)
(j) to demonstrate the grammatical relationship between one word, group or clause and another, particularly when they are uninflected.

I have listed the purposes of word order (have they been listed before?) to sensitise the translator to them, as I suspect they are often ignored (e.g. in Paepcke's translation of Pascal cited above) unless they are integrated with the divergent grammatical rules of the two languages. Frequently there is a clash between grammar and stress (the latter indicated by word order) and stress is sacrificed, although it could be preserved by a slight grammatical or lexical change: *Les positions successives que nous montrent les kinétoscopes,* 'The successive positions shown us by the kinetoscopes'. *Es folgt nun ein Konzert,* 'Now we have a concert'.

At other times, a parenthesis is needlessly displaced *(Sans doute s'est-il trompé),* 'He's mistaken, without a doubt'. At others, in informative texts, long sentences beginning with lists and concluding with verbs have their word order unnecessarily retained. In an expressive text there are often good reasons for preserving an idiosyncratic word order, but the translator has to do this wittingly. In other common cases, transferred word order can often impair the logic and the clarity of a text.

What worries me most (apart from the translation of *kahl* and *pfiff*) is the neglect of word order, for instance in Christa Wolf's simple description of Leipzig: *Uber die kahlen Plätze, die wir passierten pfiff noch der Wind . . . (Nachdenken uber Christa T,* p. 25) by the *poet* Christopher Middleton: 'We crossed the empty squares where the wind was still blowing' (p. 33) ('Over the bleak squares we were crossing, the wind still whistled . . .').

Culture

A feature of the SL culture may be an obtrusive factor in a 'persuasive' text translated for a different type of readership. Take an extract from a glamorous travel brochure for Jesolo (near Venice) showing a picture of an attractive woman: 'Jesolo can be reached so easily that my husband is able to come and see me every week-end and each time he finds me more and more sun-tanned'. (Vestiges of a conspicuous consumption culture of a past age — or recursive?) The omission of the last clause might improve the translation and help to increase the number of visitors to Jesolo, which is the purpose of the original as well as the translation.

However, the most evident form of cultural interference in translation is the transference of SL cultural words, and even more, of SL vogue words in general. The decision whether to transfer is usually pre-empted by the media rather than the translators and a discussion of the arguments would break the bounds of this essay.

Third Language

Third language interference is usually due to the translator's knowledge of another language exceeding his or her knowledge of the source language and is normally translationese. In the UK, it is rather common in universities and schools where students translate from German several years after translating from French.

Conclusion

Most problems in translation will finally reflect some kind of difference of attitude towards 'free' and 'literal' translation, and interference is no exception. Crudely, the *ciblistes* or 'targeteers' (the *Zielsprachler?*) condemn interference; the *sourciers* or 'sourcerers' (*ausgangssprachler?*) do not. In principle, if one believes in deverbalising before translating (Seleskovitch, Delisle, etc.) and considers a translation should be an independent, autonomous text, one should condemn interference. But in fact a translation can be an independent, autonomous text and still contain inroads of interference. Historically countries have benefited from interference in translation as from other effects of language contact, though they have also suffered appreciably from translationese. One has to balance one argument against another.

I think translation theory's most important task is to narrow the gap (it will never be closed) between the two approaches and methods and here interference is a sensitive touchstone, indeed a critical factor: when it is accepted that interference has its virtues as well as its vices, we shall be a little nearer to agreeing how to evaluate a good translation.

7 Word and Text: Words and their Degree of Context in Translation

Visibly and linguistically, words are put into context by their collocations, their grammatical functions and their position in the word order of a sentence. Outside language, invisibly and referentially they are within a context of a real or an imagined situation, a cultural background, a topic and a shared experience with the reader. The thesis of this paper is that there are varying degrees of each type of linguistic and referential context that bear on words; that in a text, some words are more context-dependent or bound than others and that their correspondents in translation also have degrees of context-dependency which may not be the same as those in the source language (SL) text; thirdly, that all single words have an independent meaning of some kind — their most common or core meaning results approximately from the mean of the sum of their present day uses. The core meaning of a word denoting an object or a physical action is the definition of the immediate visual mental picture the word conjures up. Words denoting qualities, concepts or mental activities conjure up mental pictures more slowly, often arising directly from their physical correspondents (e.g. 'communism', 'liberalism') in a country or a political meeting.

Finally there are words of thought, feeling, imagination and morality whose core meaning may be derived from a sum of examples, in a linguistic as well as situational context, where the connotations may even have replaced the denotation ('heaven', 'hell', etc.) but which nevertheless have autonomous, extracontextual translatable meanings. At the same time, while all words can be said to have independent separate meanings of some kind, words within semantic fields are substantially and more strongly distinguished from each other, often contrastively, by their place or value within a network of sense-relations (say 'soft' and 'mild', 'free' and 'independent').

All words can be translated independently of their context and text; and this type of isolated translation normally serves as a 'control' or yardstick of their contextual meaning.

Before going into the subject I should mention that these propositions go against the prevailing linguistic wind. At the end of the 1960s I was told there was a top level British Council meeting on EFL to decide whether the word or the sentence should be regarded as the basic unit of language or meaning, and the sentence won by one vote. In 1988, the word would get no votes at all. The prevailing wisdom is that the word has value only within or as a component of a sentence. Even more expansively, the sentence itself is 'valid' only as a component of a glorified text (as Richard Boston (1988) wrote 'Books don't exist any more. They're called texts, and you don't read them. You deconstruct them'), thus further devaluing the word. Text linguistics and the relatively new linguistic discipline of pragmatics, 'the study of how utterances have meanings in situations' (Leech, 1983), or 'the study of language from the point of view of the user (Crystal, 1988) — it seems a bit late to be coming to this study, and to make such a mouthful of the commonplace co-operative Gricean principles, 'be clear, be relevant, be brief, etc.' which sound so much like stale and obvious exam hints for writing boring essays — I recapitulate, text linguistics and pragmatics, with their emphasis on the force rather than the sense; the function rather than the description; the communication rather than the composition; have also helped to diminish the word — we are back again to Goethe's Faust trying to translate the Greek *logos,* dismissing 'word', 'sense' and 'strength' successively (the sequence is subtle and deliberate) and arriving finally at 'deed' or 'act' *(die Tat)* in anticipation of Austin and Searle's speech-acts. In fact Goethe in his emphasis on action and usefulness was often as dismissive of words as Hamlet.

The main thesis of this paper being that words are more or less affected by their contexts, and, insistently, often less so rather than more so, and often by nothing more than by the grammatical colligation (to revive a forgotten Firthian term) now sometimes called the syntagm, or the lexical collocation, I have first to define types of words as well as natures of context.

I begin with bound form morphemes as prefixes, suffixes or word-roots; they are dependent only on the words of which they form a part unaffected by any other area of context. They have specific meanings which are universal rather than cultural and are therefore literally translatable *(pace* Halliday in Halliday, McKintosh and Stevens (1964), who says they are not); if they are Greco-Latin they are often transferred in translation thus 'mega-', 'macro-', 'dys-', 'eu-', '-fer', '-nect-', 'dat-', '-junct', '-ism', '-ist', '-ity'. Morphemes as inflections are linguistically dependent on or affected by the roots with which they constitute words.

I now come to words, which for translation purposes I define as any single, isolable, meaningful units of language — 'isolable' in the sense that there are spaces on either side of them when they are written — I leave aside the vast literature on their definition. I think that all words have extra-contextual meanings and contextual senses; sometimes these two types of meaning are identical — occasionally they appear to be remote from each other but there is always some connection between the two. Extra-contextual core meaning has more impact than the various contextual senses of a word. Assuming some bilingual knowledge, I think that the most accurate and concise method of analysing meaning is through translation — monolingual definitions and paraphrases are clumsy and long-winded in comparison. Many books on linguistics and semantics implicitly acknowledge this proposition by example, though 'Translation' rarely figures in their tables of contents, their subject indexes or their introductions.

Function-words, such as 'that', 'after' and 'when', are entirely bound to their linguistic context, and normally to the grammatical rules of their languages. They have powerful and general meanings — it is incorrect to state that lexical words carry the major semantic content. They are merely more specific. The idea that function-words have little meaning is a vestige of the once current idea that grammar and meaning like linguistics and semantics are unrelated. The opaqueness and alien nature of terms like 'gerund' 'supine' 'nominative' appear to encourage such an idea, to which case-grammar is to some extent a reaction. Translation of function-words into bound morphemes is often a measure of the degree of analyticity or syntheticity of a language, but the degree of context remains constant. Function-words have universal meanings and are normally independent of cultural or subject contexts, but certain semi-functional prepositions, such as 'notwithstanding', 'herewith', *au niveau de, côté, dans le cadre de,* are more or less tied to particular degrees of formality of language, and have topic connotations which may or may not be preserved in translation. Function-words often have a large number of meanings and are tied to their linguistic and referential contexts.

At the other end of the scale, we have technical terms and brand names, which are semantically independent, normally translated or transferred one-for-one and free of linguistic as well as situational and topic context. The more specialised, the more complicated, even the larger a technical term, the more likely it is to be semantically independent, often a Greco-Latin internationalism, apart from slight naturalising of spellings and suffixes in many European languages: thus, 'haematology', 'oedema'. Such words are independent of linguistic context, but lack of shared experience with the readership may require them to be explained as well as transferred in translation particularly if they are neologisms recording new inventions or discoveries, e.g. 'groundprox', 'swingometer'. Translators also have to be careful not to render terms like *foetopathie* (F) by 'dictionary words' such as 'foetopathy' (foetal disease), which are never used.

Further, many common concept words have technical senses, which may be apparent only from the topic context, or the whole text. Thus a concept-word such as 'force' has two senses in physics; 'mass' has a conceptual sense in physics and a concrete sense in mining; 'matter' two conceptual senses in philosophy and a concrete sense in printing; 'element' has a large number of technical senses.

Often, such words will be independent of linguistic, situational or cultural context, but entirely dependent on subject context. In contrast numerous common object words like 'bit', 'jack', 'puddle', 'skull', 'strings' also have technical senses which are dependent more often on the situational than the subject (whole text) context, and are confusing if they at the same time are meaningful in their everyday sense.

Lastly, there are the technical Greco-Latinisms which are different in various languages — 'inductor' (E), *inductance* (F), 'reactor', *réactance* (F), etc., which, when they vary (e.g. *reacteur)* are entirely topic-bound (see Maillot, 1981).

I come to common words, the, say 3,500 words in any language that are in themselves neutral as regards formality, subject, personality of speaker, situation, such words as 'come', 'go', 'chair', 'table' 'rose'. Normally these have a basic extra-contextual meaning based not on their etymology but usually on the frequency of their present-day use. This is their primary central or core meaning. John Sinclair (1987) in his Introduction to the superb *Cobuild Dictionary* states that some common words have very little independent meaning, quoting 'bet' as an example. Its most common use is in the collocation 'I bet', meaning to add conviction to a statement 'I bet he won't come'. I think this is a 'freak' example, confined to one idiom, since in most people's minds it means to 'wager', 'predict', etc. and this is (of course) the first sense given in his dictionary. (Compare: *wahr, vero,* in *nicht wahr, non è vero.*)

Now, I think that the words for most common objects are normally fairly independent of the various types of context: a rose is a rose is a rose, except when it is a sprinking rose, a gem or an emblem, which is relatively rarely; a table is usually a table, but here there are more exceptions: a statistical table, a plateau, a sounding-board.

The problem is worst for translators, who have to ask themselves: what kind of a 'chair' *(fauteuil* or *chaise?)*, what kind of a 'hill' *(Berg* or *Hügel)* or 'car' it is — this is usually a matter of cultural or international context, and the more specific the object, the more independent of linguistic and situational context it becomes, provided the readership is appropriately specialised. (Unfortunately for the translator the readership is by and large the most binding form of context.)

Words for parts of the body are usually independent of all contexts unless they are used figuratively ('arm' as weapon) — in principle, any concrete word can be used figuratively — but in various languages some referents do not cover the same area (Russian 'arm' and 'hand'). I believe that in most texts and the illustrative text, there are a great many objects where you find satisfactory meaning equivalence more or less independent of context — and I am talking about word equivalence, not text equivalence. They are rather obvious but we may note 'vote', 'signature', 'secretary', 'performance', 'events', 'snubs', 'ambition' — not particularly concrete words, but could they mean anything else? And they are all translated literally here. I suggest that the most powerful contextual influence on words is the collocation: the noun that affects the sense of its adjective ('a hard core', 'a pretty sight'); the noun that affects the verb ('deliver a lecture', 'the milk churns', 'the door creaks', *'passer un contrat')*; the verb that affects its adverb ('die hard', 'think hard'). In the illustrative text there are *'collecter des signatures', 'subir des avanies, 'tenir en laisse', 'les avis divergent'*, etc.

Again, institutional like technical terms are rarely affected by their various contexts. *OPA* is 'take-over bid', *ministre de la République:* 'government minister', *le premier tour de l'élection présidentielle*: 'first round of the Presidential elections' and so on. *'Élysée'* is the Élysée (the Presidency) but the other familiar alternative term the Palais Bourbon, being not so familiar to English readers, becomes the National Assembly. Le Pen, Stirbois and Mégret all have to be explained to the readers, since the translator assumes that their knowledge is not shared with the SL readers, and so the explanation becomes the translation.

In general, verbs are much less numerous than nouns, less often assigned to particular topics or subjects, less particularised; a restricted number of them are more commonly used than nouns, beginning with auxiliaries, modals and the 16 verbs that used to be known in Basic English as operators, moving on to the common human physical and mental activities, many of which may be figuratively allotted to inanimate objects ('The year has seen, known', etc.). Such verbs enter rather obviously into collocations, often varying dramatically in different languages *'prononcer un discours'*; *'eine Rede halten'*; 'deliver a speech'); they are more determined by linguistic context than are nouns, and are less marked culturally. When they denote obvious physical actions ('sob', 'sigh', 'weep', 'laugh', 'smile' — all these words have perfect translation equivalence in many languages) they are virtually context free. However, the enormous variety/ range of senses of 30 or 40 common verbs in most languages (think of 'pass', 'move', *assurer*, 'break', *mettre, legen,* etc.) suggest they have a large number of collocations which are subject to topic as well as to the wider linguistic context.

They are often subject to the degree of formality, technicality (difficulty) and emotional warmth of the text: for example, 'supplicate', 'beg', 'adjure', 'implore', 'beseech', 'invoke', 'apostrophise', 'solicit'.

Lastly, take adverbs, which may be divided into functional and lexical words. Adverbs of time and place are functional and are virtually context free. Note on the specimen text (pp. 93–96): *invariablement, toujours* (primary sense), *aujourd'hui, bref, le plus longtemps possible,* etc., all translated neat with perfect equivalence. Adjectives and adverbs of quality are more nuancé, more difficult to characterise; in the specimen text they tend to be parenthetical and *non-gradable* and are again translated straight: *clairement, évident, évidemment, carrément, paradoxicalement.* More commonly, a quality (say 'interesting') is subject to a word that expresses cultural situational and individual criteria (say 'highly') and is gradable. Quality has more 'feel' than objects or actions, is more personal and less solid showing the intrusion of the life of the mind. What follows from this is that these words are subject to fewer outside constraints, change their meaning, notoriously become false friends between one language and another, as in words like 'loyal', 'sincere', 'frank', 'brutal', 'prudent', 'complacent', 'sufficient', 'exact', 'perfect', 'important', 'feeble', 'sage', sliding away from their meanings (note the vicissitudes of 'nice'). Many words of quality ('sophisticated', 'foolhardy', 'flippant', 'wanton', 'precipitate', the 'untranslatables') combine senses which to get anywhere near accuracy sometimes have to be separated out when rendered in another language. These are the words most dependent on at least situational context since, in order to convince, the qualities they denote come out in the text. *Traitement énergique* may become 'enthusiastic treatment', if 'energetic' sounds too violent for the patient. So in the specimen text (not a text where words are all that important), *enviable* (line 7) may be given extra force by the rendering 'no mean', though it is hard to see, even as 'feeling tone' what 'determined' (line 83) has to do with *fantastique* (line 107), which is almost a 'replica' of 'fantastic'. Possibly the translator got tired after so many close and skilful renderings. Possibly he or she couldn't see why the take-over bid should be called 'fantastique' (*fatidique* was ignored altogether).

L'OPA du RPR sur les députés du Front national

1   A première vue, tout semble aller au mieux pour M. Le Pen. Invariablement, les sondages continuent de le situer autour de
5 10 % pour le premier tour de l'élection présidentielle. Performance enviable si l'on se sou-vient qu'en 1981, le président du Front national n'était pas parvenu
10 à collecter les cinq cents signa-tures nécessaires pour une candi-dature à l'Elysée.
      Mais que fera-t-il le 25 avril ? Cette question reste l'une des
15 inconnues majeures du scrutin. M. Le Pen s'est toujours efforcé de maintenir le suspense, mais les événéments pourraient bien décider à sa place: au lendemain
20 du premier tour, il pourrait subir quelques avanies.
      M. Le Pen aurait aujourd'hui pour unique ambition de devenir ministre de la République. Erreur:
25 « *Le Pen ne cherche pas à être ministre,* confie un de ses pro-ches, *il veut rester à la tête de son mouvement, sauver ses gens pour sauver son groupe à*
30 *l'Assemblée nationale* ». Mais même de cela, le président du Front national n'est plus assuré. Son parti est secoué, son groupe à l'Assemblée nationale se
35 déchire, celui du Parlement euro-péen, sous le coup du départ de M. Olivier d'Ormesson, est en passe d'imploser. Bref, il semble de plus en plus évident que M. Le
40 Pen aura bien des difficultés à tenir en laisse tout son monde.
      La bataille entre les durs, ten-dance Stirbois, et les modernes, courant Mégret, a repris de plus
45 belle à l'approche de l'échéance fatidique. Tous n'ont évidem-ment plus qu'une seule idée en tête: tenir le plus longtemps pos-sible sur leur siège de parlemen-
50 taire, mais les avis divergent sur la méthode.
      Les durs ont clairement choisi de favoriser M. François Mitter-rand, dans l'espoir d'un retour au
55 scrutin proportionnel. C'est la consigne du secrétaire du groupe FN à l'Assemblée, M. Jean-Yves Le Gallou. Curieusement, M. Le Pen ne fait rien aujourd'hui pour
60 contrarier cette tendance dure de son parti. Au contraire, son direct-teur de campagne, M. Bruno Mégret, est aujourd'hui carré-ment pris en tenaille par le secré-
65 taire général, M. Stirbois, qui vient de lancer ses hommes-liges à Marseille pour y préparer son parachutage, et M. François Bachelot directeur de la campa-
70 gne sur Paris et qui nourrit déjà des ambitions pour les élections municipales dans la capitale. Stirbois-Bachelot, voilà le couple efficace qui fait, aujourd'hui, la
75 pluie et le beau temps au Front national.
      Déjà replié au Parlement de Strasbourg, M. Jean-Marie Le Chevallier, le directeur du cabinet
80 de M. Le Pen, est aussi en passe d'être lâché par celui-ci. Alors que l'on croyait l'affaire enterrée, M. Le Chevallier, accusé par les durs de livrer des informations à
85 la presse, passera lundi 14 mars, devant une commission de disci-pline. But de la manœuvre : exclure ce confident de M. Le Pen du bureau politique du Front
90 national et tenter de lui enlever

les cordons de la bourse du groupe des droites européennes. Réflexion dans l'entourage de M. Le Pen : « *Mieux vaut être le* 95 *coquin de Stirbois que l'ami du président. Stirbois protège ses coquins. Le Pen tue ses amis.* »

Combien de temps cela peut-il durer ? Certains ont commencé à 100 réagir contre cette « *politique suicidaire* » de leur mouvement. Mais, surtout, et c'est le fait le plus nouveau, le Front national fait, depuis quelques jours, l'objet 105 d'une fantastique OPA déclenchée par le RPR. Les discours récents de MM. Chirac et Pasqua sur la non-dissolution de l'Assemblée, l'immigration, les 110 valeurs familiales, la peine de mort, participent à l'évidence de cette opération de séduction et d'absorption. Le député de la Loire, M. Guy Le Jaouen a claqué 115 récemment la porte pour rejoindre le mouvement de M. Jacques Chirac. M. Edouard Frédéric-Dupont, député de Paris, mais qui tient avant tout à demeurer maire 120 de son septième arrondissement a déjà fait savoir qu'il voterait au premier tour Chirac. Jeudi 10 mars, c'était le président du groupe FN du conseil régional du 125 Nord-Pas-de-Calais, M. Jean Durieux, qui démissionnait pour protester à son tour contre la « *radicalisation* » du mouvement.

Au Palais-Bourbon, le groupe 130 FN n'est plus fort maintenant que de 32 membres. Deux défections suffiraient à le détruire. Une dizaine de députés paraissent manœuvrables qui pourraient 135 rejoindre le RPR ou sa succursale, le CNI, de M. Yvon Briant qui vient d'être financièrement renfloué par M. Chirac: MM. Charles de Chambrun, François Porteu de 140 la Morandière, Pierre Sergent, Jean-Claude Martinez, Pascal Arrighi, Guy Herlory, Michel de Rostolan, Jean Roussel, Mme Yann Piat. Mais il ne semble 145 pas que le RPR soit décidé à déclencher cette opération de déstabilisation avant d'être assuré, le soir du premier tour, de la présence au second de 150 M. Chirac.

Cette opération pourra d'autant plus aisément réussir, que le Front national est de surcroît aux prises avec de réelles 155 difficultés financières. M. Pierre Ceyrac a dû se rendre précipitamment aux Philippines et en Corée du Sud pour solliciter les pourvoyeurs de fonds moonistes. 160 Problèmes internes, hésitation sur la stratégie, difficultés financières : paradoxalement, un bon score de M. Le Pen, le 24 avril, risque fort de sonner pour lui la fin 165 de bien des illusions.

Daniel Carton

Specimen text — French (from *Le Monde,* 12th March 1988)

Chirac bids for FN Support

1 AT FIRST GLANCE everything seems to be going very well for Front National leader Jean-Marie Le Pen. Polls invariably continue 5 to give his party 10 per cent of the votes in the first round of the presidential election. No mean performance considering that in 1981, Le Pen failed to get the 500 10 signatures (of elective officials)

necessary for filing his candidature to the Elysée.

But what will he do on April 25? This is one of the election's big unknowns. Le Pen has always tried to keep everybody guessing, but events could well decide things for him: the day after the first round of voting, he could suffer a few snubs.

It is a mistake to think Le Pen's sole ambition today is to become a government minister. "Le Pen isn't trying to become a minister," a close aide told me. "He wants to remain at the head of his movement, save his people in order to save his group at the National Assembly." But the president of the Front National is not assured even of that. His party has been rocked, his parliamentary group at the National Assembly torn, and his group at the European Parliament is in imminent danger of collapsing since Olivier d'Ormesson's departure. In short, it is becoming ever more obvious that Le Pen would be hard put to keep everybody in his party in line.

As the election deadline draws closer, the struggle between hardliners like Front National Secretary-General Jean Stirbois and "progressives" like the party's campaign manager, Bruno Mégret, is becoming fiercer. They are all evidently obsessed by just one thing – holding on to their parliamentary seats as long as possible – but disagree on the methods.

The hardliners have clearly decided to tilt towards Mitterrand, hoping he will restore proportional representation. These are the instructions given by the FN group secretary at the Assembly, Jean-Yves Le Gallou. Strangely, Le Pen is presently doing nothing to counter his party's hardline tendency. On the other hand, his campaign manager Bruno Mégret is caught squarely between Stirbois, who recently ordered his faithful henchmen in Marseilles to prepare the ground for him to contest a seat there, and the party's Paris district campaign manager, François Bachelot, who is already eyeing the capital's upcoming municipal elections. Stirbois and Bachelot are the two who carry the most weight in the FN.

How long will all this in-fighting last? Some are beginning to react against their party's "suicidal" behaviour. But the new development is that in the last few days the FN has become the object of a determined takeover bid from Jacques Chirac's Rassemblement Pour la République (RPR). Recent declarations by Prime Minister Jacques Chirac and Interior Minister Charles Pasqua on not dissolving parliament (in case Chirac wins), immigration, family values and capital punishment are all indications of this campaign to win over and absorb the FN.

Guy Le Jaouen, the FN member for the Loire, recently quit his party and joined the RPR. Edouard Frédéric-Dupont, an FN member for Paris, who is particularly anxious to keep his job as mayor of Paris's 7th arrondissement, has already made it known he intends to vote for Chirac in the first round. On March 10, it was the FN group in the Nord/Pas-de-Calais regional council, Jean Durieux who left the party in protest against what he called its "radicalisation".

The FN Parliamentary Party in the National Assembly is now

down to 32 members. Two more defections and the FN will be deprived of the right to constitute a parliamentary group. Ten FN 115 members appear to be wavering and might go over to either the RPR or its branch group, Yvon Briant's CNI (Centre National des Indépendants) which has just been 120 given financial help by Chirac. It appears, however, that the RPR has decided to launch its bid to destablilise the Front National even before being sure of Chirac's 125 presence in the second round of the election.

The operation could succeed all the more easily as the Front National is also grappling with 130 serious financial difficulties. Pierre Ceyrac had to make hurried trips to the Philippines and South Korea to talk to Moon money managers. 135 The Front National has internal problems, a shaky strategy and financial difficulties: paradoxically, if Le Pen makes a good showing on April 24, it is very likely to mean 140 the end of many illusions for him.

Daniel Carton

Specimen text — English (from *The Guardian Weekly*, 27th March 1988)

Standard phrases, particularly if they are parenthetical *(à premiere vue), si l'on se souvient que* (7–8) as well as idioms such as *faire la pluie et le beau temps* (73–4)) are internally determined by linguistic context, but not much affected by external context, except in as far as register (degree of formality) is concerned. Thus 'considering that' is slightly less emphatic than *si l'on se souvient que.* For *faire la pluie et le beau temps* there is a choice of hoary idioms ('rule the roost', 'be the big boss', 'the big noise') and 'carry most weight' tones down the sense but avoids the cliché. Context sits lightly on such idioms, and in translation the tension between accuracy and neatness — the more polished way of saying between 'literal' and 'free' — is not perhaps as significant as in more authoritative and reference-bound stretches of text.

Before summarising my thesis, I have to mention another type of context discussed by Firbas (1979). This is the context of experience, which for translation purposes I may redefine as the common previous knowledge shared by writer and readership if the translation is to be effective. The *ad hoc* context of immediate experience (situational context) and the *ad hoc* linguistic context are both a part of the context of experience since the TL readership (Firbas's listener) becomes aware of them as the text unfolds. The old information (theme) in the text is context dependent, whilst the new (the rheme) is relatively context-independent. Paradoxically, in translation, the old information, although it is context dependent can be paraphrased, since its semantic content is already known to the readership; the new information, however, which is context-independent has to be rendered precisely. Thus in the dialogue 'What did Bob do? Bob went to the window', the second 'Bob' is context-dependent and could be replaced by 'he' or 'your friend', etc. which would not destroy the main point of the message. On the other hand a 'context-independent' stretch of text, particularly if it carries the maximum emphasis or communicative dynamism has to be rendered as accurately as possible, which means given the same emphasis as well as the same 'meaning' — the syntax as such is never of any importance in translation equivalence — note in the specimen text. *Sur la non-dissolution* (108) becomes 'on not dissolving' which is its equivalent. Such exact translation of the theme (old information) may be desirable (why translate freely if literally is just as good?) but is not essential. Again it is worth noting that the noun-object is relatively more important than the verb if the new information/theme consists of a verb and its object as in 'they have built dikes, roads and bridges' — the emphasis is on the object, which is particularised by the verb (Firbas calls it 'an absolutely essential amplification of the verb'). In practice, you can translate 'build' indifferently by *bâtir* or *construire,* but *digues, routes et ponts* are important — in principle there should be no options ('the goal of action is more important than the action').

Concept-words which are also internationalisms, and often slogan words, have to be considered both syntagmatically, i.e. in their linguistic and topic contexts, and paradigmatically; often their 'intrinsic' meaning is more powerful than their contextual meaning; they have independent force. A concept such as 'corporatism' or 'syndicalism' has to be checked for its various senses in the SL and the TL cultures; and in particular, for whether it is being applied in a positive, negative or value-free sense. Obviously translators have to be careful how they deal with words like 'liberalism', 'radicalism' and 'anarchism'; they may have to interpolate depending on the functions and readership of their translations. Further, many non-political concept-words (take 'structuralism') are differently defined in encyclopaedias and dictionaries in any two languages, but careful examination of the differences is likely to give more of the meaning to the translator than both the immediate (the 'narrow scene' — Firbas) and the wider (text) context, which will be used to refine the sense. Thus 'corporatism' may simply refer to the 'corporatism or association' of each profession and trade after the 1992 single market, and be translated as such.

Concept-words have deep associations both personal and social, which may also be described as paradigmatic rather than syntagmatic, which touch off meanings that go beyond the definitions allotted to them in dictionaries, and connect only tenuously with the words they join to form sentences. Leaving aside words with personal associations, these are the words with deep collective cultural and moral associations which defy their contexts, which are as though immune from their contexts, which contain their own world. I take a tiny example and put it against the views of a 'text-bound translation' critic, Neubert (1986). Here is Thomas Mann's sentence: *Der Künstler als Gesellschaftskritiker das ist ja schon der politisierte, der politisierende Künstler* (Neubert, 1986: 85–105) where I take 'the artist as critic of society', the politicised, the politicising (possibly the 'politicking') artist to be mandatory equivalences, leaving the functional colloquial *das ist ja schon* for variant translations: 'is really', 'is at once', 'is himself already', 'must be', 'has got to be', 'is inevitably'. (I prefer the last.) Not so Neubert. He doesn't discuss the creative possibilities of *das ist ja schon*. Before settling for 'artist' he plays with 'writer' as *Künstler* because (a) Mann was only referring to writers, and (b) 'artist' in English is often 'painter', but so he is in German, the two words virtually correspond in every sense except where *Künstler* connotes 'competence' rather than 'artistry'.

In Neubert's version *politisierte, politisierende* becomes everything but 'politicised', 'politicising'. Through a process of dizzying lateral thinking we are led through 'politically moulded and politically minded/influenced/ driven by and aiming at/making/pursuing politics' to 'an object, indeed an agent, a creature and a creator of politics', without a moment's return to the banal back-translation test, which suggests that if Mann had wanted to say any of these things, he would have used different German words. (Words are an embarrassment to many text-linguistic translation theorists.) As for 'politicised, politicking', it's not mentioned, but 'politicised, politicising', according to Neubert, is impossible, as 'the strongly pejorative meaning of the German verb is detrimental to the verbal sense "influenced or moulded by politics" and "making politics" intended by Mann'. 'I can't make sense of this sentence.' Does Neubert mean that Mann used the wrong German words? Or is he referring to the English (not the German) sense of 'politi- cise', to discuss politics, to make political) i.e. is this a typing error, or a slip of the mind? In any event, it's mistaken, 'politicise' is no more pejorative than the German *politisieren,* and here it is only the context that can fix the sense (there are many) of both words. Again, *Gesellschaftskritiker* is weakly translated as 'social critic' *(Sozialkritiker),* in a passage where the emphasis is on 'society'. From such failed *(missglückte)* examples, a text-bound trans- lation theorist obviously goes on to state that 'the only translation unit is the whole text', which has its own tiny truth.

However, what I am trying to establish is that the word has its own iden- tity, its resonance, its value. Devaluing the word in the text is like devaluing the individual in society. Syntax connects its meaning to the text, but the word is a vertical or paradigmatic as well as a horizontal or syntagmatic phenomenon. Its vertical direction gives it a prototypical meaning, as Aitchison (1986) has shown and its aura/scope defines its limits suggesting that *heikel* can be translated in many senses, but it won't stretch to 'insidious' whatever the context. A word like 'dream' or 'home' or 'socialism', when foregrounded, has behind it a collective memory that may be more powerful than all its connections with its text.

In any text — syntax, word order, form, exact word-correspondence and so on have no *intrinsic* importance at all in translation. All that is important is the transfer of meaning, but if two languages use the same syntax, word order, form, correspondent words all with equal frequency and currency, it is perverse not to take advantage of these correspondences in the appropriate places, when so many other things in the same text are different.

The readership is, I suppose, the most persistent contextual factor in writing and in translation, though even more so in speaking. For the translator, the readership is often problematic. Translating periodicals, non-literary books, advertisements, notices, one assesses the motivation, knowledge, intelligence of the readership, perhaps of varieties of readerships. Translating for an agency, the agency may be a barrier between the translator and the readership. Translating a literary work, one translates first for oneself, but if one wants the translation to be read, one cannot quite forget the readers. In fact the more authoritative the text, the fewer concessions to the readership can be made, and if the text is strictly form-bound, there is not even room to make such concessions by explaining or occasionally by interpreting. (But all literary translation is interpreting.) Any 'concessions' for the readership are outside the translation, in notes, glossaries, prefaces — the reverse of translating down to the readership is expecting them to do some homework. Further, the more authoritative, the more form-bound the text, the greater the semantic importance and the richness of each word, the more significant the word order, the syntax, the pauses between the words, the more the text goes temporarily into the background, though it remains the important binding factor. (In great music it is similar — the notes are so packed they have separate identities, and the pauses, as Mozart wrote, are most eloquent of all.)

But given the fact that readers are individuals, that the same reader will make different readings at different times, that often no one knows who the reader is going to be, it is no wonder that the literary translator is sometimes tempted to give the readership up, and just translate for himself. No context is so tiresome as the readership context; all contexts are a form of restraint and constraint.

Conclusion

No word 'is an island entire to itself' and if we accept that there are a large and complex number of types of context, viz. linguistic, situational, subjective, cultural, listener or readership, even dictionary, even 'spurious' contexts (words in made-up sentences without the implications of utterance — the term, quoted by Firbas (1979) is A. Svoboda's), then no word is ever out of context — some words are realistically more in context, i.e. more affected by their neighbours, than others. Most out of context is a word uttered at random, or as part of a random list. Most in context is a function-word that is part of a conversation, that is determined syntactically, situationally and both by the speaker and the listener. If it is a lexical word, it may also be determined by its cultural context. I have attempted to show that between these extremes, there are a large number of variations.

Secondly, no SL word and its TL correspondent have perfect extra-contextual translation equivalence, but there are perhaps tens of thousands of monosemous technical terms which have virtual extracontextual translation equivalence — the only difference in currency is that they may be used a little more frequently in one language than in another. Contextually, not only words but also groups, collocations, sentences, proverbs may be in perfect translation equivalence — not all that many but more than most people think. A good translation equivalence for a text is always possible and what the translator primarily aims for.

Contrary to the prevailing wisdom, many single SL words in texts often have perfect translation equivalence, referentially and pragmatically, with their TL correspondents, whatever their degree of context, but the perfect translation of a text — and therefore perfect translation equivalence for texts — does not exist.

8 Translation and Mis-translation: The Review, the Revision, and the Appraisal of a Translation

Any generalisation about translation is relative. Since the concept of an ideal or perfect translation is illusory, the concept of translation equivalence can only be an approximation. Paradoxically it is only at the level of reference, of apparently (!) extra-mental universal extracultural reality, of objects and, to a lesser extent of actions and events, of single nouns and verbs, and *not* texts, that translation and mis-translation and translation equivalence are 'on firm ground', *auf festem Boden, terra firma,* but not *terre ferme* — the metaphor is significant. Seen as material objects, the sun, the moon and the stars are perfectly translated. As soon as you introduce actions, say 'run', 'walk', 'move', 'drop', however, universal, dreadful ambiguities assail us. *How* do we walk? Where or where *to* do we walk? Is it a habit or a single act, or does it finish? What is the aspect? The translator starts fumbling. If he is concerned with an accurate description, he has to expand his version, thus losing the equivalent concise impact. As soon as the sun, the moon and the stars become figurative or symbols of light or life, darkness or virginity and brightness or excellence, or religious therefore universal or cultural symbols, the translation may become increasingly an approximation. However, if a translation is to be merely *functional* and, say, crudely 'prices rose or climbed or increased or went up', the translation can be equally general (it doesn't much matter what descriptive word is used) — it will be 100% successful, even though the niceties of equivalent description and register may be missing. It comes to this: if you are trying to translate/ describe the real world of facts you can and should be accurate. The more the facts are modified by qualities, then by cultural limitations, thus by figurative associations, then the ins and outs of the author's thinking, then by the onomatopoeic sound in their expression, the more approximate your achievement becomes, the more remote from the complexities of the source language text. Only if you are intent on translating a simple message or intention, the unadorned facts and figures (no wonder the grey prose of statistical reports is so easy and so literal to translate) is your translation 'totally' successful. Most translations are in the graduated area between correct translation and mis-translation, but at least, mis-translation is usually demonstrable and always unnecessary. A figurative *Schub* may be 'drive', 'push', 'shove', 'impetus' or 'thrust', but it cannot stretch to a 'burst' in any context.

I want to illustrate my argument by considering the translation of a passage from Hermann Hesse's *Steppenwolf* (see pp. 112–114). There are two ways of conducting such a review, and one is incomplete without the other: the analytical and the functional.

An analytical approach starts within sentence-correspondence, where common objects such as 'old books' (line 4), 'gout attacks' (27/28), 'a hot bath' (7) have their obvious one-to-one equivalents. At this stage one also notes that *Aktiengesellschaften* (35) 'joint stock companies' is translated as 'vampires of finance' (32/33) and one can only assume that the translator considered its use symbolical rather than figurative, supported by 'sucked dry' (32) *ausgesogen* (36).

There appears to be no mis-translation due to ignorance of German, but *Lebenskunst* (3) ('art', perhaps 'style of living') as 'way of life' (2/3), *schöne, zarte, kostbare* (13) ('lively, tender, precious') reduced to 'the loveliest' (11), *die Tage schmecken* (29) ('taste the days') as 'know the days' (27), *krass* (46) ('blatant') as 'disgusting' (43) show an extraordinary lexical cavalierness, driving the semantic range of these words beyond their justifiable limits.

In translated works of fiction, mistakes of reality are usually harder to pinpoint than in factual reports, but whilst Hesse keeps Harry Holler as *älterer Mensch* the translator wavers between 'elderly' and 'middle-aged'.

When we come to mistakes of usage, we have to distinguish the author's idiolect from normal social language. '*Das Lesen in den alten Büchern, das Liegen im warmen Bad*' (15/16) is normal German; why 'the reading of the old books, the lying in the warm bath' (13/14), when the gerund is so readily available in English and non-existent in German — therefore 'reading old books, lying in a warm (or hot?) bath'. Why, in the second line, translate *mit* ('with') so pompously as 'in accordance with' (2)? Why the simple '*normal und gewohnt*' (20) ('normal and usual') as the archaic is 'fallen to my lot' (18)? Why *blechern* (37) as 'brazen' (34) (figurative) when the word is 'brassy' (physical)?

The SLT consists of three sentences, two in the first, one in the second paragraph. The translation has 15 sentences in the first paragraph, two in the second. Even granting that German has longer and more complex sentences than English, it is hard to justify these divergences, as well as the disparity of treatment between the two paragraphs. Hesse, like Thomas Mann in German, or Aragon or Proust in French, uses exceptionally long sentences, and I think these have to be preserved. Further there is an alternative of commas, short pauses or breath gaps, and semi-colons, longer ones, cunningly reflecting the elderly man's thoughts running between an account of his day's routine and the contrasts between his monotonous and his bad days racked by physical pain or morose thoughts about the state of his part of the world.

In the first paragraph, the translator has had to introduce several of the sentences with connecting words such as 'That was', 'So was', 'But, taken all in all', 'No, it had not even', 'Rather it had been' which make rather more decisive breaks than the SLT, and add redundant shades of meaning. This is a case of text linguistics *avant l'heure.*

Such are perhaps the main features of any comparison, and they include some salient mis-translations. And as I reread the text and, as it were, revise the translation, I am appraising and evaluating the SL text. The more I study it, the more packed with meaning it appears, denotatively, connotatively and phonaesthetically — J. R. Firth's beautiful word for the aesthetics of language sound has still not got beyond the linguistics dictionaries. And the more the translation seems to be full of unnecessary inaccuracies. Mind you, there are also felicities: *wie eben die Tage so vergehen* (1) as 'just as days (do) go by' (1); though the unique English emphatic present is missed; *in den Himmel gezeichnet* (14) as 'pencilled against the sky' (12) — (here as often, a fresh metaphor can concentrate meaning); 'every nerve of eye and ear' (29/30) for *jede Tätigkeit von Auge und Ohr* (31/32) is a find, since whilst the German is strange, it is not absurd, whilst 'any activity, movement, even business of eye and ear' is ridiculous and therefore goes beyond the limits of good literal translation. Any literal translation that makes you giggle (in spite of many readings) because of its sound or its sense, has to be avoided; again *teuflisch aus einer Freude zur Qual* (31/32) as 'with a fiendish delight in torture' (30) — *auf Schritt und Tritt* (38) (dog with persistence) (35) — *sachlich* (27) a quintessential German word is nicely translated as 'matter-of-factly' (26) — this is the kind of decent *(sauber)* translation which should immediately establish the credentials of a translator who knows his German, who knows his English, whose faulty translation may be due to what I would consider a mistaken theory of translation, which W. Sorrell probably did not even formulate — hence the need for translators to write prefaces to all books they translate. (It is all a matter of discussion. Similarly bad language teaching is sometimes due to bad linguistics which the teacher is not even aware of.) Again *entgegengrinst* (39) as 'grins back at us' (34) although *grinsen (höhnisch, boshaft, schadenfroh* says the Wahrig) is usually much nastier than the friendly 'grin'.

Where we start wrestling with the text is in its many descriptive words that have metalingual, sonic, figurative problems, as well as etymological roots.

Immediately in the first line we have: *ich hatte ihn herumgebracht, hatte ihn sanft umgebracht,* which Sorrell kills off with the simple 'I had killed it (the day)' — though 'I had killed it off', 'I had softly killed it' would hint at a metalingual transfer, whilst 'I had got through it, I had done for it' would distinguish the meaning and retain the German's physical quality — some semantic loss is inevitable, but not as much as Sorrell's.

Schüchtern (3) has 'scared' etymologically behind it but one cannot go beyond 'shy' and Sorrell has 'withdrawn' (2); for *gewälzt* (4) of books Sorrell's 'peruse' (3) loses all physicalness — the image is of someone turning them over, rolling, poring over them eagerly — the waltz is there. Again with *die Schmerzen sich überlisten ließen* (7) a compromise is inevitable. 'Consented to disappear' (6) is tame, 'let themselves be slily outwitted' (by the powder), 'were being slily outwitted' would fail if it sounded ridiculous — it doesn't to me. *Die Gedankenübungen weggelassen* (11/12) on the other hand is well balanced in the translation with *Atemübungen* (11), absorbing *aus Bequemlichkeit* (12) as 'found it convenient to' (10).

I have tried to simultaneously illustrate the basic problems of translation criticism and revision which apply whenever translation is not narrowly functional, reproducing information only. The lexical unit of translation is usually a collocation or a group; in German, the grammatical unit of translation is likely to be a participial phrase or a group — their shift always causes less semantic disruption than a lexical transfer, but a change in emphasis is likely with the inevitable change in word order.

Secondly, there is a tendency to undertranslate, viz. to normalise by generalising, to understate, in all translation but particularly in literary translation. In non-literary translation, the translators are so intent on reproducing all the facts that they do not hesitate to expand the passage. In literary translation economy is more important and accuracy suffers (here the translation is shorter than the original). The most dangerous feature is the translator's fear of using individual language rather than the common coin of social language; this begins in English with the easy slide from Germanic to Romance: from 'suck up' *(eingesogen)* (9) to 'absorb' (7) 'leave out' *(weggelassen)* (12) to 'omit' (10) the toning down of *Sorgen* (worry) (23) and *Kummer* (24) 'grief' or 'affliction'; and finally the fear of vivid figurative language, *die Tage schmecken* (29), twice normalised here with 'know the days' (27), where 'taste the days' is rather odder than the German (the semantic range of *schmecken* is wider than 'taste' but the compromise of 'know the taste of' is still possible.) I take it as another touchstone of a good translation of an authoritative text, that any important metaphor, however audacious, however culturally bound, for example, Professor Neubert's well known example 'Shall I compare thee to a summer's day?' translated into, say, Arabic or Xhosa, the most widely spoken language in South Africa, 'summer' must be translated as 'summer'. It is the reader's job to do the necessary homework. This also applies to the 'lease' of summer in the next line, but (a) it may not be possible — 'leases' are unknown in many languages, (b) the metaphor is not as important.

Note that I have been discussing some lexical and grammatical points of correspondence between the SL and TL text. Such a discussion may be a transitory stage between the main process of translating and the evaluation of the translation. Thus revision, the last stage of translating, which takes up between a half and two-thirds of total translating time, unless the SLT is exceptionally easy and dull, is parallel with the process of evaluation. There are two basic procedures: (a) a reading of the translation without looking at the original, as an independent piece of writing, and (b) the meticulous comparison of the version with its original.

It is often said that a translation should not read like a translation. As a warning against inadvertent interference (*grinsen* is the only example in the Hesse piece) or translationese say ('For those who do not like competition, there will be the opportunity of corroborant swimming or to be dragged by the waves, being on their wind-surfing board'), this injunction is valid and salutary. However, when an authoritative text is linguistically innovatory, its translation is likely to be so, and if the translator-reviser or the critic keeps thinking that a translation should not appear to be one (it is anyway artificial, Brecht would laugh at it) he or she will be impairing the original's impact by normalising it. Parts of Mervyn Peake in English or any other language should read like a translation. What is clear is that in an independent reading, apart from removing traces of inadvertent interference (the translator's interference, especially of metaphor, will enliven the target language) will, if appropriate, assure the reviser and critic that the piece gives some pleasure and satisfaction.

Equally important is a close parallel reading of the translation with the original: this is not only to ensure that no word — sentence — paragraph in the original has been overlooked or forgotten (as usually happens) but to ensure that every punctuation mark (including bold face or the German spaced letters), figure or word in the original has been accounted for (not necessarily translated) in the translation. This process is a part of the translator's, reviser's and critic's continual two-way journey: they never look up a word *(morphéique)* in a bilingual dictionary ('morphetic') without checking its status and its TL equivalent's status in SL and TL monolingual dictionaries ('nocturnal'). Further, they go continually back to the SL text during revision for fresh insights and angles. In translation the SL text is never 'deverbalised', as it is in simultaneous interpretation. That is the basic difference between the two skills which has to be taken into account in any theorising. In interpretation you can't go back, either to the SL text or to your own.

However, the most important task in revising and evaluating is to review the grammatic and lexical deviations from the SL text in the translation. In many instances this is done in the light of the translator's approach to the whole text. But looked at analytically, it becomes a pragmatic comparison of grammatical and lexical correspondences as well as their underlying referential and figurative associations. After all allowances have been made for grammatical transpositions and the different semantic ranges of SL and TL lexical units that correspond imperfectly, I find mistrust and fear of literal translation can be used as a yardstick. The legitimacy of appropriate literal translation is I think the most important and controversial issue in translation. I suggest the following reasons why many translators and writers on translation avoid it on principle.

1. They associate it with 'translationese' — i.e. literal translation that makes little sense or is unnatural.
2. They want to leave their own mark on the translation, to be more colloquial, informal, idiomatic, elegant than the original.
3. They have been trained in a tradition that puts a premium on judicious clichés or 'literary' phrases (recommended by teachers of Latin and Classical Greek prose) and avoids the use of TL words that (a) look like the corresponding SL words (therefore *vertu* should never be translated as 'virtue'), (b) have obvious extracontextual one to one equivalents (so *Tugend* shouldn't be translated as 'virtue') — an elegant variation is always better.
4. The prevailing influence of *text linguistics* and of real or imaginary textual constraints moves them away from the smaller stretches of the text to the text as a translation unit. Correspondences get lost.

5. They believe that invariably the message is more important than the meaning, the function than the substance.
6. They believe that one should translate what the writer thinks or wants to say, not what he writes or actually says (hermeneutic translation).
7. They think that literal translation is humdrum and too easy.
8. They have been penalised at school and university for translating literally.

Normally, only the grey language of semi-official, commercial or technical texts can be translated literally for long. In fact the skill of translating most texts lies in the alternation on the one hand of literal or rule-governed and on the other of 'ludic' creative translation — 'rule-governed' is used in the sense of conforming to the grammatical shifts, lexical equivalences and retention of emphasis (as investigated in functional sentence perspective) apparent between the two languages — such translation is governed by 'rules', but in this or that instance, the rules often conflict. And in many cases, there is a choice between literal and 'rule-governed' translation thus: a small example: Suzanne Guillemin-Flescher (unpublished lecture) notes that when assertions are translated from French to English, English tends to qualify the assertions, thus: *Je ne vous prends pas au sérieux,* 'I know you don't mean that seriously' where 'I can't take you seriously', though literal is as good, or in *Je ne suis pas aveugle,* 'I'm not blind, you know' — the qualifier could easily be dispensed with. The above is an example of 'cultural' translation illustrating an apparent English tendency to temper, which could well be exposed by literal translation. (The role of literal translation in cutting through cultural shams and prejudices into a universal humanity — the literal truth — has still to be discussed.)

A translation problem exists not only when a deviation from literal translation is required, which usually then leaves open a choice from amongst various translation procedures, but also when, after the various procedural options have been reviewed, one returns to a literal translation which no longer appears as outrageous as at first onset. Thus, in the Hesse piece, at first sight, the three adjectives with the triple noun-compound in *schöne, zarte, kostbare Federwölkchenmuster* (13/14) alarmed the translator, but the trailing length of 'lovely, tender, sumptuous patterns of feathery wisps of cloud' is not really alarming, expresses the pleasure of the elderly gout-ridden man on his walk, and is really, after all *(ja)* what Hesse wrote, compensating even for some sound effects. Hesse follows with *Das war sehr hübsch* (15) possibly 'That was very nice', which Sorrell outrageously translates as 'was very delightful' (13), which is outside the range of *hübsch*. Here as often, a translator has been afraid of the literal truth — whether it is the prosaic facts or the unfamiliar metaphor. (Unfortunately 'literal' in English, not in French or German, connotes narrow-mindedness, dullness, and pedantry as well as accuracy.)

In evaluation and revision, one has to look hard at interference which is as ambivalent a factor in translation as is interlanguage in language learning. Clearly when we revise or evaluate, we have to correct or fault all instances of interference (cultural, lexical, grammatical, or word order, from the SL or a third language) — where it distorts the sense or inappropriately breaks the register of the translation, and certainly if it has crept in without the translator being aware of it. Even here there are borderline cases. Interference can be used creatively, by a child, a second language-learner, and by a translator in 'semantic' and 'communicative' translation. It is a means not only of cultural (instanced in word-transfer) but of 'universal' linguistic enrichment. Some translations and languages would profit from the literal translation of foreign proverbs, even if there is already a TL near-equivalent: 'it fits like a fist on the eye', 'other countries, other customs' — 'that's striking a blow into water', 'I wish you a lucky hand as we Germans say' — there is no reason why universal proverbs should remain within one language. Again, idioms can be translated and desexed: 'He's no longer the youngest'. 'See you' already exists, 'hear you (again)' from *Aufwiederhören* is overdue. The lack of *Bon appétit* in English has been often commented on, and since this is a cultural gap, not always a courtesy gap, it ought to be filled. 'Enjoy your meal' is starting to fill it. The translator's deliberate use of interference is often shocking and clumsy but it may be salutary, as a direct approach to meaning. The alternative is paraphrase or the search for the thought behind the words, which is often arbitrary and hermeneutic. To return to the Hesse text, you get *Aktiengesellschaften* hermeneutically and unnecessarily translated as 'vampires of finance'. I'd rather not.

I have attempted here to indicate some analytical *Ansätze* (an amazing holdall word) for the revision and the appraisal of a translation. I have tried to show what I mean by translation and mis-translation concretely, in the wistful hope that those who think about translation, those on the narrow *Übersetzungswissenschaftler* circuit, are more likely to agree about big things if they can first agree about small things. Because that is what all this is, an attempt to seek agreement. As 'scientists' we are rather pathetic, because we have fewer points of agreement than the linguists whose parasites we partially are; compare the translators and the literary critics who feed on the writers. And now that I turn to the second and essential part of my subject, a functional or general approach to the revision and appraisal of a translation, I am pursued by questions which cannot be answered in any general terms: What is translated? Is it what the author writes? (Yes?) Is it what the author means? (Rarely?) And is this to be moderated by the facts as the translator knows them? Yes. And is this to be 'filtered', to use Juliane House's term, in such a way that it is both comprehensible and stylistically agreeable to the putative readership? (It depends.) And is it to be presented as an idiomatic message, or as a close rendering of the original or as a hermeneutic rendering of the thought behind the words, the *vouloir dire*? When does a *version* become a *perversion*? These two terms can be transferred into German and most Romance languages. Such questions become irrelevant only when the text is in the realm of grey facts where there is a clear gap between correct translation and mis-translation, successful and failed translation.

In choosing to identify now some functional aspects of the Hesse text, I realise that my criteria may be considered subjective. Much of what I say, however, merely underpins my analytical comments, which are more apparently objective.

The intention of the Hesse text is clear — to convey the typical observations, experiences and feelings of an elderly, neurotic, pessimistic, gout-ridden educated man — written as notes *(Aufzeichnungen)* — in a moment of leisure and release from pain. The writing is correspondingly leisurely, emphasising states rather than movements, qualities rather than actions. Hence the heaped adjectives, the parentheses, the commas, even a certain stress on the unique vowel-like 'l' sound — *lesen, liegen, leidliche, laue* and other suggestive or standard sound effects *(auf Schritt und Tritt)* (38), which here as often are sacrificed in the translation. A functional analysis such as this one could be prolonged, but not profitably.

The cardinal question is 'how to translate'. Perhaps we could agree that in a text such as this one, an authoritative and also an expressive text, the manner is as important as the matter; the translator has to empathise with the writer, to reproduce in language the impact of the text on himself. The putative effect on the putative readers of the translation, the referential truth of what the writer states (is the earth sucked up by joint stock companies?) are here of secondary importance. In any event, if this text is translated for an educated readership in at least Europe, there are barely any cultural problems of period or region. *Aktiengesellschaften* do not exist in Eastern Europe, but they are well understood. On the other hand, if one insists say that German prefers long sentences, heaped up adjectives and 'physical' Germanic words and makes great play with its prefixes where English prefers short sentences, fewer adjectives and more Greco-Latinisms, and that the translator must show this difference in any type of text, by chopping up the sentences, smoothing out the adjectives, skirting the assonance and the word-play and so on, one is going to produce, not a completely different — I don't think Sorrell has harmed Hesse's work or his reputation — but a somewhat different translation.

If we cannot agree on what a good translation is, how can we produce a basic course on principles and methods of translation, let alone on translation theory, such as is the small but essential core component of any academic or professional translation course?

My problem is that I think I know what a good translation is, but I doubt whether many people would agree with me. Thus R. de Beaugrande: 'As every translator knows, two texts in different languages may mean the same thing, and yet bear scant outward resemblances in terms of any "material properties"'. If this means what I think it means, that translation correspondences often only exist at text level, then I certainly don't know it, and I'm a translator too.

Again, if a translation is regarded only as a cultural or ideological object, a genre in the TL's polysystem, it has no scientific character, and any comparison between translation and original becomes otiose.

Again, you may think it legitimate to liven up a text, to write consistently colloquial language while the original is sober and deadpan, translating Camus' *Il faisait beau* as 'It was a blazing hot summer afternoon'; or you may like Paepcke, a most stimulating writer, translate Pierre-Henri Simon's *Je n'ai pas eu beaucoup de chance* as *Mir war das Schicksal nie besonders gewogen*. Or you may, like Neubert, translate Goethe's *Das Übersetzen ist eines der wichtigsten und würdigsten Geschäfte in dem gesamten Weltwesen* as 'Translation is one of the most important and honoured professions in the world'.

Or you may have a behaviouristic view of translation, like Catford's 'replacement of SL textual by equivalent TL textual material', and virtually ignore the text level.

Or you may follow Benjamin, Nabokov, Roland Sussex, Bruno Bettelheim, Gasset, and believe that words are more important than texts, but that is not very likely, is it?

Or, more concretely, take my *pièce témoin* my 'reference text'. Whilst I believe that Sorrell's knowledge of German is fine and his English sensitive, the theory of translation that emerges is that felicity is more important than fidelity; that the translator should impose a personal idea of good style — the three glorious sisters: brevity, clarity, simplicity — on to the original; that wayward German language which might enrich the English language must be safely normalised; that SL sentence and therefore speech rhythms should be sacrificed, if they go on too long (1–7); that precise metaphors like *Aktiengesellschaften* have to be 'interpreted', i.e. translated into something ghoulish, ridiculous and conventional like 'vampires of finance'; that a translation should never read like a translation.

Now, I disagree fundamentally with all the propositions I have enumerated, both generally and in the concrete Hesse case. In the concrete instance I think the Hesse translation is serviceable, catches the spirit of the original, has excellent stretches *(zum Gipfel der Unleidlichkeit getrieben* (39/40) 'focused to the last pitch of the intolerable' (36/37) and is, if anything, *too* concise (shorter than the original!). From my point of view, most of the inaccuracies are unnecessary, and if he had observed my own theory of translation or my principles and methods of translation Sorrell would have produced an incomparably better translation than any I could do. I need hardly add that translation is for discussion — Walter Sorrell (1963) is perfectly entitled to his views but I wonder if he would or could infer them. It's all very well for translators to say 'I translate; let others theorise'. We are not going to get any basic syllabus on Principles and Methods of Translation until translators *(translators, not* translation theorists, *not* teachers), can externalise their translating, that is generalise their practice explicitly and so discuss, and so come to a minimum agreement.

In contrast, as a view I can agree with, I take Galen Strawson's review of Michel Tournier's *Gilles and Jeanne* (translated by Alan Sheridan) in an issue of *The Observer* of March 1987. He points out that *faon* ('fawn') is translated as 'farmhand' *(valet de ferme)*; *cou* ('neck') as 'backside' *(cul)*; *jurer avec* ('incongruous with') as 'swear at' *(jurer contre)*. He disapproves of elegant variations such as 'clouds that constantly formed and reformed at the behest of wind and rain' for *nuées déchiquetées par le vent et la pluie* ('heavy clouds tattered by wind and rain'). Note that Galen Strawson can check a translation even at the word rank, without reference even to the collocation, let alone the whole text.

As it is, I can only finish by defining what I think is good translation. A translation has to be as accurate as possible, as economical as possible, in denotation and in connotation, referentially and pragmatically. The accuracy relates to the SL text, either to the author's meaning, or to the objective truth that is encompassed by the text, or to this objective truth adapted to the intellectual and emotional comprehension of the readership which the translator and/or the client has in mind. That is the principle of a good translation; where it plainly starts falling short, it is a mis-translation.

Finally, it is a text that is translated. But texts can't be measured, words can. And Weinrich's apophthegm: 'Translated words always lie, but translated texts only lie when they are badly translated', which I quoted so approvingly 14 years ago, is, in its first part, a sweeping and misleading generalisation, it is mainly wrong, it is an invitation to inaccuracy.

Appendix

An extract from Der *Steppenwolf* by Hermann Hesse
Suhrkamp (Gesammelte Werke, 1947) pp. 40–1.

1 Der Tag war vergangen, wie eben die Tage so vergehen, ich
  hatte ihn herumgebracht, hatte ihn sanft umgebracht, mit
  meiner primitiven und schüchternen Art von Lebenskunst;
  ich hatte einige Stunden gearbeitet, alte Bücher gewälzt,
5 ich hatte zwei Stunden lang Schmerzen gehabt, wie ältere
  Leute sie eben haben, hatte ein Pulver genommen und mich
  gefreut, daß die Schmerzen sich überlisten ließen, hatte
  in einem heißen Bad gelegen und die liebe Wärme
  eingesogen, hatte dreimal die Post empfangen und all die
10 entbehrlichen Briefe und Drucksachen durchgesehen, hatte
  meine Atemübungen gemacht, die Gedankenübungen aber heute
  aus Bequemlichkeit weggelassen, war eine Stunde spazieren
  gewesen   und   hatte   schöne,   zarte,   kostbare
  Federwölkchenmuster in den Himmel gezeichnet gefunden.
15 Das war sehr hübsch, ebenso wie das Lesen in den alten
  Büchern, wie das Liegen im warmen Bad, aber – alles in
  allem – war es nicht gerade ein entzückender, nicht eben
  ein strahlender, ein Glücks- und Freudentag gewesen,
  sondern eben einer von diesen Tagen, wie sie für mich nun
20 seit langer Zeit die normalen und gewohnten sein sollten:
  maßvoll angenehme, durchaus erträgliche, leidliche, laue
  Tage eines älteren unzufriedenen Herrn, Tage ohne
  besondere Schmerzen, ohne besondere Sorgen, ohne
  eigentlichen Kummer, ohne Verzweiflung, Tage, an welchen
25 selbst die Frage, ob es nicht an der Zeit sei, dem
  Beispiel Adalbert Stifters zu folgen und beim Rasieren zu
  verunglücken, ohne Aufregung oder Angstgefühle sachlich
  und ruhig erwogen wird.
  Wer die anderen Tage geschmeckt hat, die bösen, die mit
30 den Gichtanfällen oder die mit jenem schlimmen, hinter
  den Augäpfeln festgewurzelten, teuflisch jede Tätigkeit
  von Auge und Ohr aus einer Freude zur Qual verhexenden
  Kopfweh, oder jene Tage des Seelensterbens, jene argen
  Tage der inneren Leere und Verzweiflung, an denen uns,
35 inmitten der zerstörten und von Aktiengesellschaften
  ausgesogenen Erde, die Menschenwelt und sogenannte Kultur
  in   ihrem   verlogenen   und   gemeinen   blechernen

Jahrmarktsglanz auf Schritt und Tritt wie ein Brechmittel
entgegengrinst, konzentriert und zum Gipfel der
40 Unleidlichkeit getrieben im eigenen kranken Ich – wer
jene Höllentage geschmeckt hat, der ist mit solchen
Normal- und Halbundhalbtagen gleich dem heutigen sehr zu-
frieden, dankbar sitzt er am warmen Ofen, dankbar stellt
er beim Lesen des Morgenblattes fest, daß auch heute
45 wieder kein Krieg ausgebrochen, keine neue Diktatur
errichtet, keine besonders krasse Schweinerei in Politik
und Wirtschaft aufgedeckt worden ist.

1 The day had gone by just as days go by, I had killed it
in accordance with my primitive and withdrawn way of
life. I had worked for an hour or two and perused the
pages of old books. I had had pains for two hours, as
5 elderly people do. I had taken a powder and been very
glad when the pains consented to disappear. I had lain in
a hot bath and absorbed its kindly warmth. Three times
the post had come with undesired letters and circulars to
look through. I had done my breathing exercises, but
10 found it convenient today to omit the thought exercises.
I had been for an hour's walk and seen the loveliest
feathery cloud patterns pencilled against the sky. That
was very delightful. So was the reading of the old books.
So was the lying in the warm bath. But, taken all in all,
15 it had not been exactly a day of rapture. No, it had not
even been a day brightened with happiness and joy.
Rather, it had been just one of those days which for a
long while now had fallen to my lot; the moderately
pleasant, the wholly bearable and tolerable, lukewarm
20 days of a discontented middle-aged man; days without
special pains, without special cares, without particular
worry, without despair; days on which the question
whether the time has not come to follow the example of
Adalbert Stifter and have a fatal accident while shaving
25 should not be considered without agitation or anxiety
quietly and matter-of-factly.
He who has known the other days, the angry ones of gout
attacks, or those with that wicked headache rooted behind
the eyeballs that casts a spell on every nerve of eye and
30 ear with a fiendish delight in torture, or those soul-
destroying, evil days of inward emptiness and despair,
when, on this ravaged earth, sucked dry by the vampires
of finance, the world of men and of so-called culture
grins back at us with the lying, vulgar, brazen glamour
35 of a Fair and dogs us with the persistence of an emetic,
and when all is concentrated and focused to the last
pitch of the intolerable upon your own sick self — he who
has known these hellish days may be content indeed with

normal half-and-half days like today. Thankfully you sit
40 by the warm stove, thankfully you assure yourself as you
read your morning paper that another day has come and no
war broken out again, no new dictatorship has been set
up, no particularly disgusting scandal been unveiled in
the worlds of politics or finance.

Translation by Basil Creighton (1929)
Revised by Walter Sorrell (1963)
Penguin Classics (1982) pp. 33–4

9 Pragmatic Translation and Literalism

I make the basic assumption that provided a source language text contains no misstatements of fact, is competently written, and has to be fully translated rather than summarised or functionally reorientated, one's purpose in translating it is to be referentially and pragmatically accurate.

I see this as the base line of translation; the fact that the translator of non-literary texts more often than not has to work on inaccurate and poorly written texts, and has various resources to cope with these deficiencies is not relevant here. My purpose is to discuss the base line.

I need say little here about referential accuracy in translation. It is often approximate, often difficult. Languages cut up reality in different ways, and whilst figures, standard units, parts of the body, general features of nature, are universal, many ecological features as well as objects of common use are culturally modified. In any event, translation as description is always more approximate therefore less accurate than functional translation, which is why a description can sometimes be tactfully clarified by a statement of function: objects of similar dimensions can be distinguished by a mention of their purposes, e.g. vase, urn, jar, pot, jug, bowl, vessel, receptacle.

In foreign cultures, these objects usually look rather different, and require a different taxonomy or hierarchy of nomenclature, but there is no difficulty in matching purpose to purpose, so that 'jar', 'jug', 'pot', *jarre, pot, broc, cruche, Glas, Topf, Krug,* can be plainly marked for water, jam, milk, beer, etc. as appropriate. Again, the borderlines between many culturally tinged features of various sizes are fuzzy: hills, towns, streams, animals, people, flowers, birds — when does one object become or grow into another? The border, the no man's land, is often vague and each language is apt to decide differently.

And again, the more that descriptions move from the physical to the mental and the moral, the more they encroach on the pragmatic aspect of translation. The majority of people may know what good and evil, right and wrong, slavery, beauty and so on are, but here too culture influences mental and moral judgement and infringes on language.

The second element in translation is the pragmatic. 'Pragmatic translation' is a part of the title of this conference,[1] but I do not know in what sense the organisers intended it. 'Pragmatic' may mean 'advocating behaviour that is dictated more by practical consequences than by theory or dogma', in which case we could be discussing practical translation, translation which successfully fulfils its purpose; such translation is a desirable aim provided that the purpose is clear, e.g. to reproduce the information in the source language (SL) text, to 'transfer' the persuasive power of a notice or a tourist brochure into another language culture as efficiently as possible. When you are either trying to recreate publicity, or to show how publicity is framed in the SL, you ask the client, who may be the retailer or an advertising agent. But in other cases, where the SL text is written for various types of readership, or is an imaginative text, the purpose may not be all that clear. There may be many purposes or no particular purpose — what does the translator do then? Secondly, 'pragmatic' can mean 'concerned with immediate practicalities or expedience' (often in a negative sense — 'his approach was pragmatic rather than principled') in which case 'pragmatic translation' could be regarded as selective as well as functional. In this sense, which is being urged on West German universities in the important memorandum produced by the co-ordination committee *Praxis und Lehre* and translated in the current *Meta,* published by the Federal Association of German Translators (BDÜ) in 1986, the language of the original may be of little importance, and the translator may simply have to answer a few pertinent questions as concisely as possible — and again, 'pragmatic' may simply be opposed to 'literary', as in Delisle's (1980) *Analyse du Discours.*

Or again, pragmatic, an adjective deriving from pragmatism, pragmatics or praxis, may stress experiential and objective truth rather than the subjective statement used as the *Vorlage* or model to be processed, and here 'pragmatic translation' may result in a bold ideological transformation. I won't go into the depths of this; it may mean anything from reducing a text to its basic facts to St Paul's 'seeing through a glass darkly' (1 Corinthians: 3.11).

As I am using 'pragmatic' as one of the *two* factors in translation, I cannot talk of 'pragmatic' translation in isolation, but I have to state my own definition of 'pragmatic', which derives from Charles Morris and ultimately from Peirce.

'Pragmatic' denotes the reader's or readership's reception of the translation, as opposed to 'referential', which denotes the relationship between the translation and the extra-linguistic reality it describes.

I contrast this definition with that of Geoffrey Leech (1981): 'Pragmatics is the study of how utterances have meanings in situations', which is contrasted with 'semantics', denoting meaning in a general sense that is not linked to particular receptors in particular situations. Whilst I would suggest that 'pragmatic' includes the 'permanent' characteristics of the receptors (their education, job, knowledge, etc.) its main emphasis is situational, that is the ability of the translation to stimulate the appropriate frame of mind and therefore the comprehension of the readership through a particular text. It is largely tentative and presumptive — the various maxims and principles so fashionably discussed in the pragmatics literature are rather marginal and obvious (Grice's exam-hints: be clear, brief, relevant, etc.) but emotional tone — emphasis, metaphors, words of feeling — is predominant in examining the pragmatic factor in translation. Whilst one can state that in principle, 'clear' is a referential but 'pellucid' is a pragmatic word, there is no guarantee that one reader is, or all readers are, going to react correspondingly.

If one translates a sentence such as *un Grec est quelqu'un qui habite la Grèce* as 'a Greek is someone who lives in Greece' this is an almost entirely referential statement and one need make no assumptions about the readers except that they are literate. Unless the sentence appears in an emotive context, the translation is purely referential, it has no pragmatic element. And if one translates a sentence such as *Les entreprises françaises ont fait preuve d'une remarquable capacité de mener des recherches fondamentales, à l'aide de budgets assez faibles* as 'French companies have shown a remarkable capacity for conducting fundamental research with fairly small research budgets', one assumes the readers have a measure of general education, but the sentence is referential unless it is read by 'interested' persons, e.g. some French company's research staff.

The pragmatic factor therefore has two elements: the first is relatively extra-contextual, and relates to the reader's characteristics at the time of reading: of these, subject knowledge, linguistic level, SL cultural familiarity, job, are likely to be more important than social class, age, sex, and the time distance from the compilation of the SL text. If you look at the illustrative text, the SL like the target language (TL) readership is only likely to be emotionally involved if they feel strongly about some leading statement and this is hardly predictable, in a period of (even in France) waning patriotism. But if the SL text affects the whole readership, the translator of publicity or public notices has to bear this in mind, since these are the pragmatic text types where the success of the translation can be assessed only by the readership's subsequent behaviour.

If I now consider the relationship between the language of the SL text and the readership, I first have to point out that this relationship depends on the latter's sensitivity to language, and if this is dulled, the relationship may not be all that important. Nevertheless, a translator assumes this sensitivity even when it doesn't exist.

1 L'OTAN face
à M. Gorbatchev

Le vrai héros du
sommet de l'alliance atlantique;
5 qui s'est terminé le jeudi 3 mars à
Bruxelles, n'a été ni Mme Thatcher pugnace comme à son habi-
tude ni le président Reagan, par-
ticulièrement discret ni le
10 « couple infernal » Mitterrand–
Chirac. Non, celui qui était pré-
sent dans tous les esprits c'est
M. Gorbatchev.

En effet le secrétaire général
15 du Parti communiste soviétique
et sa nouvelle politique de désarmement posent problème à
l'alliance. Finis les heureux
temps ou il était aisé d'anticiper
20 les mouvements diplomatiques
et stratégiques de Moscou.
L'adversaire est devenu infini-
ment plus subtil dans l'art d'innover, de surprendre, d'enfoncer
25 un coin dans une solidarité atlantique toujours vulnérable aux
égoismes nationaux.

Subtil certes,
mais M. Gorbatchev n'est-il pas
30 sincère lorsqu'il affirme vouloir
soulager son pays d'une sur-
charge militaire paralysante pour
se consacrer à la remise en ordre
d'une économie chaotique ?
35 M. Mitterrand a raison, lorsqu'on
lui pose la question de refuser
d'y répondre. Qui peut savoir ce
qui est réellement dans la tête
d'un homme qui n'est de toute
40 façon pas arrivé au pouvoir par
inadvertance ? Force est donc de
le juger sur ses actes.

Deux tests seront cruciaux de
ce point de vue pour l'avenir des
45 relations Est–Ouest. Le premier
ne concerne pas directement
l'Occident, mais il devrait per-
mettre de se faire une idée de la
volonté de M. Gorbatchev de
50 corriger les « erreurs du passé ».

C'est de l'Afghanistan qu'il
s'agit, dont l'évacuation par les
troupes soviétiques ferait beaucoup pour convaincre l'opinion
55 mondiale que de nouvelles analyses ont enfin cours à Moscou.

La seconde matière de l'examen de passage auquel il faut
soumettre M. Gorbatchev, ce
60 sont les négociations sur le
désarmement conventionnel. Ce
sont les armes classiques, qui, en
effet rendent la guerre possible,
et il serait dangereux d'encoura-
65 ger les rêves de dénucléarisation
de l'Europe occidentale tant que
ne sera pas effacée la supériorité
du pacte de Varsovie dans le
domaine de l'armement conven-
70 tionnel. C'est l'idée-force du
sommet de Bruxelles, et les Seize
se doivent de mettre M. Gorbatchev au pied de ce mur-là.

Ils n'y parvien-
75 dront que s'ils réussissent à
conjuguer ouverture d'esprit et
fermeté. Les deux postures,
illustrées ici par MM. Mitterrand
et Chirac, au niveau européen
80 par le chancelier Kohl et
Mme Thatcher, ne sont pas forcé-
ment contradictoires. Elles
devraient même être complémentaires, l'une ou l'autre pré-
85 valant en fonction du comportement de Moscou.

Au-delà d'arrière-pensées
électorales, M. Mitterrand: l'a
compris qui a passablement
90 gommé ses précédentes déclarations hostiles à la modernisation
des forces nucléaires de l'OTAN
pour insister sur la nécessité de
définir une « stratégie pour le
95 désarmement »· M. Chirac aussi,
qui affirme aujourd'hui n'avoir
plus aucune réserve à l'égard des
positions du chef de l'Etat, qu'il
soupçonnait d'accepter un peu
100 vite l'argumentation de M. Gorbatchev.

Specimen text — French (from *Le Monde*, 5th March 1988)

1 How to be open-minded and still firm

THE REAL STAR at the Atlantic Alliance summit which ended on 5 March 3 in Brussels was neither Margaret Thatcher, who was as pugnacious as ever, nor Ronald Reagan, who was particularly discreet, nor even that "infernal 10 couple" of Mitterrand and Chirac. No, the one who was on everybody's mind was Mikhail Gorbachev.

15 The Secretary-General of the Communist Party of the Soviet Union and his new disarmament policy have in fact presented the Alliance with a problem. Gone are those balmy days when it was so 20 easy to anticipate Moscow's diplomatic and strategic moves. The adversary has become infinitely more wily in devising new things, springing surprises and nicking 25 Atlantic solidarity which is still vulnerable to considerations of selfish national interest.

Wily he may well be, but isn't Gorbachev being sincere when he 30 says he wants to relieve his country of crippling military over-expenditure and get down to sorting out its economic mess? François Mitterrand is right to 35 refuse to answer the question. How can anyone know what is really going on in the mind of a man who, in any case, did not gain power by inadvertence? We must then nec- 40 essarily judge him on his deeds.

Here, two tests will be crucial for East–West relations. The first does not directly concern the West, but it should permit us to get some 45 idea of Gorbachev's determination to correct the "mistakes of the past". This is Afghanistan, where the withdrawal of Soviet troops will go a long way towards con- 50 vincing world opinion that new analyses are at last being made in Moscow.

The second test to which Gorbachev will have to be put is the 55 negotiations on conventional disarmament. These are conventional weapons which in fact make war possible, and it would be dangerous to encourage dreams of a 60 denuclearised Europe so long as the Warsaw powers maintain their superiority in conventional weapons. That was the key idea at the Brussels summit and the 16 will 65 have to push Gorbachev up against this particular wall.

They will succeed here only if they successfully join together in being both open-minded and firm. 70 The two attitudes, illustrated in France by Mitterrand and Chirac, and at the European level by West German Chancellor Helmut Kohl and British Prime Minister Mar- 75 garet Thatcher, are not necessarily mutually exclusive. They should even be complementary, with one or the other prevailing, depending on the line Moscow is taking.

80 Electoral considerations aside, Mitterrand has realised this and has somewhat backed off from his previous declarations objecting to modernising NATO's nuclear 85 forces. He is now insisting on the need for laying down "a strategy for disarmament". Jacques Chirac has also shifted his position and is saying today that he has no 90 reservations about the attitude of Mitterrand, whom he previously suspected of being too ready to 93 take Gorbachev at his word.

Specimen text — English (from *Guardian Weekly,* March 1988)

Normally the syntax predominantly sets the tone of any pragmatic relationship: action is pointed by verbs; description by nouns and adjectives or adverbs of quality; dialogue by forms of address and tags; injunctions by imperatives or rhetorical questions; urgency and speed by brief sentences; leisureliness or meditation by long ones. Unusual word order indicates stress, emphasis, liveliness. The argumentative strident tone of the specimen text on pp. 118–19 set by the negative–positive sequences (*ni. . . ni. . . — non, celui qui était, c'est* (lines 6–12); *ne concerne pas . . . mais il devrait* (6–7, 4–5); *ne sont pas contradictoires. Elles devraient même être complémentaires* (81–4) — even the last sentence goes from negative to positive to negative, with a positive-negative sequence (28–9); each succeeding sentence contrasts with the next. There is opening stress in the word order shifts notably in the *c'est* sentences, but also in *Finis les heureux temps* (18) and *Subtil, certes* (28) *Non, celui qui était* (11) *force est* (41), all admirably reproduced in 'gone are those balmy days' (18), 'Wily he may well be' (28), 'No, the one who was' (11), 'We must then necessarily' (39). The sentences are bold statements, self-contained, but clearly interrelated, uncluttered by clauses with the exception of the adjectival clause, the specially privileged subordinate clause of French syntax, so often related to the even more privileged emphatic *c'est* or *ce sont.* The two rhetorical questions (29, 38) and the inversions help to force a view on the readership. Note also how, as often, the translator converts two verbs *innover, surprendre* (23, 24) into 'empty verbs plus (verb) nouns', 'devising new things', 'springing surprises' which strengthens the emphasis. The paradox of the subject–verb–complement sequence is that the stress is on the complement which is appropriate when the verb is a copula (John is *strong*), but may be inappropriate if the stress is on the action 'He murdered his enemies' and can be remedied if the object is an unstressed pronoun: 'He *mur*dered them', or the verb is converted to 'empty verb plus verb noun': 'He committed several murders'.

Stress which is intimately connected both with syntax and word order, is an essential element in pragmatic effect. Looking at the first sentence in the specimen text on p. 119, the English translation follows every rise and fall of the principal French tone-groups, culminating in the 'nor *even that* "infernal couple" of Mitterand and Chirac' (9/10) (alternatively, infernal couple, Mitterand and Chirac). (*Infernal* has a connotation of 'insupportable' and 'incompatible couple' may be closer.)

Note that I am here positing a 'universal' word order or *Ordo naturalis.* I assume that

(a) the natural sequence of a proposition is from given (or old) to new information, from theme to rheme, which is also the natural sequence of explanation or teaching; but if rheme precedes theme, a degree of pragmatic expectation or tension is imposed on the sentence, which should be reflected in the sentence: e.g. 'suddenly a man came into the room', *soudain un homme est entré dans la salle.* In languages that have no definite or indefinite article a change of word order is automatically required;

(b) that grammatically the natural word order of a sentence is subject–verb–complement, which follows the natural order of thought;

(c) that the main stress in this word order will be on the lexical part or head-word of the complement, provided it contains the new information or rheme (therefore, in 'The man on everybody's mind was Gorbachev', stress is on 'Gorbachev' as it is in the French);

(d) that every language has its own lexical, grammatical, word-ordering resources for putting stress on a non-final group of the sentence, which will normally entail a change or an interruption in the natural word order — the spoken language obtains the stress by an increase in sound volume. This will to a greater or lesser degree produce an emotive effect;

(e) that the reason why many languages (e.g. Latin or German) do not follow the subject–verb–complement natural word order is that its scribes — the clerks, the priests, the ideological hegemony — have imposed an unnatural grammar on the illiterate masses for them to acquire.

Many of the above are intuitive statements, but I do not think there is anything in the classical essays by Firbas (1979) and Greenberg (1963) that contradicts them.

In 'referential translation' the word order is normal; in 'pragmatic' translation it is often upset by particular stresses.

In all examples the functional perspective (or the thematic structure) of each sentence is important. In another sentence, such as *Dies zeigt ein Blick auf jede Landkarte* there is a choice between the intonation ('this is clear if one takes a glance at any map') and the 'lexicogrammar', ('a glance at any map shows this clearly') which displaces the theme ('this') to the end of the sentence. Here I think the choice is in the taste area (I use 'taste area' in contrast with the science — where there's no choice — skill and art area), but in principle I prefer literal translation of thematic structure to literal translation (or even literal approximation) of lexicogrammar in expressive and persuasive texts. In informative texts, where the pragmatic factor is less important, the lexis, i.e. the close description of objects and processes, is more important than the reproduction of the thematic structure.

After the interplay of syntax, word order and stress, metaphor is normally the most powerful pragmatic factor in translation. Metaphor is language's main resource for conveying strong feeling; at present, in many European languages, even amongst the ideological hegemony, sexual and scatological have replaced religious metaphors to express the most vehement feelings. Original and standard metaphors are strongest in taboo and colloquial language; in scientific and descriptive language metaphor is equally important, but it is likely to be spatial or temporal as an aid to reference. Lastly, metaphor is language's main resort for conveying the world of the mind and, with sound-effect in a lesser role, for demonstrating the wealth of the life of the senses: (taste, smell and touch are mainly demonstrated through metaphor — and sound through onomatopoea — though the senses also have a small store of 'literal' technical terms). The pragmatic effect of metaphor in the most emotive types of texts — poetry, advertising, propaganda, metaphysical or religious writing — needs no illustration; the needless evasion or dilution of metaphor is one of the worst features of much poetry translation — needless to say it goes hand in hand with the fear of literalism.

If we now look at the specimen text on pp. 118–19 it seems to me that *enfoncer un coin* (lines 24–5) is the strongest metaphor and to translate it as 'nick' is rather neat but feeble, since a literal translation ('drive a wedge into') would produce a perfect equivalence. A second 'strong' metaphor *mettre au pied de ce mur-là* (72–4) is successfully and literally rendered as 'push up against this particular wall' (65–6). A third, *gommer ses déclarations* (90) a rubber image that appears with much use to be moving from 'delete' to 'moderate', is cleverly given as 'back off from' (82). The more informal English journalese lends itself to phrasal verbs, which are usually metaphorical. The remaining metaphors are unremarkable, but incline to a more 'popular' pragmatic effect, thus *héros* (3) becomes 'star' (3); *heureux* (19), 'balmy' (19); *surprendre* (24), 'springing surprises' (24); *se consacrer à* (33), 'get down to' (32); *paralysant* (32), 'crippling' (31); *remise en ordre d'une économie chaotique* (33–4), 'sorting out an economic mess' (33); *ferait beaucoup* (53), 'go a long way' (49); *conjuguer* (76), 'join together' (68); *le comportement de Moscou* (85–6), 'the line Moscow is taking' (79). Note also the supplementary: 'Chirac has also shifted his position' (88). *Accepter l'argumentation* (99–100), 'take at his word' (93). These English standard metaphors are warm, familiar, simple, homely, on the whole more physical and concrete than the French. (This illustrates a translation tendency to allow free play in an exercise where the precise words used in the translation, just as their correspondents in the original, are not all that important.)

Again, in the title, the translator, by extrapolating *ouverture d'esprit* (76) and *fermeté* (77) from the SL text, has produced a more intriguing effect than the original 'Nato facing Gorbachev'.

Note also that 'wily' (23, 28) is a bold and vivid translation of *subtil,* but that 'test' (53) hardly reaches *examen de passage* (57–8) ('aptitude test'?), and 'withdrawal' (48) is not the same as *'évacuation'* (52), a typical under-translation.

In this piece, syntax, word order and metaphor adequately take care of pragmatic effect; here there is no need for SL and TL readerships to identify. But in persuasive and more universal texts the translator requires other pragmatic resources relating to words as meaning and/or sound: on the one hand, unusual words, unusual metaphors, unusual collocations, neologisms to produce an arresting effect; on the other, alliterations, the most ancient, common and natural of the sound resources (note even here *pose problème* (17) — the p's are *sec* and *saccadé* (Grammont (1949) a lovely book), 'springing surprises', the s's are sexy), only the first has an alliterative correspondent, 'present with a problem'. I repeat: metaphor, alliteration, onomatopoeia, assonance, rhyme, rhythm (the play of stresses) metre — all these as well as conveying meaning appeal to the readership's senses.

Readership is like context: it can never be completely ignored, but it is more important on some occasions than on others. If the readership consists of one client, it is all-important, and you can normally elicit his or her requirements in detail, in particular, whether technical terms (*lordose,* 'hollow back'; *éthylique,* ('alcoholic') or institutional terms (*AMG,* free prescriptions) have to be simplified. If your client is a middle person, and you are translating for their customers who are your readers, you ask for all possible information about the readership, and you may have to strike your own balance about their knowledge, and make use of couplets such as *usines* ('laboratories') or 'corpus' (body of linguistic data). At the other extreme, you have a subtle dense expressive text, such as a poem where the putative and guestimate reception of the readership is irrelevant, where you can only attempt to assess your personal reception of the text.

Between these extremes, there are many variations, many compromises. A translator sometimes has to find a middle way between many masters: not only the author and the readership, but his own intuition, the middle'man' or middleperson (agent, publisher, employer, authority).

Above all, there is the problem of the identity of the readership. Translating a manual of instructions for a far away country (and I don't mean Czechoslovakia), what does one know of their technical linguistic or cultural skill knowledge expertise? Translating an advertisement, who is going to buy the product, a mass or a minority market? Translating a notice or a manual, how are you going to attract attention to it? The presentation (print, illustrations, logo, etc.) may be more important than the translation, the medium more than the message. Sometimes you not only have to guess what type of readership your translation will interest or attract or persuade, you have to swivel your translation towards the readership, to pay constant attention to the effects of positive, negative and value-free words that cannot be swamped by their contexts.

I have attempted to review some of the pragmatic factors in translation, which are closely bound to the readership, the factors that take the text into the target language literature and work towards its absorption into another convention and often another tradition. This is not limited to the canonical or the alternative literature but may absorb all the influences of the media, the generalisations of computer languages, the internationalisation of communication, instantiated in convergent Common Market language. Thus excessive pragmatics tend to rob the target language text of its translational character, and obviously, if the genius or the particular of the foreign language is to be preserved, cleanly and straight, only two procedures can preserve it — transference and literal translation.

Just as 'linguistic science' now seems to be a dusty old-fashioned expression, so the 'Science of Translation' (the title of Wilss' (1982) book) is a false translation of *Ubersetzungs — wissenschaft* and Brian Harris's (1988) 'translatology' appears to be a non-starter. Few people even or ever refer to the scientific element in translation. If words are considered to have no meaning outside their texts or their sentences, their situations, it appears difficult to find a criterion for a translation, let alone an aim.

Yet if one is discussing the full translation of a worthwhile text of some importance, there can be no *primary* aim but accuracy, which may itself be some kind of compromise between the referential and the pragmatic factor (the content and the style, the matter and the manner), and if one looks for a yardstick, a general basis to judge a translation, there is nothing concrete but literal translation. When you ask how close, how faithful, how true a version is in relation to the original, you can have nothing else in mind except the 'spirit' of the original, which is the reverse of concrete. Vinay & Darbelnet (1958) saw this thirty years ago, when they wrote, at the conclusion of their great book:

> On doit arriver a ne s'écarter de la littéralite que pour satisfaire aux exigences de la langue d'arrivée . . . On ne doit pratiquer la traduction oblique qu'à bon escient, dans des limites nettement définies. On doit rester littéral tant qu'on ne fait pas violence à la langue d'arrivée.

On ne s'écarte de la littéralité que pour des raisons de structure ou de
méta-linguistique et on s'assure alors que le sens est sauvegardé.
(Vinay & Darbelnet, 1958: 268)

(The passage was brilliantly recalled by Jean Maillot in *Traduire,* March
1988.) As I see it, the scientific principle in translation could not be better
expressed than it is here, though I think there is a corollary: in an authoritative and/or serious literary text, any violence done to the norms of the SL has
to be reflected in translation by violence done to the norms of the TL.

Further, Vinay & Darbelnet (1958) rightly point out that whilst the
word is rarely the unit of accurate translation, it is wrong to suggest, as did
Gide, that one should translate sentences rather than words; normally the
sentence as a unit is much too wide *(l'ampleur d'une phrase entière).* If that
is so, it is absurd to talk about translating texts rather than words.

If one accepts literalism in the above sense as the scientific principle of
a full translation, one has to make many qualifications, of which the first
is that translation is not a science, it is a craft and an art, and is at the
last revision, within certain narrow limits, often just a question of taste.
Secondly, the more concentrated, the more authoritative, the more studied,
the more 'important' the language of a text, the more meaningful become
the individual words of the text and *pari passu*, in parallel, their translation.
In such a text, each word is charged with meaning, the translator like the
writer beforehand, is wrestling with words; words are so strong that the context falls temporarily into the background. Words become like notes in
chamber-music, expressively important vertically (paradigmatically) in
their associations and etymology, as well as horizontally (syntagmatically).
In a run-of-the-mill text, on the other hand, the message is direct,
unadorned, but the language, like Benjamin's memorable cloak, is looser,
more otiose, more dispensable. One comes to a stage where, as in the case
of my deliberately chosen specimen text, one feels one might as well translate literally but it is not a matter of importance, since one wants to be
accurate but a paraphrase would do as well.

So, if one applies the literalism yardstick to the specimen text, one notes
how in most cases, not only the facts and the main syntax but also the quality
words that state the feeling of the text, have been retained precisely to maintain the pragmatic quality: thus 'pugnacious', 'particularly discreet', 'vulnerable', 'sincere', 'inadvertence', 'crucial', 'dangerous' and others shine
through from the original. Whilst 'nicking' Atlantic solidarity (lines 24–5) is
a neat but feeble version of the literal 'driving a wedge into Atlantic solidarity', the translation of *contradictoires* (82) as 'mutually exclusive' (76) *(ne
s'excluent pas l'une l'autre)* is markedly an improvement on the original.

Here then, literalism is a form of control on the 'style'. The message is secure, accuracy in every verbal detail is not important, but inaccuracy in detail is unnecessary rather than elegant. The translator usually shows commendable restraint in resisting the all too common temptation to convert straightforward literal language into clichés, but note that *héros* (3) becomes 'star' (3); *heureux* (18), 'balmy' (19), and *accepter l'argumentation* (99–100), 'take at his word' (93), admittedly close to the taste area. (Some translators can't resist translating *j'ai à vous parler* by the cliché 'I want a word with you'.)

Certainly there are informative texts where one is faithful to the author not out of loyalty to the author (the author's precise style is hardly worth it), but simply out of loyalty to one's client and the readership (who, one assumes, want to know exactly what the author wrote), and from a training in accurate translation.

Conclusion

Vinay & Darbelnet (1958) wanted translators to keep to direct translation (loans, through translation, literal translation) where this could be done without violence to the norms of the target language, and only revert to indirect translation, i.e. all the arts and crafts (the 'strategies' — yuck) — of translation where this became necessary. The fact that they mistrusted literal translation (see Vinay & Darbelnet, 1958: 89) and have been criticised by Wilss (1982) for so doing shows that they were no slaves of *transcodage*.

There are, in fact, two approaches to translation and to translating, and this first one we may call bottom to top. In practice, this is where the translator starts translating immediately. It has the excitement and adventure of immediate practice, of getting the feeling-tone of the text at once, of learning and erring through experience. It is a literalist approach, where we plough ahead and stop, usually sentence by sentence, at places where literal translation won't do. My definition of a translation-problem is where literal translation fails and we have to consider a number of choices, or procedures, guided by a reasoned perception of a number of contextual factors, which can finally be confirmed only by a reading of the whole text. More often than not, the grammatical problems can be solved instinctively without reflection through readily available transpositions or shifts: crudely, *ils jouent,* they play, they are playing, they do play; lexical problems (one word into one word won't go) require more deliberation, offer a larger number of choices: crudely, 'neat' may become *concis, propre, soigné, fin, bref, habile, net, clair, adroit, pur, sec,* etc., 'encyclopaedia' problems (*OPA* as 'take-over bid') depend on one's provisional assessment of the readership; cohesive problems are subject to sentence and paragraph sequencing. That is the humdrum, scientific literalist approach to translating and its problems, which not infrequently includes literal translation as a solution, when its first strangeness has worn off in the translator's mind, or if the translator thinks of it as a possible TL acquisition (*Fingerspitzengefühl für Sprache:* 'a finger-tip feeling for language' — what's so *German* about that? or 'speak oneself out' — *sich aussprechen*).

The second approach to translating and translation is top to bottom, which every translation teacher recommends and the poor students follow, but perhaps few instinctive translators practise: this means reading the text two or three times before we start, and I concede that if the text is a technical maze to the translator, he or she would be rash *not* to pursue it. Here we assess not the particular but the general problems of the text: first the topic, then the language, and concomitantly the appalling readership, then the register, then the tone down to a dwindling number of other factors, figura-tive or denotative, fact or fiction (is the 'street' a real 'street' or a 'path', 'a goal', a 'road' etc.?).

Both approaches are valid; top to bottom, with its absurdity, text as translation unit, is at present overblown. Bottom to top, that starts as literal and soon gives up, is more objective, more specific, more scientific, the *contrôle* of a translation, the back translation test (BTT), that can easily be abused, that can degenerate into translationese, is at present neglected in the literature. But against the potential licence of pragmatics, hermeneutics, the *vouloir dire,* the sub-text, the spirit, the *génie de la langue,* it's the only buffer, the only sense and common sense.

What I see as the most urgent objective in translation studies, trans-lation theory and more pertinently, translation teaching is to bring these two approaches and methods a little closer together — they will never be unified — most translators are and always will be instinctively either *sourciers* or *ciblistes* (Ladmiral's clever terms), source — or target-orientated ('sourcer-ers' or 'targeteers'?) — and this is natural. What is harmful is extremist state-ments on either side, and these come now from the *ciblistes,* as no *sourcier* would want to emulate Benjamin or Nabokov. The task is important, as it not only has a bearing on standards of translation, but also on the various stages of translating and therefore on translation teaching. I see this as more profitable than 'objectively recording and scientifically analysing what trans-lators do' or 'maximising the individuality of the process', whatever that may mean; or naively regarding the 'immediate' approach (i.e. 'begin to translate at once') which is frowned upon by so many translation teachers, as a 'sharp dose of realism'. (Quotations all from Brian Harris, 1988.)

What is likely to at least bring the two approaches (and methods) closer together is first to relate them to text-types, readerships and other contextual factors; secondly, to bear in mind that stretches of text of whatever length have meaning, and the translator is only concerned with meaning transfer; thirdly, in the critical third stage of revising, to read the translation as an independent, autonomous, spontaneous text, as well as to read it sentence by sentence, side by side, with the original, and thereby not foregoing, as the interpreter has to, the advantage of all the information that rereadings of the original can continue to offer; fourthly, to exploit the contrasted insights of text linguistics as well as of literal translation; lastly to aim for the 'closest possible' (Nida) translation, which normally indicates a sheaf rather than a point of intersection between the two methods. If a closer agreement can be reached on the approach, choices will remain, but they will be a little narrower, and eventually translations may become more accurate.

Note

1. Pragmatic translation in Canada, Windsor, Canada, 1988.

10 Teaching Translation

Introduction

I approach my subject, teaching translation, rather apprehensively. To my knowledge, there is hardly any literature on it. Simon Chau (1984) has written a brilliant doctoral dissertation entitled *Aspects of Translation Pedagogy,* but essentially this describes and evaluates various approaches to translation theory syllabuses, with further discussion of useful exercises preparatory to and parallel with translation itself. In addition, there is some discussion of the qualities required of the trainee student and a brief note on the qualities required of the translation teacher, consisting merely of a list of remarks by Wilss and a quote from Keiser about teachers of interpretation who have never even had to interpret professionally at an international conference. And among the over 400 items in the *Translation Teaching Bibliography*, of which I may have read one-third, I can see little hint of a discussion of the business of teaching a translation class, of going through a text. I tried to do this in a paper I read in Aarhus (Newmark, 1980), which was, as they say, unnoticed in the literature. This time I have to enter the delicate area of how to teach and how to learn. It is a hot potato. I may give offence, many of my remarks will be considered trivial and below the dignity of a scholar and an academic, *verb. sap.,* indeed. I propose also to relate my description of teaching rather loosely to some problems of translation.

What is Required of the Translation Teacher?

Teaching translation, you have first to be organised in your class procedures, which includes informing your students of them: they have to have copies of your syllabus, and the opportunity of commenting on it; they, rather than the legendary French education minister, have to know what

129

they will be doing with you next week; further, you have to acquaint them with the names and location of all the main relevant up-to-date reference books — the various types of fact-books *(Sachbücher)* — *il faut être absolument moderne* (Rimbaud) — as well as the various word-books (the monolingual are more useful than the bilingual), such as dictionaries, thesauruses, glossaries, books about translation, collocation dictionaries, and you have to demonstrate how to use them — in no subject are reference books so important — latest editions always. Any reference book can be useful, provided you know its limitations; you have to state your own preferences — why, for instance, the *Collins Dictionary* is more useful than the *Concise Oxford Dictionary* for the translator; why the Merriam-Webster is a short cut across many bilingual problems (look up *hamartia* — a Greek term meaning 'defect of character' which you might find in a Spanish or Russian or German learned text); the uses of the *Cobuild* for all non-technical words.

Secondly, you have to be punctual when you start, consigning the holy academic quarter of an hour (*quart d'heure académique, akademische Viertelstunde* — strange that only in English is the expression unfamiliar) to the dustbin and finishing the class so as not to keep the next teacher waiting.

Thirdly, you need a certain confidence, particularly when admitting mistakes, or teaching students more gifted than yourself, that you still have enough experience and expertise to impart to them.

I think the translation teacher should have a *fortiori,* preferably from professional experience, the four professional translator's skills, all of which can be acquired if the motive and the milieu are there: (a) sensitivity, fingertip feeling for written and spoken language, the ability to discriminate nuances of the language of your habitual use, and to write elegantly, neatly, plainly, tersely and naturally in a number of stylistic registers; (b) a wide knowledge of your language and culture of habitual use including an extensive vocabulary and the basic institutional and geographic facts, and as a teacher, the metalanguage derived from a grounding in linguistics to describe and categorise linguistic terms; (c) a good if temporary knowledge of the topic(s) — I teach a translation topic by way of exemplification on the ground that I see the problems better than the expert; (d) knowledge of two or three foreign languages and cultures. The last two skills are sometimes in inverse proportion: the more technical the text, the less important the knowledge of the foreign language and its culture, and vice versa.

I suggest for the sake of controversy that the success of any translation course must depend 65% on the personality of the teacher, 20% on the course design and 15% on the course materials.

Personality first. In a classroom, it's hard to say where personality finishes and teaching technique begins. You have to find your own teaching style. Some people are laid-back, calm, patient, cool, tidy, natural, spontaneous, can turn it on at a moment, and they are first-rate. For me, patience has always been a vice, an excuse for inactivity and laziness, and impatience a virtue; I want to get on, to move fast, but I answer any question straight at any level, however irrelevant.

I have to make a lot of notes before I take a class, I prepare more than I need as I'm afraid of drying up, I often go beyond my notes at the risk of straying to points I don't remember too well where I don't know the facts properly. I always bring in a dictionary partly to show I'm the reverse of infallible. I take a note of questions I can't answer properly and fully and deal with them next time.

Operationally, the ability of teachers to make their students work hard and purposefully is a function of their personalities; magnetism, charm, charisma, etc. have nothing directly to do with it, but openness and friendliness have. Most decent teachers may be laid-back or exhibitionists or actors, giving a performance for each lesson that is rarely applauded and little appreciated, simply taken for granted, and remembered gratefully only 30 or 40 years later. Now something new is required: the disposition to invite collaboration and participation is more important than the old-fashioned performance! This is still an aspect of 'personality', and as personality I include: (1) personal qualities that are attractive as well as compulsive, (2) professional qualities and experience which are reflected in course design and choice of materials, (3) general knowledge of culture. The personal qualities include those of any good teacher as well as of any translator: energy, curiosity, enthusiasm, ability to work at speed against a deadline, meticulousness in the smallest details, punctuation, sign language, figures, checking that every word and sign in the original is accounted for, scrupulousness, admitting that any informed guess is 'not found'.

Whilst the teacher's main job is in the selection, translation, assessment and exploitation of texts, he or she also has to teach two important subjects which I can only touch on briefly: (a) note-taking, (b) revision. Sometimes students write translation notes on their returned translations. I try to discourage this, as they never look at them again. I encourage them to bring notebooks, and compile (a) grammatical, (b) lexical, (c) cultural notes under separate heads, say transpositions, synonyms, neologisms, institutional terms, proper nouns. If they do not take them down and learn them, they will forget everything. Students often regard hand-outs as a substitute for note-taking. They encourage passivity.

When it comes to revision, this often takes up at least half of all translating time. But this is a huge subject, which I discuss in Chapter 8.

As a translation teacher, your personality is expressed in your attitude:
your job is to help a wide range of students, many *brighter* than you are —
'bright' usually has no one-to-one FL equivalent. It is a combination of intelligence, quickness, imagination, observation, *(gescheit — advisé),* whilst at
least 20% may be dull (again a no-equivalent word), below the 'desired standard'. These are the ones in whose favour you discriminate positively. You
both serve your students and guide them, tactfully, which is a modern definition of leadership. You set the tone for a collaboration — 'this is so, isn't it?'
leading on to 'Yes, but . . .', as F. R. Leavis put it. In other words, again,
translation is for discussion. Whilst the plain mistakes of fact and language
can normally be identified, the area of usage in social language is more delicate (does one say 'Please desist' seriously?).

Teaching Various Kinds of Texts and Problems

There are many cases where general cohesive stereotypes in the source
language (SL) will not fit in the translation: as a title 'Observations on
planing work' is absurd in an English text book. Sentences that begin: 'It is
evident that . . .', 'Let us say that . . .', 'It is the movement given to the
table which determines . . .', 'Let us note that . . .', 'It's a question of . . .',
'We recall that . . .' (all of these are literal translations from a French
machine-tool manual), whilst perfectly acceptable in various contexts,
would not be natural in an English machine-tool manual.

There is often the question of how much extra 'encyclopaedia' information or explanation is required for the target language readership, not only
for cultural, but also for technical data: how is a specialist English readership
to guess that an 'amnesiac cerebral eclipse' or an 'amnesiac ictus' probably
refers to 'transient global amnesia', unless the translator makes the sugges-
tion in a square bracket note? Further, there may be ambiguous or obscure
sentences to be elucidated and interpreted and beyond that, there is always
the taste area. Many structures and lexical units, whilst they differ in meaning extracontextually or virtually or potentially are synonymous or at least
equivalent and interchangeable in actual context.

Ironically, while a translation has to be accurate, it is only approximate,
it can always be changed, even at its best. At its last stage, it is a question of
style, whether it is non-literary or literary, anonymous or authoritative.
More generally, since no text translation is perfect, correct, ideal — but

often needs have literally no semantic loss — any idea of dictating a fair copy *(Reinschrift, copie au net)* or a model translation, for so long the obsession of schools, is out of place. A translation is never finished, it is always slightly but significantly dependent on the interpretant (in C. S. Peirce's sense) or different interpretants, or the same one at another point of time and mood.

So the translation teacher, faced with a class and a text to be discussed, has a formidable task. He has to have a different plan for each text. Always first he has to ensure that the text is understood linguistically and referentially (i.e. that everyone knows what it is about in reality, and can gist it), the writer's intention, the main themes, and who it is addressed to: the title may be allusive ('One man's city') rather than descriptive ('In London'), and a descriptive title ('London') may conceal an intention ('avoid London'), giving the translator the option of recasting the title, providing the text is not authoritative.

Understanding the text and its themes means reducing the language to its reference-points in reality, which means not only simplifying but as it were dementalising it, treating it as an object without a spectator, dehumanising it, so that temporarily (before we go back to the SL text) the 'Old Lady of Threadneedle Street', becomes the Bank of England, *melilot* becomes sweet clover, 'the American authors' becomes 'Link and his colleagues'. Thus the teacher has to clarify meaning at all stretches of the text, from text and paragraph to word and morpheme (e.g. 'dys-', 'thym-', '-ase'). Where the teacher is useful is not simply in pin-pointing problems in their contexts, but in generalising them, in assessing how often a particular type of problem occurs. The text is not just a piece to be gone through and translated as happens in many translation classes, but it is a *pièce-témoin,* a reference object or exhibit.

Personally, I have a lesson for today for most classes, beginning with the role of the readership and what, if anything, we are going to do for them. Then I select from the text two or three important general problems and lead in with these: it may be the meaning of italics, which can be used to emphasise in French and German, but maybe are translated by bold face in English, or the ways of translating verb-nouns, or the distinctions between informal and colloquial styles, or even, teaching the SL (which I'm not meant to), to summarise *(rappeler)* the delicate structures and meanings of say: *tel:* 'like', 'such', 'any', 'one', 'a particular', 'a given someone or other', 'such and such', 'take for example' . . . Now, assuming the text has been done as homework and corrected, the discussion that follows is the staple of any translation class. Someone will start with the first sentence, and I have to point out that other things come first: it may be the source, the publisher, the title, the author and his position, the first foot-note, the paragraph head-ing — we have to settle what to translate, what to transfer or what to transfer and to translate, with reference to house-style, and not retranslate a translated quote. The translator has to account for, not necessarily translate, every word in the text. (Here the type of exam paper which gives texts without titles, let alone authors, sources and dates, is not helpful — these data should always be given at school and university level.)

As we proceed through the piece, sentence by sentence — since however expandable or contractable the unit of translation may be, the unit of translating is normally the sentence — I have to assign the sentences, and *a fortiori* put translation problems to the students I judge capable of *almost* or just capable of dealing with them, not quite too difficult nor quite too easy, that make them have to think, that make them 'take the strain'.

The ability to put the right questions is dependent on your judgement of character as well as capacity; it is one of the bases of a good teacher–student relationship. In Scandinavia, the cult of the silent student has to disappear. It baffles comprehension.

The teaching technique during the class reflects translating activity. The relation between words and things has to be continuously verified: abbreviations, acronyms, figures, metaphors, names, neologisms, terms of art, symbols, jargon, gobbledegook, familiar alternatives — all have to be made factually plain, all have to be assessed in terms of frequency and register. There is rarely a sentence that does not have to pass between one of the tensions of translating: on the one hand an accurate rendering of nuances of meaning, which includes factors of emphasis as well as a recognition of deliberate sound effects in the original and undesirable sound effects in the translation, and on the other, the attempt to follow the appropriate natural usage based on frequency, which tends to expand and weaken the force of the original (*La grève est une source d'exaltation* — 'a strike is a means of arousing feelings'). If the text is well-written as well as authoritative, the tension between meaning and natural usage may be replaced by the tension between meaning and aesthetic sense which stretches over the articulation as well as the sound of words and sentences. Always the teacher has to point out problems at every level of difficulty, from the interpretation of connotations ('negotiations stalled' — temporarily, deliberately, unexpectedly, violently stopped?) for the subtler students to the indication of true and false friends for the less subtle. You can't be teaching all the people all the time, but you have to be teaching all the people at least 75% of their time — otherwise they'll say (the most damaging comment) they got nothing out of the class.

The peculiar quality of the translation teacher (and this is where translation 'theory' can at least assist) is to know how and when to generalise from the particular and to follow the generalisation with further particulars. You don't let *d'usage courant* be translated as 'currently used' without pointing out that the shift from 'verb–noun plus adjective' to 'adverb plus adjective' is frequent in translation from Romance languages, and you follow with several other examples, however artificial (an 'artificial', i.e. 'without the implications of utterance' example is better than no example at all), and again, you distinguish fast trains from swift, quick, rapid, speedy, fleet trains — alas, no velocitudinous trains. You have to 'teach about' sometimes, but this teaching about, as in language teaching, has to be brief, simple and clear — there is still a text to be translated, to be got through. In fact I mis-time often (so combining intensive with extensive) which means having to take over the translation of the last few paragraphs of the text, pouncing a few questions in the middle, or asking for questions afterwards. (I rarely get through more than 250 words in an hour.)

It is essential, as I see it, to vary informative or 'anonymous' with 'classical' authoritative texts. In authoritative texts, manner and matter are equally important in principle, they include any definitive statement as well as imaginative literature. In informative texts, the content and the intention are more important than the form of the original, and if the form of the original is deficient, it has to be improved. The translation of an authoritative text has to be closer than that of the average technical, commercial or scientific text. I have found that if a translation course consists almost exclusively of 'subjects' such as electronics, computers, drugs, finance, chemical engineering etc. the students are at sea if they are suddenly faced with a text by a leading statesman, a guru or an innovative novelist. Inevitably, some of the texts you choose have to be routine, as are many of the texts your students will be translating, written in that dreary semi-official reporting style, both commercial and technical, not far off jargon, which is all too easy to translate almost literally. You know what I mean: *Das Jahr 1981 war durch den stagnierenden Markt für Schweißelektroden beeinflußt,* 'Business in 1981 felt the effects of the stagnant market for welding electrodes'.

Fortunately there is usually plenty to discuss about the choices and decisions to be made in translating even the most lifeless metaphorless texts, but you have to take care not to invent translation problems where they are nothing but matters of taste.

Text-translation is normally 'full' translation, covering the entire SL text, with varying emphasis on its message (language as speech-act), the stretches of its semantic texture, and sometimes even its *vouloir-dire* rather than what was actually written (the unholy hermeneutic alliance between Seleskovitch and Paepcke). But full translation should be occasionally varied with partial translation: gisting, abstracting, summarising, sight translation, functional translation, i.e. responding merely to a question or two from the client: e.g. is the drug successful or not? Here (too) translation should be 100% successful.

I have suggested that 35% of the success of a course depends on the planning of the curriculum and the choice of the materials. The two go together. The curriculum may be distributed evenly over the three main text areas: literary, institutional and scientific-technological, in a first degree course; in a professional course, of say ten syllabuses, it will be restricted to a few topics, and the variety lies in making sure that the main heads within each topic are covered; the choice is in the variety of registers: research papers, professional journals, text books, manuals, technical reports — well and badly written, preferably from local firms — popularising works, quality papers, tabloids, advertisements, case histories, thus a wide range of diffi-culty of subject and formality of language. The common factor in all topics is business — that is, commerce, finance, marketing — with institutional terms introduced in a fair proportion of the texts. Most texts should be up to date in topic as well as in language, it is no good using a text about an opaque planer if that type was abandoned in 1986. One is always looking for challenging texts, texts that have difficulties of language as well as of topic, problems where literal translation is not feasible and imagination as well as linguistic skill is required.

Take care not to select a translation (where problems have usually already been ironed out) as your text, but if you do, turn it into a translation criticism exercise.

Whilst literary texts are appropriate only in courses where there is a secure demand (from applicants and/or employers), some established authoritative 'classics' in the topic which have a broad humanities base should be included in some courses; texts about art, literature and music may have a nice combination of innovative language and technical challenge which can be introduced as an occasional alternative to the main subject texts. There are some writers who require continuous 'creative' translation, whose complexity and richness of thought and language appears to defy translation (it doesn't), and it may be useful to make a list of them within your area. But it is a mistake to set such texts continuously and to discuss translation mainly at this exalted level, making their subtlety an excuse for fantastically clever and wayward translations allegedly concentrating on the thought (the 'message' or 'communication' would be an inferior word for them), rather than the words of the original, as does Fritz Paepcke (1986), who is otherwise a rich and rewarding writer, subtly stressing the play and the rule elements in translation.

Teaching Translation — A New Profession

Teaching translation, like translating, is a new profession, and it needs clarification from two points of view: first, it needs distinguishing from teaching translation within language teaching, where it has so long played a dubious role hovering between the aims of literary good style, language enrichment, and avoiding the literal truth; secondly, it needs distinguishing within conventional university teaching, which in the humanities in the UK has for long been a non-subject without a literature (no one writes even about how to teach the 'upper' forms of schools), a poor second to research, an ancillary activity for dons, lecturers and masters. (Trevelyan's relief at finding only three students before him at his second lecture is legendary: 'Now I can write another book'.)

Teaching such a necessary but tricky subject as translation which is at once a skill, a science, an art and an area of taste has to be discussed, particularly when there are veteran professionals who think it cannot be taught or learned, and academics who resent such rude mechanicals at a university. ('Why is there no full-time course or diploma at Oxbridge?', I was once naïvely asked.)

Often the translation teacher practises the systematic routines of a craft teacher. He does not lecture: he teaches in a classroom. The difference is (here he resembles the literary critic) that every text presents a new task that challenges his resourcefulness. He is teaching, not a new subject (translation was the staple, first of classics, then of so-called 'modern' (what a word) language teaching), but an old one that has been transformed in the last twenty years, when professional translation courses may be said to have started. (The first, appropriately for its international significance, was in Geneva.) The subject that used to be 'academic' in a grammar school sense is now basically a craft subject in a technical college sense, but stretches to areas of linguistics, language philosophy, language criticism and cultural studies.

SL and TL cultural backgrounds are essential subjects in a university translation course. They must not be confused with the old-fashioned 'Life and Institutions' class. Their basis is solid economic geography, a conspectus of a country's industrial services and agricultural centres related to demography, social and political factors, as well as to scientific and cultural achievements. This is followed by a description of national institutions: central and local government, corporations, the churches, utilities, education, arts centres and the current philosophies which guide and assail them. The three basic translation procedures: transference, TL cultural adaptation, 'universal' sense, that is a functional and descriptive equivalent, underlie any cultural background course. Only universal sense makes translation possible.

The translation teacher has to be able to draw on cultural backgrounds readily during a text-based class. (In the UK at any rate, most students are geographically and culturally uninformed, they also ignore diagrams.) Further, translation teachers should use their second and third languages to make brief analogies and contrasts as illustrations, normally using both literal and close translations (*gewiss* may translate as 'admittedly', compare *certes,* literally also 'certainly', often there is nothing 'certain' about either) to underline their points. Similarly, they need linguistics and translation theory, not only because when they teach translation they are, like language teachers teaching grammar, implicitly teaching a theory of language (as well as of translation) but because they need this metalanguage of lingusitic terms — stylistic, grammatical, lexical, phonological, always from a semantic perspective — for describing the numerous issues raised in translating.

Further they should have a translation specialism, enabling them to freelance from time to time, and to have experience not only of translating for money but of contacts with translation clients, companies, agencies, and bureaux, to keep in touch with the market, as well as with professional colleagues by attending workshops.

In view of the educational as well as vocational aims of this entirely new form of university teaching, the translation teacher has to be not only a solid classroom teacher, but a person of wide cultural background, normally engaged in one of the at least eight areas of translation research, viz. linguistics-based translation theory; corpus-based bilingual translation research; translation and culture; translation and society; machine translation; terminology; translating processes; translation criticism (see Newmark, 1986: 37–50).

But as in all jobs where you work with people, qualification and experience get nowhere without personality. It's a new situation: in UK schools, at one time, if you were respectable, you schoolmastered, you didn't teach. In higher education, you were a don. Don, dominus, Spanish don — ridiculous word even now; in the Chambers *Twentieth Century Dictionary:* 'a fellow of a college'; in the *Concise Oxford:* 'a head fellow or tutor of college especially at Oxford or Cambridge' — but in fact, only at Oxbridge.

Even now, at college, you're a lecturer, and you talk about pedagogy, which once meant leading children. And in the USA, everyone's a professor. And it is unscholarly to discuss punctuality, and the board's peppered with notices cancelling classes without explanation. And the cosy academic circuits are remote from the classroom.

11 Teaching About Translation

Teaching about translation in translation courses often meets with the same prejudices as teaching about language (notably about grammar) in foreign language courses. I will not rehearse all the arguments which range from condemning all abstractions to the proposition that as one learns only through practice, anything that is not practice is a waste of precious time. There is, however, a marked difference in this analogy: learning a foreign language can be begun at an early age, when grammar is taught ostensively (if at all) and simply within the child's continuous comprehension; teaching about translation, however, is as complex, divided and sophisticated an activity as much translation itself. Further, such teaching has a dual component since it comprises the study of two (or more) cultures as well as two languages. Since a full-time vocational translation programme contains a number of disparate courses, such as translation of various types of texts, backgrounds in topics and cultures, machine translation, word processing, etc., there has to be one central or core course — not in linguistics, not in translation theory, certainly not in translatology (a contrived and ponderous term) but in principles and methods of translation: a period of reflection in both senses of the word, on which all courses make an impact, and which makes its impact on all courses.

Principles and methods of translation is the core of any full-time vocational translation programme, but it is hardly a discipline or science in the sense that a term such as 'translatology' would suggest. It is based on a theory that can never be properly integrated, a subject split down the middle, primarily between the original's author and the readership of the translation. On a second level, there is the tug between the facts of the text, the truth and the translator's orientation ('sourcerer' or 'targeteer'), idiolect and ideology. On a third, there are the language norms, cultures, situations and genre traditions — non-literary or literary — in or underlying the two languages, which may also pull the translator in one direction or the other. It is a large, loose, untidy subject with a lot of grey and fuzzy areas and plenty of loose ends. For these reasons, the purpose of this focal subject, setting out from a functional theory of language, is to sensitise students to translation problems at all levels of a text-to-word hierarchy, and depending on various contextual factors to at least reduce the number of feasible solutions to the narrowest possible taste area, where there are sometimes syntactic as well as lexical options that are equally valid, particularly in a non-authoritative text. (So often it hardly matters which synonym you choose: 'agreeable', 'nice' or 'pleasant'.)

The less pregnant, dense or meaningful the words of a text, the less critical its nuances of meaning become, so that only the message or the force of the text matters — and it may be a simple one. Yet the subject of 'translation theory' is pulled together by its adherence to the truth, by its moral and critical nature, by its dedication *(consacrazione)* to understanding between and among individuals and people.

But before discussing approach, content and method, I have to say something about the qualifications and qualities of a teacher of such a course. The teacher has to have a strong attractive pervasive personality, embracing the whole classroom or the rows (the nearest rows only) occupied by the students; a voice that carries without hectoring (I have experienced too much Italian and Indian hectoring); a warm manner that invites participation; an open undogmatic tone — we are talking about a subject where there are no absolutes and few certainties, where there are probabilities and approximations, compromises and compensations, rather than laws or rules. Translation has shifted from the technical college to the university, from dilettantism to professionalism, but its many-sided nature, scientific, cultural, artistic, technical, discriminating, taste-tied requires the talents of the all-round classroom teacher rather than the scholar: to explain clearly with many translation examples; to summarise; to structure the talk ('discourse') and keep it relevant and pertinent; to give hints and references rather than erudite citations; to avoid or mock buzz-words.

A teacher has to teach translation as well as 'translation theory'; to have professional translating experience; to be able to translate from two-plus foreign languages; to have a broad eclectic knowledge of linguistics, and in particular semantics; to interest oneself in any type of text, literary as well as technical or institutional; to write one's target language (TL) economically, resourcefully and agreeably in a number of registers. The subject is new and controversial as a university discipline, and one has to be able to defend it, to state one's own views and warn where these are unorthodox or tentative.

Obedience, submissiveness, docility (note the etymology) and patience are not virtues in 1990, and a teacher has not only to demonstrate why the subject is being taught, but also why and how it will be useful. (All knowledge has to be useful.) Correspondingly students normally want to start by hearing a brief description of their subject, why it is going to be useful to them, and how their work is going to be assessed, and they want copies of the syllabus and the bibliography. I sometimes answer the first question by saying that my subject is all you ever wanted to know about translation and wish you had asked, i.e. it is not about one translation theory but the body of knowledge we have about translation; it includes the criteria for a good translation, providing a framework of reference, after distinguishing the purpose of the text and that of the translator — they may be different — for identifying the problems at any stretch of language from text through paragraph, sentence, clause, group and word to punctuation mark with stress on grammatical structures and words (metaphors, puns, eponyms, cultural words, proper names, etc.) and for matching these with the appropriate contextual factors (type of text, readership, setting, importance of problem, etc.) and translation procedures (synonyms, cultural equivalent, literal translation, compensation, etc.). In the UK there are no textbooks and few training courses on teaching for university teachers, who prefer to be called lecturers or dons, and often regard teaching as below their dignity. However, this situation is changing. Inspectors of Education (HMIs) are now reporting on polytechnics, and 'appraisal' of lecturers (often used in an economic sense — do they 'deliver'!?) has become a university buzz-word. The course is designed to be useful in various ways; at the bottom line, to assist translators creatively with every type of problem they meet. But to do this successfully there must be a theory of translation, and behind this a theory of language, which here has to be explicitly though succinctly stated. The course is not all practical: it offers an insight into the nature of translation as simulation and language as self-communion or communication in general, and in particular, for instance, the nature of metaphor, the central problem of translation, the concision of the pun (more readily translatable than is often thought) even the elemental significance of alliteration (emphasis and rhythm) and of sounds (the violence of a final k). Inevitably, teachers choose their own theory of translation and should declare themselves as instinctively 'sourcerers' (source-oriented) or 'targeteers' (target-oriented), but they have to keep open-minded, they have to show the strengths and traps of both approaches, and they have to continuously narrow the gap between them, to search for acceptability without compromising their standards. This theory component is a thin thread that runs through all the teaching.

The relationship between student and teacher is a delicate one: in the jargon, it has to be interactive, not passive. There must be no dais, no cathedra; the students must be close, have easy access, not sitting in far corners, no steep amphitheatre. But the tools are pens or word-processors (now respectable and essential for both sexes, where previously typewriters were in Britain a symbol of female inferiority). If students don't ask questions, the class is a failure. As Nida has said, there's no such thing as a silly question, there are only teachers' silly answers, like 'You ought to know that by now'. If in replying to a question, you don't produce some kind of translation example, not much is learned. In an hour-long class, all students should learn, but they cannot be learning every minute of the time; some, when they are not learning, will be internalising. My own job is to raise each student's standard, and their struggle is to improve on their yesterday's selves, not to be better than their classmates.

I think that students should regularly have a clear indication of their progress. This is possible only if their work is marked on a scale where a pass (say 4) and a distinction (say 7) are generally known, rather than the obscure Oxbridge α, β or A−, or the ambiguous 'Fair' or 'Quite good'. If the current text and its translation problems are to be discussed in class in the following week, then all fair copy corrections on the scripts are a waste of time, but there should be symbolic indicators for linguistic as well as referential mistakes; wrong usage; preference for another rendering; misspelling; linguistic sexism; wrong tenses; and 'bring this up in class unless it's been already discussed to your satisfaction'. In any event, the mark or grade is given to gladden or assure or alarm the students about their progress, not as a spur to competitiveness, since one should be competing only against oneself — or rather one's last peformance — not against others.

In my classes, the students all have an English text (I produce a new one every three or four weeks), the syllabus (based on my book *A Textbook of Translation*) and a bibliography. I prepare my classes by writing headings with notes, translation examples (new ones) and references, and reading the relevant section of my book (frequently reacting against it) and referring to the writers I most disagree with (Ladmiral, Holmes, Toury, Vermeer, Holz-Manttari, Seleskovitch, Neubert, etc.) rather than the ones I agree with (Wilss, of course). You usually learn more from your 'adversaries' than you do from your friends. (But this may apply more to politics than to works on translation.) Nida is always good to read, but for me the richest and most satisfying book on translation is Vinay & Darbelnet's *Stylistique Comparée* and the best periodical is *Meta*.

My best teaching manner is hesitant, Forsterian, 'seasoned' possibly with my stalest immature jokes, e.g. 'I never make mistakes, only slips'; 'I don't know whether this is what I'll be thinking tomorrow'; 'I change with the language'; 'I believe in the literal truth'; 'I see you're another of those faithless beauties; I prefer the plain and the true'. The majority of students are always girls. 'Principles and Methods' should be an anchor course, allowing for the diverse approaches of the other translation teachers. In my experience, students often complain about the contradictory pronounce-ments of the teachers on this post-graduate diploma course as in no other, all pitched at various points on the axis of translation as an art and as a science; as beauty and as truth; as text-bound and as word-bound. Hence translation teachers should meet at least once a term, not to determine an identity of approach, but to try to bring various approaches a little closer together; to allow for some flexibility; to acknowledge the different potential reader-ships of a translation, the various purposes and uses of a text, the limits to the meanings of words. Hence also the need for continuous refreshment, not only for teachers to do professional translations from time to time, but for students to visit translation agencies and departments in the public and private sectors for an afternoon as well as for *stages, Praktika, periodi di addestramento* and for a series of talks by practitioners — freelance trans-lators, heads of agencies, staff translators, local business people, literary translators (e.g. the fortnightly seminars at Surrey University) to give stu-dents and staff a realistic insight into conditions of work.

My insistence on a plethora of translation examples to accompany the 'Principles and Methods' course may appear surprising. A few people, from Luther to Benjamin, have written well about translation without examples, but only the demonstrated instance of a principle is going to convince or enlighten, let alone teach, most students. Say I state: 'no source language (SL) word can be translated by a semantically irrelevant TL word, unless there is an implied collocate linking the two words'. This is abstract until I produce the instance, say a case where a technical term in one language *(communication)* is translated by 'hole', a word that has no semantic con-nection with 'communication', but covers collocations in two languages: *communication intraventriculaire* and 'hole in the heart', which also demon-strates a negative to positive modulation, as there is a 'hole' (lack of communication) between the two ventricles. Thus the word for word sub-structure of a translation has to be understood, even when the final version of, say, a sentence in relation to its original appears to be remote from such a substructure. In a full, as opposed to a partial, translation, every com-ponent has to be accounted for by some component in the original — that is the scientific element in translation, and it should never be lost sight of.

The objectives of the course have been described, but what are the aims, the *finalités,* as the French put it? At the bottom line we are trying to show how to transfer knowledge, to convey information, in various styles, affected by many factors, and monitored by the truth. We demonstrate gen-eral strategies and numerous particular procedures, as well as the sheer tricks of the trade, of which there are a great many: I instance merely the various compensation procedures, often neglected in the literature, for puns, alliteration, rhyme, slang, metaphor, pregnant words — all these can be compensated, if the game is worth the candle — sometimes it isn't. Compensation is the procedure which in the last resort ensures that translation is possible. Secondly, we have to act as a guide to the continuously increasing number of reference books, both linguistic and factual, that are now being published. Instance: 'Dunhelm', a not so familiar alternative term for the Bishop or University of Durham, can apparently only be found in *Payton's Proper Names.*

Lastly, I believe the main feature of translators is that they are writers; they can write plainly, economically, gracefully, elegantly in a repertoire of registers, factual as well as emotional, popular as well as technical, official as well as slang. They respect language. Nothing is as pathetic as the technical translator or the teacher who says (one did) 'I have no pretensions to literary translation' (though he was meant to teach it). Given that literature is the broad base and storehouse of all varieties of language, the concrete manifestation of the imagination, and given that poetry — its most concentrated form is the only genre that makes use of all its resources and is technically the most difficult, spare and demanding form of composition, the link between poetry and translation is deep and indissoluble. Only a poet can translate a poem, but the result is an object lesson for any translator.

I once wrote that one can't make a bad into a good translator, but one can always help someone to improve. A good translator is distinguished early by a certain sensitivity to language; more often than not, by a determination not only to write sense but to impose an 'own' elegant style on to a mediocre (informative) original. A poor translator will translate the words as though they were isolated, will swallow any idiom or metaphor whole (*danser sur le ventre de,* 'dance on his stomach'), or will write the kind of nonsense that makes sense but that can't be visualised in any setting. Instance: 'Constructivist, he participates from 1920 in the animation of the new institutes of art of Moscow', which I could describe as Romance English for 'As a Constructivist, he helped to inspire the new Moscow art institutes from 1920 onwards'. But a creative translator (and the legitimate linguistic creativity in translation requires discussion) will be aware that there's more to *animation* than 'inspiration' and sooner or later have to introduce 'animate' to cover 'organise', 'inspire' and 'be the driving force of'. *Animateur* and *animieren* (G) are there already.

Authors, publishers, employers, examiners — they may all have to make the critical decision about who is to get the commission or the job, who is to pass — and who is not, who is to fail; who is a translator, and who isn't. The dividing line here is the reverse of clear-cut, it's as fuzzy as most things in translation. And for examiners it has to be made judiciously, partially intuitively, but on the basis of scaled marks, at the bottom, not the middle of any cluster on a list.

'Teaching about translation' means discussing translations, switching from examples to generalisations and back to examples, and in the course of the discussion, firing, inspiring students to continue, to collect examples and learn for themselves. It is a dynamic pragmatic activity, miles away from any academic study of translatology. To use Austin's terms so regrettably jargonised, teaching adds a permanent perlocutionary element to the illocution and the proposition contained in it, meaning to say that an announced principle such as my 'Translation is the only direct statement of linguistic meaning — anything in the same language is merely glossing, adding or subtracting meaning' can have no effect on the listener unless an example of statement and direct translation is contrasted first with a paraphrase or circumlocution of the original and then a translation of the paraphrase. Such teaching requires the individual effort of taking notes on a discussion rather than the reliance on the all-purpose handout.

Whilst good teaching about translation has to have all the qualities of good teaching about, say, philosophy or linguistics, indicating the main schools of thought about translation (recently, the impact of reception theory), it also has to leave a residue of details, say, how to deal with a variety of misprints or grammatical metaphors ('May found them in Spain'). This might rouse the scorn of philosophers and historians, and be seen as anti-intellectual and pedestrian. In contrast, I find it comic that there are still linguists inventing new theories of translation, with the inevitable mathematical models, flow-charts and boxed acronyms representing abstractions that will soon go 'down the memory hole' (Chomsky).

I see my subject primarily as a resource, based on a view of language where function respects essence; a source that can be referred to and used continuously, for providing information about procedures, for coping with any difficulties met with in any translation; a source that changes as varieties of language change; that can be used for gist as well as full translations; that can meet new requirements in new situations and new topics; and finally, being a repository as well as a facility, that enriches as it informs.

12 The Translation of Political Language

The trouble with the translation of political language is that it is an abstraction (rather more than most translation) of an abstraction. Ortega y Gasset, wrote: 'To create a concept is to leave reality behind' — does this mean that political translation is going to leave reality even further behind?

Whilst this paper assumes that political utterances are often translated, it should be borne in mind that political speeches are usually summarised and/or put in indirect discourses before they are shortened again and translated by reporters in news agencies, embassies or in government translation offices. Modern political books or even articles are not that frequently translated into English; whilst new translations of some political works of Marx and Engels, as I have previously noted (Newmark, 1982a) are overdue.

This paper is as much concerned with the comprehension as of the translation of political language. I believe there is not enough straight translation of political texts in the press and elsewhere. The originals are often concealed in the target language (TL) versions — for 'political' reasons.

I take it as axiomatic that politics pervades every aspect of human thought and activities to a greater or a lesser degree. We are governed by politics and politicians, democracy at one extreme, monarchy or its modern form, dictatorship, at the other — otherwise it's anarchy, which is also politics. I am not claiming that art, science, sport, education are politics; I am simply maintaining that these fields all have political implications — that those who think they can exclude, say, international chess or abstract art from politics or propaganda in the political sense, are kidding themselves. Politics is the most general and universal aspect and sphere of human activity and in its reflection in language it often appears in powerful emotive terms, or in impotent jargon.

Because politics by its nature generalises, it is suspect; it is sometimes all appearance without being. Take the sentence, 'In the 1980s the IMF will be more effective if it is less political'. (The same remark could be made of any public institution.) The meaning becomes clear only in the context *più efficace se dipende meno dagli atteggiamenti politici dei suoi stati membri più potenti.* 'Political' is given a pejorative sense, which may have to be spelt out as above in any translation.

The word 'political' needs some separate consideration. Whilst in its 'proper' use it is related to every branch of administration, it has no 'proper' separate sense and should have no separate existence. No one should be just a politician. In English, if you say 'Be careful! He may be taking up your case for political reasons', it suggests that the person's motives have nothing to do with the rights and wrongs of the matter, he is simply using you for his own ends. This pejorative debased sense of 'political' is well attested in Italian terms like *politicante,* petty politician, intriguer, schemer, *politicastro,* translated by Collins–Sansoni as 'politicaster' (a dictionary word if ever there was one — I define a 'dictionary word' as one that you find only in a dictionary) *politicone,* 'schemer, sly fox'. Italian's capacity for expressing the various negative or pejorative senses of 'political' — that is 'political' when it is divorced from any other subject — is probably unique. The English journalist Jill Tweedie has recently defined a pure politican as simply 'a liar'. In other languages, this sense of 'political' has to be translated by qualifying it with an adjective such as 'sly', 'cunning', 'stealthy'; note *ménager quelqu'un par politique,* 'dealing with using someone shrewdly/ artfully/cunningly'. Or Heseltine of Parkinson: 'He's one of my closest political friends': *è uno dei miei amici politici più intimi.* What does that mean? Isn't it a contradiction in terms? This brings us to the English term 'politic' ('a politic old scoundrel') an 'untranslatable' word (by componential analysis: *avveduto e furbo?*).

A further curiosity is that whilst English at least has the sense to distinguish between 'policy' and 'politics' (though it 'lost' polity) most European languages don't; further, the 'study/practice of the art and science of forming directing and administrating states' has little to do with 'What are your politics?' *Quali sono le tue idee politiche?* It's all the same word! and what a distance between 'related to the state' and 'affecting a person's influence or status', 'a political decision', *una decisione politica.*

The core of political language lies in abstract conceptual terms. In their most powerful form, they are found more often in slogans, catchwords, phrases, refrains, chants, titles, maxims, etc., rather than in texts, speeches, treatises, newspaper articles. They tend to be isolated, prominent, apparently extracontextual — even when they are in fact value-laden and culture-bound (some linguists — not me — would say they have no nuclear meaning, no semantic core whatsoever). Paradoxically, they appear to be easily translatable: words like capitalism, communism, socialism, democracy, revolution, collective, tend to look the same in most at least

European languages; all they require is a slight change of suffix, say for fascism, '-ism', *-isme, -ismo, -ismus, -izm,* or again, say for revolution, '-tion', *-tion* (F), *-zion* (G), *-zione* (It), *-cion* (Sp), *-tsia* (R). Because so many of these words have a common ancient Greek or ancient Latin stock, all the translator appears to have to do is to operate a slight conversion, or a virtual transference ('bourgeois', *borghese, burgues, burshuaznji*) — there are exceptions like 'society', *Gesellschaft, obshchestvo*).

However, it will be a main thesis of this paper to claim that such quick conversions are deceptive; that translators in particular have not done enough to distinguish the real cultural meanings of these conceptual words. I tend to support Hjelmslev (1971), one of the founders of modern linguistics, when he wrote that 'understanding between the West and the East' (let alone the Third World) 'is in the last analysis largely a problem of translation', and Marx (source unknown) when he wrote: 'The thief, the translator and the seller were necessary for 19th Century European colonial enterprise', rather than T. D. Weldon (1953: 44) (a brilliant writer, nevertheless) when he wrote: 'the trouble between the USA and the USSR at the moment is not that there is a shortage of competent translators'. I need hardly say that this is a relative argument; I am not trying to suggest that competent translation will lead to peace and political harmony in the world; I am merely claiming that if the translators did their job better, there might be better understanding. (Obvious examples are the, according to some, mistranslation of the Japanese Government's word *mokusatsu* — literally 'kill with silence' — as 'take no notice of' instead of 'withhold comment' prior to the dropping of the atom bomb on Hiroshima; it has been much discussed (see Butow, 1952) and the truncated translation of *Mein Kampf* omitting the most pernicious passages which was the only 'official' translation in the UK prior to the outbreak of the Second World War and the UN Resolution 242 concerning Israel's occupied territory.

I want now to look more closely at the nature of many of these key conceptual terms. Note first their tendency to grammatical personification. 'Good' (but also 'bad') positive abstract nouns tend to be feminine: take *liberté, libertà, Freiheit, svoboda:* they reek of the fraudulent idealisation of women that has characterised so much history. You have only to make a person of a positive adjective ('equal', 'just', 'good', even 'brotherly'!) to make the quality into a women (in English, this is or used to be semantic rather than grammatical, whilst Russian does alternate *-ost, -ina* and *-ota* — all feminine — with an occasional *-enie* or *-stvo*, which are neuter. Explicit political theories prefer the masculine *-ism* (the German *-ismus* is even more virile). English and Italian can make a distinction between the suffix '-ist' which is objective (e.g. Marxist, capitalist) and '-istic' which is negative

('Marxistic', 'capitalistic'). If you now preface these with the deceptive *viva, vive,* 'long live', *es lebe, da zdravstvuet,* you get a rather misleading view of these concepts. What does the translator do? Not much here — the translator has to translate. When it comes, however, to the personification of countries *La France* etc., the translator can, at least when not translating an authoritative statement (see Newmark, 1982b), encourage the tendency to 'neutralise' them. It is notable that even in French, newly formed states (Israël, le Zaïre, le Zimbabwe, le Malawi, le Botswana, le Tchad) tend to lose their (feminine) articles, or at least to acquire a 'neutral' masculine.

From there, it is a dangerous step to further personalisation to state that the State, the local authority etc., is 'good', 'treats people well'; again a translator can intervene in informative texts only by diminishing the metaphor: thus 'that State is kind to its citizens', in *quello Stato, si prende cura dei cittadini;* in authoritative texts, the metaphor has to remain.

However, the four main facts about political concepts are that they are partly culture-bound, mainly value-laden, historically conditioned and like all concepts, abstractions in spite of continuous efforts to concretise them.

A further disadvantage of concept words, outside or inside context, is that they evaluate or appraise without any terms of reference, like a poor English school report or marks. Words of appraisal like 'good' or 'just' are not meaningless, but they are vague unless they represent a value in a scale common to the writer and the reader.

Take 'democracy', now (but not 50 years ago, when it was often used negatively in opposition to order and authority — and not only by Nazis) a purr-word in the West and East, defined most grandiloquently in Abraham Lincoln's (1863) words (but at least by supplying helpful case-partners) as 'government of the people, by the people and for the people', which contains its hazy semantic core; democracy's main implication in the West is that it is dependent on the holding of frequent, free and regular elections which offer a real choice and where all but minors and the incapacitated vote. In the East, 'democracy' is also a purr-word, although the term 'people's democracy' (stage between capitalism and socialism) has gone out of use and only the GDR (the others are 'socialist' or 'popular') officially described itself as 'democratic'. In the East a sharp distinction was made between bourgeois and socialist democracy (grossly, political and economic democracy). In both forms, democracy is indirect or representative. In many Latin American countries, the intellectual hegemony (Gramscian sense) inevitably gives the term a negative connotation.

Clearly the translator translates the internationalism 'democracy' as 'democracy', and though it is a value-laden term, the translator has, within the limits to be described later, normally to preserve its core-value. However, the basic cultural difference, the emphasis on political and legal rights in the West (free expression, security, choice), and on economic rights (work, health, education) in the East as it was, is an undercurrent in political writing and has to be borne in mind in many translations. See the implication in *daß die Demokratie für Erziehung mehr aufwendet als irgendeine andere Staatsform ist geschichtlich erwiesen (Neues Deutschland, 8th May 1948)* 'that a democracy spends more money on education than any other type of state is historically evident'. This is East German — in contrast to the present tendency in the UK.

In the official communist jargon, the concept of 'democratic centralism' continues to thrive. In theory, it means that policy is proposed and voted with maximum participation at the base (grass-roots, coal-face, chalk face) whilst the centre is responsible for the unanimous execution of each decision. The theory is fudged by the GDR *Kleines Ökonomisches Wörterbuch* which defines it as the 'unity of central and scientific management on the one hand and democratic codetermination and self-responsibility of the working people on the other'. In fact, it is often a cover-word for 'monolithic', once, but no longer, a purr-word for subordination to the Party centre.

The only other term I wish to discuss under this cultural head is the universal snarl-word 'fascism'. The term, apparently coined by Mussolini in 1919, was already being used by German communists in the late 1920s to cover not only National Socialists and right-wing groups, but also 'all important bourgeois parties'. The communist sense has ever since equated fascism with almost any kind of anti-communist or revisionist movement ('Titoist clique') and has much influenced the Western sense (if there is one) which perhaps identifies fascism with any antidemocratic or authoritarian ideas, usually excluding communist ones, except in the now rare cases where fascism is identified with communism. Fascism is, I think, the messiest term in the entire world political vocabulary, and the translator in certain contexts should try to resist its extravagant use by a narrower definition.

'I was once an idealist', Mr Cecil Parkinson once stated, presumably emphasising the negative sense of the term. I once wrote to an East German friend, saying I had found more idealism and less materialism in Leipzig than in the West, for the purpose of both pleasing and shocking him. In spite of Marx, political language outside the Socialist countries is concerned with the moral rather than the philosophical senses of idealism and materialism — the moral and philosophical senses have little connection with each other. In spite of this, 'idealism' , the belief in ideals, is often patronisingly and illogically associated with youth, immaturity, lack of realism. 'Materialism' is a snarl-word, though most advertising openly panders to it.

I now discuss two political terms that require special translation. The London Wiener Library recently held an exhibition of Nazi memorabilia which included a copy of the main party newspaper, the *Völkischer Beobachter*. This was boldly and rightly translated as 'The Racialist Observer' — titles of newspapers are not normally translated, but this was required to inform the visitors. The term *völkisch* is defined in the standard Wahrig dictionary as 'relating to the people', belonging to the people, emanating from the people', a misleading definition. In fact, the term was coined only in 1875 by nationalist movements in Germany, was 'Germanised' in the sense of 'national' in 1900, was taken over by the Nazis and can be only appropriately translated as 'racialist' or 'antisemitic'.

Similarly, I regard it as misleading and irresponsible that the former South African policy of *apartheid* (literal translation: apartness) should simply be transferred and therefore become a so-called 'loan-word', therefore a component of most European languages' vocabulary, although the word's meaning is opaque. As I see it, a minimal translation of the term is: 'racial segregation and absolute white domination'; the first noun-group should be omitted in later references. It is partly due to translators' cowardice that *apartheid* can be defined and is still described as 'separate racial development' (see a disgraceful article on Education in the *Encyclopaedia Britannica*).

Further, like Arbutov, the Soviet diplomat, I criticise the transfer of *détente* into English. French no longer dominates the world diplomatic scene, the word is opaque and in English means 'relaxation of tension', and the policy should be known as such. If it is later shortened to 'relaxation' policy, so much the better. Both German and Italian have the good sense to translate the word as *Entspannung* (G), *distensione* (I) — in any event the referent must be West German in origin, but unfortunately the term has existed in English since 1908, when French dominated much English diplomatic vocabulary.

Political terms are normally value-laden — terms are either positive or negative, even when referring to objects or activities; the contrast between *Profit* and *Gewinn* (profit), *Wettbewerb* and *Konkurrenz* (competition), *Propaganda* and *Agitation* (propaganda), *Schandmauer* and *Schutzwall* (Berlin Wall), *Flüchtling und Sperrbrecher* (East German refugee), Pankow Régime — now dated — and Workers and Peasants State for GDR being well known (Lewis, 1979; Wagner, 1981). Weldon (1953) has also pointed out (rather inaccurately) that the German sentences *Das ist verbrecherisch! Durchaus nicht, es ist eine ehrenwerte Tat* if translated as 'That is criminal. Certainly not! It's an honourable deed', would have a peculiar meaning if spoken during the Nazi period, and referring to an SA gang beating up a Jew. In the hegemonistic culture of that period, the action and the term describing it, *ehrenwert*, 'honourable' would be positive. In a sane culture, it is negative; the definition of sanity which implicates the translator's responsibility will be discussed later. '

There is a certain tendency for transferred or loan words to acquire a negative meaning: thus 'régime' in English and German but not in French has an authoritarian, sometimes 'upstart' connotation; *Collins Dictionary* gives 'a fascist regime, the regime of Fidel Castro' as citations. The negative senses of 'bourgeois', which are included in French too are well-known. The word 'propaganda', originally deriving in a good sense from a Papal encyclical (*De propaganda Fide*) and retained positively by Goebbels, is always value-laden, but in all languages that have adopted it — except perhaps East German, where it is positive and contrasted with the more practical *Agitation* (cf. Russian *agitacia* and *'agitprop')* — its positive or negative connotation has to be derived from its context. 'Bureaucracy' came into mid-nineteenth century English in a negative sense (John Stuart Mill particularly) as a political system dominated by officials or functionaries (which, unlike *fonctionnaire,* is a pejorative term) and then generalised still negatively to denote any type of anonymous officialdom and red tape such as has been classically and brilliantly analysed in Kafka's novels. However, it has to be carefully distinguished from its Weberian sociological sense, which is value-free in intention, as the 'formal codification of the idea of rational organization characterizes by legal rules, a salaried administrative staff, the specialization of function, the keeping of written records and documents' (Bullock, 1981) and distinctively, 'the authority of the (non-hereditary) office, not the person'. Note that here bureaucracy can be regarded as the necessary and efficient apparatus of any type of political system or government. Note that in *Lexis* (Dubois, 1979) the term is given a mainly negative sense *(influence néfaste sur la conduite des affaires),* and that the negative sense can be reinforced by the suffix '-ism'; in the GDR, *Bürokratismus* is particularly designated for socialist failings; Ulbricht in particular characterised Stalin as the protagonist and Lenin as a bitter enemy of bureaucratism — but that wasn't until 1964, eleven years after Stalin's death.

Alec Nove (1983) has noted that 'struggle' has a negative connotation (vain, desperate, futile struggle) whilst its European counterparts: *borba, lotta, Kampf, lutte* are positive (certainly politically). However, 'struggle' has no one-to-one equivalent in other languages (to do it translator's justice, you have to do a componential analysis). 'Fight' is the nearest one-to-one equivalent, and English has the even more positive but less political 'combat' in reserve.

The term 'normalisation' is used politically to signify a return to normal friendly relations between states but notoriously attained a negative currency outside the socialist countries in 1968, when it was used by Soviet leaders to justify their invasion of Czechoslovakia. Finally, the term 'revisionist', in the Marxist sense was used to denote any deviation from official communist doctrine at any one time. It can be confusing, since it may refer indiscriminately to diametrically opposed policies, e.g. in Hungary or Czechoslovakia, where revisionists may be favouring some kind of return to the Stalinist (therefore Rakosi or Gottwald) system or to the reformist period (Nagy or Dubček) or somewhere between these poles.

However, a translator's difficulties with value-laden political concepts do not end there. Up to now, I have been discussing only the conventional wisdom to be found in standard monolingual dictionaries, some of which conflict with each other within one language. A further difficulty is idiolectal usage, that is an idiosyncratic even bizarre personal sense given to a term by a particular writer. Take the terms 'radical', 'radicalism', which exist in most European languages, including the Slavonic. When this is standardised to refer, say, to the 'radicalism' of the French Third Republic, and sometimes identified with the *Parti Républicain Radical et Socialiste,* which was notoriously neither radical nor socialist, 'radical' means perhaps 'in favour of some timid democratic reforms and anticlerical'. Again 'radical' may refer to the 'extreme' *(Webster's Dictionary)*, i.e. democratic wing of the British nineteenth century Liberals, or again in American English, 'radical' may refer to left-wing, i.e. anticapitalist views, in a more revolutionary sense than 'liberal', which favour social reforms within the capitalist system; but again, parties of the extreme right may be referred to as 'radical'. In the above cases, there may be no difficulty in sorting out the appropriate meaning. However, the term 'radical' can also be used purely as an intensifer, depending on the idiolect of the writer, and here the translator may have to normalise or interpret the word in the case of an informative or 'anonymous' text, where the personality of the writer is of little importance; in an authoritative statement, the term must be translated 'straight'.

My previous example shows that an historical sense is peculiarly important in translating political language. In fact, with the dominance of the two mass-media (TV and tabloids — in the UK at least there are no others), political language is particularly susceptible to a quick 'accept and reject', and every word as well as every person gets ten minutes of fame.

'Imperialism' started in English in 1980 as an objective description usually with positive connotations, and was identified with the expansion of civilisation. Its criticism was initiated by J. A. Hobson, the British economist, at the turn of the century and popularised by Lenin as the last stage of monopoly capitalism. But after 1945 the term 'imperialism' was absurdly most frequently bandied around by the USA against the USSR and the USSR against the USA, Soviet politicians tending to extend it to Britain and West Germany (but not to France or Italy). Again, 'anarchism' needs precise historical placing to distinguish its 'direct action' from its 'non-violent' component. Finally, contemporary political eponyms are particularly subject to swift change and decay. Whilst place-names to represent opinion as well as occupancy remain constant (e.g. Westminster, Montecitorio, Dalal Street (opinion on the Bombay Stock Exchange) used as familiar alternative terms remain fairly steady), eponyms formed from the names of prime-ministers and prominent politicians (in English, Thatcherism, the first one since 'Churchillian', Bennite, the only other, probably reflecting the word-play activities of the mass-media rather than the influence of French, where adjectives formed from proper names are much more common). Note that whilst geographical eponyms are usually replaced by the place name (Dalal Street therefore becomes *la Borsa di Bombay)* in translation, political eponyms are normally translated by a couplet, viz. the transfer of the proper name plus a definition, viz. Thatcherism, *Thatcherismo la politica della Thatcher, che implica il controllo dell'offerta monetaria per regolare l'economia* (the control of money to regulate the economy).

Some political concepts, such as 'Marxism' or 'feudalism' are hardly bound to their contexts, and therefore can usually be translated 'straight', or one-to-one, though marxism has different senses in the areas of economics (surplus value etc.), sociology (alienation etc.) or philosophy (dialectical materialism).

Notoriously, 'liberalism', *libéralisme, liberalismo, Liberalismus* is the most slippery word in the political vocabulary, mainly because the same word is used in the economic and in the human rights sense. Thus belief in freedom of thought and expression merges *(se confond avec)* with belief in the free forces of the market as the logical result of liberal ideals. Currently, prevailing thought in France, Italy and Australia tends to identify liberalism with the Right; in the UK and West Germany with the Centre; in USA (pejoratively) and Canada with the Left; and in any Marxist countries, if such exist, with bourgeois reaction. The translator therefore has to be reasonably confident that any switch of meaning from source to target language is understood.

Note also that Vačlav Havel's (1989) term for the political system in Eastern Europe from 1945 to 1990, 'post-totalitarianism', if it gains acceptance *(sich durchsetzt)*, as I think it will, will have to be glossed for some time.

Many concepts, primarily those formed from adjectives (e.g. freedom, justice, truth) and to a lesser extent those formed from verbs (liberation, exploitation, order, détente, peaceful co-existence) are implicitly bound not only to linguistic and situational contexts, but to implied case-partners, and their danger consists in the fact that the case-partners are missing! In writing on case-grammar and translation, I have suggested that the supplying of these case-partners may be obligatory, implied, optional or supplementary; that the main case-partners are, for the translator, who does what to who for what purpose? but that this can be extended to 'where', 'when', 'for what reason', 'against what', 'under what condition', etc. If we now take the political concept 'freedom', T. D. Weldon (1953) has pointed out that generally in the West, it means 'freedom *from*', say from 'State interference and fear' (with little emphasis on want) — he forgets freedom of speech, whilst in the East, it means 'freedom *to*' (indeed, 'obligation to') 'work and receive a living wage', and I would add 'to receive education and medical treatment'. Thus the radical difference of meaning between the two cultural or conditioned concepts may be said to depend on the omission of the relevant case-partners — not surprisingly, since 'freedom', is the most inflammatory word in the political vocabulary. Margaret Thatcher has rightly pointed out, for instance, that 'free health service' is a catch-phrase shorn of its case-partners. The service is 'free' to patients, but has to be paid for by tax-payers.

An amusing example of missing case-partners incorrectly filled in by a translator is the Malay translation of Churchill's call for sacrifice on the plinth of his statue in Brunei: 'I have nothing to offer you but my blood, my sweat, my tears, my toil'. Not even the context saved the translator. But other universal terms often need qualification by case-partners, as Orwell qualified 'equality' with 'some animals are more equal than others', 'justice' asks 'justice for who', and social, economic and political justice may each have entirely different case-partners, though used without them.

'Security', which Murray Edelman (1977) refers to as 'the primal political symbol', is usually well determined in its 'passive' agent but vague in its active instrument 'against who', 'against what'. The term is bandied around indiscriminately as a reason for increased nuclear weapons and sometimes pre-emptive warfare, for securing 'welfare' (another loaded term) in financial and living conditions, as well as mental and spiritual security, often overlapping with safety (*salvezza, sûreté,* narrower than *Sicherheit*), a term with implications of fear, want and threat, now more explicit in Russian (*bezopasnost,* 'without danger', which is clearer than 'care'). Security is not only a political symbol, it is a jargon-word that requires case-partners if emotion is to be followed by action.

The reverse of security in English politics is 'mob rule' *(la legge della plebaglia, governo della plebe, oclocrazia)* a time-honoured English upper-middle-class definition of 'democracy', which is now more carefully applied as a threat of excessive democracy.

Pronouns

Gill Seidel (1975) in her paper 'Ambiguity in political discourse' has shown how in French political tracts of May 1968, the pronouns *vous, nous,* and *on* are skilfully used as 'shifters', that is their referent can only be determined by their use with varying degrees of inclusiveness. In more general political terms, 'we' is the party making the statement, 'you' is the public, 'they' is the opposition, the bureaucracy, those in power, provided 'we' are in opposition. The French *on,* like the Italian impersonal reflexive, is more flexible than 'they', and can identify with 'we' or 'you'. The purpose of a political statement is to unite 'we' and 'you' against 'them'. In general terms, there is no translation problem until *vous* becomes *toi* as a more personal form of appeal.

Political Jargon

Jiri Levy (1965), a fine translation theorist, refers to 'the translators's tendency to choose a general term, whose meaning is broader than that of the original one, and in consequence is devoid of some of its specific semantic traits', this tendency to abstraction/ism! coincides with the present most common sense of jargon (which, however, is significantly omitted in English dictionaries). An example from *Rinascita,* 17th June 1983:

> Il partito di De Gasperi si indirizza oggi a tutti gli italiani chiedendone un sostegno che gli assicuri la forza indispensabile perché — al di là di ogni artificiosa distinzione tra destra e sinistra, superata dalle condizioni storiche — l'attività politica possa essere effettivamente indirizzata verso quella rigenerazione dell'economia e delle instituzioni in difetto della quale il paese non potrà guarire dall'inflazione e dell'ingovernabilità.

Now, there are several ways of translating this passage. If it is a 'sacred' text, i.e. authoritative or reproduced to show the author's personality, as is likely, it has to be translated in all its vagueness and pomposity.

> The party of De Gasperi today addresses all Italians seeking support to secure it indispensable strength so that — beyond any artificial distinc-

tion between the right and the left, which has been overtaken by historical conditions — political activity may be addressed efficiently to that
regeneration of the economy and our institutions for lack of which the
country will not be able to recover from inflation and ungovernability.

(The extract shows that the deadening predictability of political language is not confined to its main genre — Marxist literature in the Socialist
countries — the *Bruderländer*). If, however, it is an informative text, the
translator's task is to reduce it to its information:

The DC is making a broad popular appeal in regenerating the Italian
economy and its institutions, and later eliminating inflation.

If the text is vocative, that is, persuasive in intention and 'anonymous'
(unsigned, or the authorship is not important) the translator is justified in
making it persuasive, though he may want to transplant the culture, as in
theory the translation is for English readers.

The DC is making every effort to enlist support for economic and
institutional reforms which will certainly include the elimination of
inflation.

However, political jargon is usually produced by politicians or political
organisations, and it usually has to be translated straight in all its tedious-
ness.

Sometimes language in translation may reveal the true purpose of an
action. Thus in Russian the 'Industrial Relations Act' is officially referred to
as *Antiprophsojuzniji zakon*, i.e. the anti-trade union act. This is a puzzle I
ask someone to solve.

Notoriously, the term *druzhba* ('friendship') the 'word that needs
no translation' (Soviet press) is the most abused in the Soviet political
vocabulary.

Euphemisms

Already in 1946, Orwell in *Politics and the English Language* was pointing out the political tendency to adopt euphemism; the use of abstract to
replace concrete nouns, 'empty' verbs and verbal nouns to replace verbs;
Latin and Ancient Greek to replace Anglo-Saxon. Even then 'pacification'
was used for 'violence'; 'transfer of population' for 'driving out ethnic
groups'; 'rectification of frontiers' for 'aggression'; 'elimination of unreli-
able elements' for 'murder'. The Nazis had their own set of such words:
Strafexpedition ('punitive expedition'), *Staatsakt* ('state occasion'),

aufziehen ('set up') — Viktor Klemperer (1969) chronicled and explained them as they appeared in his pioneering work — and the Americans (Farb, 1974) had theirs during the Vietnam war: 'resources control program' (defoliation), 'condolence award' (grant for victims), 'navigation misdirection' (bombing error); 'new life hamlet' or 'Open Arms camp' (refugee camp). Most political registers have words to conceal the realities of unemployment: 'redundancy', 'recession', (unemployment) 'benefits'; 'resting' (acting profession), 'voluntary severance'. Euphemisms allied or identical with generalising jargon are the politician's most useful weapon for telling lies ('being economical with the truth').

Note that political language has cover-words like 'problems', 'public opinion' (the silent majority), alarm-words like 'crisis', 'chaos', 'anarchy' which translate easily into Western European countries and conceal the truth.

Metaphors

Each linguistic culture has its own set of political metaphors. Russian, being proverbially nourished on peasant proverbs more than other languages, once had its hyenas, mad dogs, cannibals, lackeys, flunkeys (this has been exaggerated), which, given the nature of their usage, may have to be modified by interpreters at international conferences. It is notorious that Krushchev's 'We'll bury you', a metaphor for the end of capitalism, was widely misunderstood as a military threat. But Russian's metaphors have more recently drowned in its political jargon.

English political metaphors are typically tamer and present few translation problems. Carlo Dondolo, following Anthony Burnett, has rightly referred to Mrs Thatcher's Churchillianism ('resolute approach') but this hardly extends to her language, which tends to centre on the Ship of State holding or setting the course.

Hudson (1978) has analysed the metaphor sets of various politicans. Many of Macmillan's numerous game-metaphors would be reduced to nonsense in translation; 'it was slow batting, not as good as a run a minute, but safe play. Stumps were drawn at about 5 p.m.', *I negoziati che si trascinavano, ma senza correre rischi si sono terminati verso le cinque.* Such frivolous metaphors could hardly be treated seriously, let alone translated semantically.

Neologisms

Political language is rich in neologism both ephemeral and permanent. The term 'wets', indicating members of Mrs Thatcher's government opposed to her social and monetarist policy was common a year ago (sometimes Keynesians), but appears to be declining for lack of referents. Therefore, in translation, the meaning has to be spelt out.

On the other hand, English for a long time needed a term for *noyautage* (1923), that is, political infiltration with the purpose of capturing the top positions in an organisation. We now have 'entryism' with this meaning.

Again *massimalismo*, in the sense of the largest possible political aims of a party (the original 'direct action' component appears to have been lost) has hardly yet entered English as 'maximalism' or French as *maximalisme*.

Italian can make a distinction between *progressivo* and the political *progressista* which would be useful in English, but we have only the vague, usually Left, 'progressive'.

'Populism', another early Russian revolutionary concept, is regaining currency in a new sense: the direct demagogic appeal of a politician at large meetings.

Acronyms and Euphony

Political language's main use of acronyms is for the titles of political parties and organisations — DC, SPD, SDP, etc. The translation is dependent on contextual factors: the motivation, and linguistic and cultural level of the readership, the house style of the setting, the importance in the SL culture (or European culture) of the referent. Thus DC may be translated as Democrazia Cristiana, the Italian Christian Democrats, the governing party, the main right wing party, etc. in an informative or vocative text.

In most political writing, jargon effectively replaces euphony, but any great political texts such as Churchill's or De Gaulle's have to preserve some of their phonaesthetic quality in translation. I have already discussed aspects of the *Communist Manifesto*'s translation (Newmark, 1982a). In the rather dated translation of Lenin's *State and Revolution,* I note that 'they omit, obliterate and distort' is a brave attempt to carry over the 'ayut' sounds that terminate the three Russian verbs, which give them powerful rhyming effect.

Collocations

One characteristic of political language is that it tends to collocations that are repeated so often that they become clichés, therefore weaker in force, giving them the same dull thud as many abstractions. (The tendency to compound, noted by Orwell, has a similar effect). Thus 'warmly praise', 'loudly applaud', 'stick firmly', 'overriding priority', 'fight hard', 'fundamental truth', 'great tasks', 'reject totally', 'hard choice', 'we face the challenge'. Note that many of these collocations have *less* force than their pseudo-intensifiers, which a better speaker than Mrs Thatcher would have omitted, and that they don't usually bear one-to-one translation, but they have to be translated in all their banality (not difficult) when they form part of an authoritative statement.

Whatever the local requirements of this or that translating task, translators must have an ultimate point of reference for all their work. This point of reference is, in my opinion, the principles of the Universal Declaration of Human Rights. In 1948, the UN decided that everyone is entitled to all rights and freedoms without distinctions such as race, colour, gender, language, religion, political opinion, national or social origin, property or birth. Now, in 1984, it is necessary to add mental or physical condition (unless virtually incapacitated), age (over 17) and sexual orientation — always provided that the persons concerned are not actively challenging these distinctions of which the most important for the translator is gender rather than race. That is the translator's professional and social responsibility.

Whether this responsibility is regarded as objective or subjective is a matter of opinion. In one sense it is a wager, a *pari*, a personal declaration of faith. In another, there is so much continuously increasing and accumulating evidence that it must be identified with objective human progress, to which there is no alternative. Does this mean that the translator should refuse to translate, say, *Mein Kampf,* the most concrete negation of human rights that has ever been composed? No way.

I think translators have to translate anything they feel competent to translate, but their tasks may include sensitising their clients to misleading or untrue statements in a text. The problem inevitably arises in political texts, since, in principle, politics is an extension of ethics, and political acts are also moral acts.

Political writing is likely to be 'sacred', and therefore translators cannot interfere with the text, though they can and should reduce the sexism in language by discreetly replacing 'he' or 'his' with 'they' or 'their', 'man' and 'mankind' with 'women and men' (compare De Gaulle's *Françaises, Français*), or with 'humanity' and 'people' where appropriate. In other cases of concealed prejudice, they can and should only intervene by writing a separate comment, either in detailed notes, or, better, in an introduction, which in any event, they should write whenever they are translating a book or a text of any size, which will make it more difficult for reviewers to ignore them, as reviewers often do. (In order to unsex or desex the above sentence, I have had to put the subject in the plural, and, to make it unambiguous, to repeat the word 'review'). A 'moral' comment would be superfluous if one were confident that any likely reader were already alerted to the prejudices of a text.

In particular in respect of political texts, the translators' neutrality is a myth. Their aim may be as transparent as glass in the actual translation, but even more than members of other professions, since one of their aims is to promote understanding beween nations, they have social and moral responsibilities, to humanity as well as to language. For hundreds of years, translation was a transmission-belt of high culture. Only in this century has it a further task to disseminate knowledge and understanding among all peoples.

Acknowledgement

I thank Tom Newmark, Peter Whiteway and Mary FitzGerald for helpful suggestions.

13 Translation as an Instrument of Linguistic, Cultural and Literary Criticism

Introduction

Translation can be a weapon, a cutting tool, a hatchet. Such characterisation may surprise. We are told too often that translations should be smooth, natural, elegant; or that translation distorts, betrays, is in more than one sense a false friend; or that it is a glass, impersonal, anonymous, transparent gauze. And that is so, sometimes. But translation has various functions. In the eyes of translators of religious works, from Luther to the martyr Dolet to the modern translators of the Koran and the Bible, translation is a weapon for truth. In the eyes of some political thinkers such as Engels, who supervised many translations of Marx's works and his own, it was a weapon for communism. Similarly the United Nation Charter and the Universal Declaration of Human Rights, universally translated, to which translators subscribe, is a weapon for morality. And of course translation is continuously used as an instrument for diffusing knowledge and technology.

However, I propose to discuss translations as a weapon in another sense, as a critical instrument turned on the source language text — therefore as an implicit, indirect critical tool — a text that is suddenly stripped of much of its own culture and all its own language, that is exposed to the harsh light of a different culture and language, and perhaps, if you believe in them (I do), to some universal truths and morality and common sense. As I wrote that, I was listening to a prime example, a close broadcast translation of the transcript of a meeting of the Soviet Composers Union's meeting of 1948, where Shostakovich and others were accused of being traitors and enemies of the people, writing chamber music for a mere handful of people, 'spitting in the face of the noble proletariat'. Perhaps, to many Soviets, it sounded different at the time . . .

Criticism of Translations

We can criticise a translation using three points of reference. In the first place, if it is translated closely at the author's level, it is exposed to a different language, culture and literary or non-literary tradition. It may be open to criticism for jarring with the readers' concept of natural usage or social language, because it makes us laugh or feel embarrassed when this wsn't the author's intention (which is a common first reaction to close translation). Secondly, if the translation conforms broadly to target language norms, and the translation follows what the author might supposedly have written had he been a master of the target language, not what he actually wrote, the only way to assess the deficiencies of the translation is to examine the linguistic differences between it and the original. The third form of criticism is basically non-linguistic, but may underscore both the first and the second: it is to examine the translation and with it the original in relation to the truth, the material facts, and moral and aesthetic principles, so that the translation is evaluated as an independent free-standing work.

The Link Between Linguistics and Literature

Translation can bridge the gap between the two disciplines of linguistics and literature. In the UK this gap has had a chequered and disturbing history. When philology turned into linguistics in the 1920s and 1930s under the impulse in their different ways of such figures as Saussure and Bloomfield, it also turned away from literary or religious texts to the spoken language and to non-literary models (Fries was the paradigm here) and proclaimed itself as the science of language. Literature was abandoned as material to be evaluated as well as analysed, and literary criticism was different, it was an art (however, Jakobson and the Prague School among linguists preserved the link between linguistics and literature). In translation there was a not dissimilar evolution, a turning away from literary to non-literary texts. Moreover, most writing about translation before the middle of this century was about literature — nothing else was respectable. Nowadays I think the theorising about translating is as much about non-literary as about literary texts, and the quantity of translated non-literary far exceeds that of literary texts. In fact, in some countries (13 of the International Federation of Translators' (FIT) 62 member countries), translators are separated in two organitions, technical and literary, and sometimes view each other with regrettable suspicion. In the UK there has been a history of mistrust between the established discipline of literary criticism and the relatively new linguistics. Under the impulse of Leavis, the most powerful English literary critic of the mid-century, much literary criticism took 'life' or shared moral experience as its main criterion for the value and perceptiveness of works of literature, and rejected much of the familiar technical apparatus of literary criticism as useless jargon — as an incestuous turning to metalanguage. Leavis in fact denied the use of linguistics in literary criticism. British linguists, however, were never as resolutely anti-literary as the Americans — Halliday has produced sensitive analyses of Yeats and William Golding; and Quirk, Roger Fowler and Geoffrey Leech have brought linguistics and literary criticism closer together. Nevertheless you don't see much trace of linguistic jargon remaining. The few philosophical figures, way behind Barthes and Derrida, to span this gap in Britain have perhaps been Terence Hawkes and Terry Eagleton.

Now I am suggesting that translation is a kind of uncovering, that it suddenly exposes culture, 'art' and language to the cool wind of common sense, to literary and linguistic criticism in a different cultural climate, or should I here say 'space'? With some temerity, I give a scrap example from Michel Foucault — by a scrap example, I mean an example that is inadequate, and may not be representative, but may give a better flavour of what I mean, rather than some sweeping generalisation that requires particular substantiation, such as saying that Edgar Allan Poe and Charles Morgan appear to be more impressive in French than in their native English.

By way of illustration, I take the following post-modernist passage:

Il faut faire l'histoire de cet autre tour de folie, — de cet autre tour par lequel les hommes, dans le geste de raison souveraine qui enferme leur voisin, communiquent et se reconnaissent à travers le langage sans merci de la non-folie; retrouver le moment de cette conjuration, avant qu'elle n'ait été définitivement établie dans le règne de la vérité, avant qu'elle n'ait été ranimée par le lyrisme de la protestation. Tâcher de rejoindre, dans l'histoire, ce degré zéro de l'histoire de la folie, où elle est expérience indifférenciée, expérience non encore partagée du partage lui-même. Décrire, dès l'origine de sa courbure, cet "autre tour", qui, de part et d'autre de son geste, laisse retomber, choses désormais extérieures, sourdes à tout échange, et comme mortes l'une à l'autre, la Raison et la Folie. (Foucault, 1976.)

Here then is Foucault and Richard Howard's translation:

We have yet to write the history of that other form of madness, by which men, in an act of sovereign reason, confine their neighbors, and communicate and recognize each other through the merciless language of non-madness; to define the moment of this conspiracy before it was permanently established in the 'realm' of truth, before it was revived by the lyricism of protest. We must try to return, in history, to that zero point in the course of madness at which madness is an undifferentiated experience, a not yet divided experience of division itself. We must describe, from the start of its trajectory, that 'other form' which relegates Reason and Madness to one side or the other of its action as things henceforth external, deaf to all exchange, and as though dead to one another. (Howard, 1988.)

The translation we may safely say, couldn't have been written in English; there is no English tradition behind it. It is a bare uninspiring translation, rightly sounding like a translation. French words have more nuances and connotations than English words; they have more semantic space to cover, since the vocabulary is so much smaller than the English. Nevertheless, the remarkable feature here is how closely the translator embraces the text, both in lexis and grammar. Howard barely interprets Foucault: the irony in 'sovereign reason' and 'merciless language of non-madness' is left to stand as it is. No attempt is made to gloss madness as an 'undifferentiated experience' when it was still indistinct from reason.

What is exposed in the Foucault text, what stands out more clearly in English than in French, is the description of the historical act, the conspiracy to divide Madness and Reason (why separate the idiots from the sane?) in such abstract terms and concepts, usually without agents, so that the reader has to grope to understand it and to place it historically; take the 'lyricism of protest' — who were the protesters? why was the protest lyrical? who were they protesting against? Presumably the conspirators, but who were the conspirators? What is 'a not yet divided experience of division itself? Is this the beginning of the other 'form' or 'stage' of madness, when it starts to separate off from 'reason'? Translation into a less abstract language, a language that at its best is not so prone to nominalising its verbs, nor to leaving them without case-partners (look at the pregnant symbols of division — *courbure, partage, coupure, rupture* — all without case-partners) functions as a critical instrument, or perhaps a cold douche.

Admittedly, the literary and cultural tradition behind Foucault makes it easier for the French reader to divine and perhaps accept such a passage; when it is translated, however, it is suddenly exposed to a more empirical judgement, to a universal resource of common sense. Or, as Richard Cobb would say (in *Sunday Times*, 9.1.89) 'it doesn't wear so well in the cold light of English . . . It all sounds profound but it shows up rather lamely in translation'. If I may, not for the first time, translate the polite, ironical and perceptive Cobb, this means 'it may sound profound, but it is rubbish'. Not surpisingly, Anthony Quinton refers to Foucault's 'tremulous' hint of emancipating the oppressed — the good intention is obscured in a cloud of abstractions.

Compare, now, a more recent guru, Jean Baudrillard, whose message is conveyed through continuous metaphor laced in abstraction, with a minimum of concrete observation — here's a scrap: 'anorexic culture, a culture of disgust, of expulsion, of anthropoaemia *(sic)*, of rejection'. Baudrillard is merely the latest of a line of thinkers that draw more on the pragmatic than on the referential, which is another way of saying that they are strong on connotations and short on denotations. When they are well translated, they sound all too much like translations.

Take again:

Popular proverbs foresee more than they assert;
Le proverbe populaire prévoit beaucoup plus qu'il n'affirme;

they remain the speech of a humanity which is making itself, not one
Il reste la parole d'une humanité qui se fait, non

which is.
qui est.

(R. Barthes, 1957)

If this means anything, I assume it is that popular proverbs hold for the future as well as the present and so will go on being repeated; as Alan Duff (1981) has pointed out of another of Barthes's passages, it is a pompous vacuous statement, but in French, the vacuity is 'disguised' in brevity, sharp contrasts, pregnant verbs, positives and negatives — the classical style. In English, writers don't usually express themselves in such simplistic aphorisms — after Bacon in fact the genre is not taken up again till Wilde, whilst in French a long line stretches from Pascal and La Rochefoucauld through La Bruyère and Chamfort to Camus, Malraux and Char. Semantic or close translation exposes Barthes's maxims linguistically and as a piece of literature; communicative or social translation would make it sound more natural, but also more banal.

I take it as axiomatic that many close transfers of meaning from one language to another will potentially or in fact cause some kind of jolt or clash or shock: most obviously, culture shock: the bread and the coffee you get in Namur is not the same as you get in Birmingham, unless the supermarkets have now made them so. So the French and English words appear to be referring to slightly different objects. At other times, the jolt may be linguistic. You get a French passage: *Les questions du traducteur obligent le théoricien à remettre sans cesse son ouvrage sur le métier. L'important pour l'un et l'autre, est de ne pas se contenter de vivre l'acquis* (Margot, 1979: 339), which you might translate as: 'The translator's questions compel the theoreticians to continually improve their work. The important thing for all of them is not just to mark time.' Both French phrases, *remettre son ouvrage sur le métier* and *vivre l'acquis* are more vivid than the trite English versions, and could be brought nearer as 'rework their ideas' and 'live on one's experience'. In two languages, there is a frequent clash in the degree of freshness and concreteness with which an idea is expressed; each language has its own idioms which the translator is afraid to translate literally. It appears feeble to translate *sich aussprechen* as 'give vent to one's feelings', but what would you say if I said 'I'm going to speak myself out'? That's for discussion.

I had intended to take as my main example of translation as an instrument of literary criticism a French translation of Anne Brontë's masterpiece, *The Tenant of Wildfell Hall.* This is a clumsily constructed, clumsily written novel, with long straggling sentences and stiff dialogue, with heavy parentheses that appear to be remote from the rhythms of normal speech, as well as rather conventional collocations ('no trifling sacrifice', 'throng and bustle', 'cherished predilections') and the kind of literary language and standard metaphors ('cast a cloud') one would expect from a mid-Victorian middle-class woman, with an emphasis on feelings and fine sentiments. Anne Brontë, however, was not concerned with literary values, only with telling the truth and her emotion smashes the clichés. This is a novel which, in translation into a modern idiom, with a reduction of gush and a more straightforward syntax could perhaps become an improvement on its main theme, the tyranny of a husband over a wife who leaves him. Translation could, I suspect, act as a concentrating medium, an instrument of creative literary and linguistic criticism of this novel, which would be naturally enhanced by the requirement to convert from literary into modern colloquial but not 'idiomatic' usage. But this impressive work has never been translated into French.

The idea of adapting or abbreviating a classic is controversial and cannot be resolved by argument. It is possible that it can be done more successfully in translation.

Translation as an Instrument of Literary and Linguistic Criticism

Translation is an instrument of both literary and linguistic criticism when, for instance, a bloated rhetorical passage within a long rhetorical tradition, say in Arabic or Italian, goes over the top. Take any erotic passage by Moravia or D'Annunzio:

> As if the seal of treasure there intact,
> On the plump pubis and the hollowed groin
> The clinging droplets in the curly fleece
> Glittered like dew in some resplendent fern.

(D'Annunzio, 1980)

The Italian is smoother, more mellifluous:

> *E sul ventre brilla — suggel d'intatte*
> *richezze — l'ombellico e su l'emerso*
> *pube e ne l'incavato inguine attratte*
> *scintillaron le gocciole tra il crespo*
> *vello come rugiade tra un bel cespo.*

From Venera d'acqua dolce
G. D'Annunzio (translation Willoughby Higson)

Note here that translation revives a tiresome literary tradition by showing it up in another language, where, divested of this tradition, the words are more lubricious than erotic. In fact here the translator, Willoughby Higson, has done a tactful if sickly job; in the original the droplets glitter in her frizzy hair like dew in a beautiful tuft of grass.

Cultural Translation

I preface my discussion of cultural translation by pointing out that in any cultural problem, the translator has three basic choices: to keep the source language (SL) culture (say *Matignon*); to convert to the target language (TL) culture (the 'French Downing Street'); or to select a neutral international, inter-cultural term ('the French Prime Minister or his office') — within each of the three choices, there are various alternatives, and two or three of the procedures (couplets, triplets) may well be combined in one translation.

Secondly, when one makes any kind of choice (and there is a choice at most stages of translation, which is a problem-solving activity), one is implicitly making a criticism simply by preferring one procedure to another. Most languages retain vestiges of old cultural beliefs — the sun rises, the sun and virtue are female, a country is a woman, qualities are personified, 'considering' is in origin looking at the stars, etc., and if this is 'corrected' in the TL that is hardly cultural criticism. Countless metaphors remain in most languages testifying to the wickedness but also the goodness of animals. Now they are a convenience hard to get rid of but they still do residual 'harm'. The sexism that is rooted in most languages is another matter and the translator has to make a contribution towards its reduction (by translating into non-sexist language within the limits of natural usage); there are well established procedures for, for instance, 'desexing' man by using plurals, impersonal forms (one), generic terms (people, person, subject, individual, etc.) but if they become too obtrusive, the language becomes unnatural, which is self-defeating and counter-productive. Further, there are special problems in translating texts, ancient or modern, where sexism and ageism (the child as an object, the elderly as implicitly senile and handicapped) is in the accepted culture as well as in the language. F. R. Leavis (1958), a great élitist literary critic, writing a fine searching essay on 'The Great Books and a Liberal Education', could still write thoughtlessly of his undergraduates: 'These *men* are very highly selected', 'they find an especially good man', 'a man may leave the university' but he makes one reference to 'his or her' and the fact that his wife, Q. D. Leavis, collaborated with him in many books (though she did complain of his underestimation of her after his death) should justify the translation of 'man' as *l'étudiant* if not *les étudiants*.

Sexism raises the question of the other prejudices embedded in language which often remain obstinately a part of colloquial language: class (lower class), physical health (crippled), mental health (still 'safely' identified with stupidity (idiotic, imbecile), race (the word itself now unscientific or taboo), 'sexual orientation' (this current term in English equal opportunities advertisements sounds absurdly euphemistic ('straight', 'bent'), ageism (wrapped around in 'our seniors' and 'our juniors' or 'children' at school aged 18) — not to mention all the euphemisms for war, death, sex, cruelty, excretion, etc.

The question here is how translators are to deal with the verbal manifestations of such prejudices. Are translators to become instruments of moral criticism? There is no single answer but the first point is that they should not ignore prejudice, they have to be aware of it. Translators are no longer, as I've said, invisible glass, pale reflections and echoes, neutral, faceless, etc. — they never were, except in some people's ideal of a translator. Secondly, if these manifestations of prejudice appear in an authoritative text, ancient or modern, they should normally be reproduced (as accurately as possible) in the translation and the necessary criticisms made in the translator's preface, or, in an extreme case (perhaps Hitler's *Mein Kampf*) in footnotes, unless the translator is confident that the readership will not be misled.

In an authoritative text, a close translation of a passage objected to (say 'parts of Jordan conquered *(sic)* in 1967 and therefore recognized internationally as now belonging to Israel') is essential as an integral part of a text and as evidence or justification for the translator's *'sic'* in square brackets, which draws attention to the opprobrious anachronism of 'conquering' land. This is neater than a footnote at the bottom of a page, end of chapter or text, and is as far as translators can usually go and *must* go as they are not licensed to engage in a polemic with their text.

In a non-authoritative text, a translator has more right to modify adapt or delete but not distort passages likely to be offensive to the new readership; there may for instance be taboo words or swear words. Here translation is being used not as an instrument of criticism but to keep the readership's sympathetic understanding, which is in many instances a *sine qua non* in translation. *Sakrament noch mal, Mon Dieu,* goat, *Ziege,* 'bitch', could all be mistranslated and thereby alienate the readership. They are merely evidence of cultural history, past cultural attitudes; but translation is into present language.

Much has been written about cultural translation, *pace* Brewer (1988) who states that 'treatises on the theory of translation generally give short shrift to the transmission of culture as an aspect of the art of translation' but not much about translation as cultural criticism. Indeed, many translators, even those who recognise its interpretative or hermeneutic function, would deny that translators are critics. Now I could discuss this on a general moral level (I have done so) by pointing out that translators subscribe to the Nairobi Convention, and implicitly to the various international human rights conventions; they have a duty either to refuse the commission, or to make the infringements clear to any reader through a preface or footnotes.

Translators are sometimes even required to exercise cultural criticism by their country's censorship. Thus Iago's 'Your daughter and the Moor are now making the beast with two backs' (*Othello* I.1.) has had to be translated by an astrological metaphor into Marathi, which could be regarded as an indirect criticism of the Maharathra state's censorship laws.

In my opinion, if an original passage that is to be translated is so abstract and vague that it may mean anything or nothing, it is the translator's duty to translate it literally (but allowing for the standard grammatical transpositions) leaving it to the reader to decide whether it means anything or nothing. Thus, from *Le Somnambulisme* (Montplaisir & Demers, 1983: 691–20):

In our opinion this sleep-walking condition indicates that when the instincts are roused, they fail to integrate owing to the dream's hallucinatory process, since the arousal of the instincts is necessarily eliminated in an extra psychic space outside.

A notre avis, il s'agit d'un échec de l'intégration de l'excitation pulsionnelle par le processus hallucinatoire du rêve, l'excitation devant alors se liquider dans un espace extra-psychique au dehors.

I realise the alternative view is that the translator must try to make better sense of, i.e. interpret, the passage, but this narrows the semantic range of the passage, and increases the likelihood of misinterpretation. The compromise is to couple the smooth rendering ('nerve movements') for the general reader who wants to know what the author in fact wrote *(comportement moteur)*.

When translators change the image of a metaphor, they may do it for several reasons. If the SL metaphor is a standard metaphor which does not exist in the TL, they have to change it whether it is universal, e.g. 'in the cold light of the day', à *tête reposée*, 'in a new light', *mit andern Augen sehen*, or cultural, 'carrying coals to Newcastle' (a cultural fossil), *porter de l'eau à la rivière*. If it is a bizarre metaphor in an informative text, they may change it because they think it inappropriate; *la démographie galope* — 'there's a population explosion' and thereby they are implicitly criticising the SL original.

Lastly, if translators change the image in an original universal metaphor in an authoritative text, they are weakening the original, and are themselves subject to criticism. Thus Polish and Bulgarian translators change 'dew' to 'mist' or 'smoke' in

O that this too too solid flesh would melt
Thaw and resolved itself into a dew.   *(Hamlet* 1.2)

Rather more obviously, an exaggerated metaphor in an informative text, *La thèse de l'épargne victime de l'inflation* can be toned down as 'the idea that savings are eliminated (or suffer) due to inflation'. Therefore once again metaphor is a touchstone of translation, in the sense that the literary translator who is shy of translating an original metaphor is either a coward or a critic.

I close by pointing out that there is research to be done in this field, which hinges on the accuracy of the translation in relation to the original. I think it is profitable to consider translation as an instrument of criticism,

particularly of distortion and deficiency, such as is apparent in so much published translation (Stuart Gilbert jigging up Camus, Constance Garnett
depressing Checkhov, etc.). I think such studies more profitable, and likely
to stimulate an improvement in translation quality and to fulfil translation's
progressive and socially responsible role, than their antithesis, the study of
translation reception, which ignores the values of the original and is limited
to the sociology of translating. Translation reception theory is centred in
The Netherlands, Belgium and Israel, and though seeing translation as
target-oriented, has no target except the study of the past. It is concerned
with changing tastes rather than values. I am not denying that, to adapt
Jauss's definition of reception theory, it is interesting to see a translation in
terms of its impact on its contemporaries. This is an academic contribution
to the study of literary taste, but it tends to devalue the translation as an
important document and to ignore the original altogether. Thus if we simply
study the impact of Stuart Gilbert's translations of *La Peste* and *L'Etranger*
on their Anglo-Saxon readers, what do we find? First that they have sold
enormously and have been much appreciated; secondly that the readership
has been unaware that, if I may oversimplify, the style of the original is terse,
usually formal and classical, while that of the translation is bright, emotional
and colloquial, conforming to Stuart Gilbert's idea of snappy writing. So
what does this tell us? (a) Possibly that a poor translation cannot keep a good
book down, and this is normally true; (b) the only thing that is quite enough
to wreck a translation is one or more fundamental errors of fact or figures,
or for drama, the continuous phony dialect (as in Hauptmann's case); (c) the
impact of Camus was first on professional critics and academics rather than
a readership; these have ensured the enormous Anglo-Saxon readership for
Camus regardless of the quality of the translation, which many of them have
hardly bothered to read let alone comment on (there are some exceptions)
(reviews of translations normally ignore the translator); (d) in relation to
popularity, content carries far more weight than form, whether in works of
art or in trash, whether in translation or in original. After that cynical conclusion, you may wonder what is the point of reception theory, which is both
rather theoretical and passive, and what is the point of translation criticism,
which is active but doesn't seem to make a great deal of difference. I would
have to reply that translation criticism as well as translation sociology are
always the concern of a minority or an élite which is exercised over the larger
and democratic diffusion of the values it upholds (the only way to reconcile
élitism and democracy is to see the élite as a pressure group striving to
increase its own numbers — in fact this is how Nietzsche saw it).

Bad writing is bad writing in any language, however well or however
badly it is translated. Nothing could be more naïve than the excuse of a trans-

lation theorist who, when I declined to review his book (written in English) on the ground that my view would be unfavourable, wrote back to say that English wasn't his native language. When I talk about bad writing, I don't mean deficient grammar or misused words; I mean overused words, overused collocations, newly and excessively suffixed words ('-tualise', '-tuality', '-tability', '-tionalisation', '-ticity', '-nismic', '-tistic', '-timisation', '-tational', 'conceptuality', 'problematise', 'analytico-referential', 'aestheticise', 'recommodification', and add 'interact', 'interface'), the overbloated abstractions that substitute for the small kernels of thinking; and in 1988 when there is less awareness of Latin, these easily translated suffixes sound rawer in English or German than in French, where they originated. They indicate the abstractions and images which, paralleling the media, replace reality. It is my contention that close translation can expose such writing — as language for its imprecision, as literature for its lack of correspondence with reality (no, not for 'ugliness' — that's an illusion). This is the 'monstrous rhetoric of post-modernism' (Bradfield, 1988), the pretentious rubbish which translation into empirical English should pulverise, but which intellectual English humbugs take seriously. And again, the value of writing cannot be equated with the quality of a culture. Romanticism, for instance, which has many forms, but may be said to centre on one individual's emotional relationship with another or with nature, is characteristic of various cultures at various periods, but the value of this or that romantic work depends on its truth to shared experience of life and on its artistic qualities, not on its 'culture'. In fact, when it is translated, and necessarily denuded of its phonaesthetic properties, it may be exposed for the poor and vacuous thing it is. I shall be treading on a few corns with my scrap example:

> *La mort et la beauté sont deux choses profondes*
> *Qui contiennent tant d'ombre et d'azur qu'on dirait*
> *Deux soeurs également terribles et fécondes*
> *Ayant la même énigme et le même secret.*

If I translate this first quatrain of a Hugolian sonnet is is only to show that when English is divested of the French poetic clichés and their literary or cultural associations (and *ondes, sombre forêt, divin abîme, gouffre* are to follow), it is as trite as the French. 'Death and beauty are two deep things which contain so much shade and azure that they look like two equally terrible and fertile sisters, having the same enigma and the same secret.' I am simply saying that a French reader, inebriated by a surfeit of this cloying inverted language, balancing the words in each line, can apparently go on deceiving his pupils that this is poetry, but when it is stripped of its sound effects and the words so often linked to this cultural period, when it is transferred into another language, there is nothing there, it's empty. There is no instrument of language that is so piercing and revealing as translation. No wonder that in the Middle Ages the scribes, the cultural hegemony, used Latin with its deliberately complicated grammar as a cloak to ensure that the sacred texts were not popularised, not revealed. But translation, if it is naturalised, if it is continually made to conform to the TL culture, can also be the instrument of a source language hegemony, can be anodine, unrecognisable, docile. Oddly, the best example of such translation is the 'To be or not to be' monologue, so brilliantly analysed by Tytler in 1790, turning Hamlet into a freethinker. However, the purpose of my paper is more militant: to use translation not for sociological purposes but as a critical instrument of literature, culture and language — in the service of better understanding.

Unless literary translation becomes accurate, unless its scientific component is recognised, it will continue to be regarded, as many see it now, merely as cultural history. It would be generally agreed that medical, technical, legal translation would be a disaster, if its main stress were not on accuracy. When political speeches and statements are mistranslated (and translation may well uncover a misstatement of fact as well) there is an outcry, sometimes historic. A literary text, where connotations are more important than denotations, as the latter only exist ultimately in the writer's mind, and the other resources of language are more frequently and continuously used, is more complex, not necessarily more difficult to translate than a non-literary text; translation can barely expose its phonaesthetic properties (alliteration, the most ancient and powerful, onomatopoea, assonance, rhyme, metre) since more often than not it can only echo or hint at many of them. It often sacrifices them unless of course phonaesthetic properties have priority over connotation as well as reference, and no moral purpose exists, as in nonsense and 'pure' aesthetic literature such as surrealism.

Outside the two extremes, however, which are non-literary and phonaesthetic texts, I think that literal translation has a powerful critical function, which can be exercised when 'classics' are retranslated, but more powerfully on contemporary texts; the most important function here is not linguistic, literary or cultural, but moral. Imagine Spanish bull-fighting texts, fox-hunting texts, managerial finance worshipping texts, suddenly wrenched from their cultural traditions, exposed closely and coldly to common sense, to the lay reader, to the critic. In this intensive period of translation, where transparency or glasnost or honesty comes into its own, so would sobriety.

References

AITCHISON, J. 1986, *Words in the Mind*. London: Blackwell.

AL-CHALABI, S. A. 1979, *Bibliography of Translation and Dictionaries*. Al Jahidh: Baghdad.

ALKSNIS, IVARS 1981, The hazard of translation. *Parallèles*. Geneva University.

BARTHES, R. 1957, *Mythologies*. Paris: Gallimard.

BENJAMIN, W. 1955, *Die Aufgabe des Übersetzers. Gesammelte Schriften*. Frankfurt/ M: Suhrkamp.

— 1979, The task of the translator. In H. ARENDT (ed.) *Illustrations*. London: Fontana.

BETTELHEIM, B. 1983, *Freud and Man's Soul*. London: Chatto and Windus.

BOOTHMAN, D. 1983, Problems of translating political Italian. *Incorporated Linguist* 22, 4.

BOSTON, R. 1988, Article in *The Guardian* 15th April 1988.

BOYS, ROBERT 1979, The translator's calling. *Times Literary Suppplement* 7th December 1979.

BRADFIELD, SCOTT 1988, Word abuse. *Times Educational Supplement* 21st October 1988.

BREWER, T. 1988, The role of culture in successful translation. In P. TALGERI and S. B. VERMA (eds) *Literature in Translation*. London: Sangan.

BULLOCK, A. 1981, *Fontana Dictionary of Contemporary Modern Thought*. London: Fontana.

BUTOR, M. 1957, *L'Emploi du temps*. Paris: Editions de Minuit.

BUTOW, R. J. C. 1952, *Japan's Decision to Surrender*. Stanford: Stanford University Press.

CATFORD, J. C. 1965, *A Linguistic Theory of Translation*. Oxford: Blackwell.

CHAU, S. 1984, Aspects of translation pedagogy. Unpublished PhD thesis, Edinburgh University.

CHUKOVSKY, K. 1984, *A High Art. The Art of Translation*. Translated by L. G. LEIGHTON. Knoxville: University of Tennessee Press.

CONGRAT-BUTLAR, S. 1985, *Translation and Translators: An International Directory and Guide*. New York.

CRYSTAL, D. 1988, Pragmatics. In ALAN BULLOCK and O. STALLYBRASS (eds) *Fontana Dictionary of Modern Thought*. London: Fontana.

DEENEY, J. J. and CHAU, SIMON 1984, *ECCE Translator's Manual*. Hong Kong: Chinese University.

DELISLE, J. 1980, *Analyse du Discours*. Ottawa: University of Ottawa Press.

DERRIDA, J. 1980, Des tours de Babel. In J. GRAHAM (ed.) *Difference in Translation*. Ithica: Cornell University Press.

DODSON, C. J. 1967, *Language Teaching and the Bilingual Method*. London: Pitman.

DUBOIS J., 1979, *Lexis*. Paris: Larousse.

DUFF, ALAN 1981, *The Third Language*. Oxford: Pergamon.

EDELMAN, M. 1977, *Political Language*. London: Academic Press.

FARB, P. 1974, *Word Play*. London: Cape.

FIRBAS, J. 1972, On the interplay of prosodic and non-prosodic means of functional sentence perspective. In V. FRIED (ed.) *The Prague School of Linguistics and Language Teaching*. Oxford: OUP.

— 1979, A functional view of *ordo naturalis*. *BRNO Studies in English* 13, 29–39.

FLEW, ANTONY 1981, *Dictionary of Philosophy*. London: Macmillan.

FOUCAULT, 1976, *Histoire de la Folie*. Paris: Gallimard.

FRAWLEY, W. (ed.) 1984, *Translation: Linguistic, Philosophical and Literary Perspectives*. Newark: University of Delaware Press.

GOETHE, J. W. VON (1808) *Faust Part I*. 1224–37.

GRAHAM, J. (ed.) 1985, *Difference in Translation*. Ithaca: Cornell University Press.

GRAMMONT, M. 1949, *Petit Traité de versification française*. Paris: Armand Colin.

GREENBERG, J. H. (ed.) 1963, *Universals of Language*. Cambridge, Mass.: MIT Press.

HAAS, W. 1962, The theory of translation. In C. H. R. PARKINSON (ed.) *The Theory of Meaning*. London: Oxford University Press.

HALLIDAY, M. A. K. 1974, In H. PARRET, *Discussing Language*. The Hague, Mouton.

— 1985, *Introduction to Functional Grammar*. London: Edward Arnold.

HALLIDAY, M. A. K. and HASAN, R. 1975, *Cohesion in English*. London: Longmans.

HALLIDAY, M. A. K. and MCINTOSH, A. 1967 *Patterns of Language. Papers in General Descriptive and Applied Linguistics*. London: Longmans.

HALLIDAY, M. A. K., MCINTOSH, A. and STREVENS, P. 1964, *The Linguistic Sciences and Language Teaching*. London: Longmans.

HARRIS, B. 1988, What I really meant by translatology. *TTR*. 1/2 University of Quebec at Trois Rivières.

HASAN, R. 1968, *Grammatical Cohesion in Spoken and Written English*. London: Longmans.

HAVEL, VACLAV 1989, *Living in Truth*. London: Faber & Faber.

HAVRANEK, B. 1964, The functional differentiation of the standard language. In J. VACHEK (ed.) *A Prague School Reader in Linguistics*. Bloomington.

HENDERSON, JOHN, 1987, Personality and the linguist: A comparison of the personality profiles of professional translators and conference interpreters. Unpublished PhD Thesis, Bradford University.

HERMANS, T. (ed.) 1985, *The Manipulation of Literature*. London: Croom Helm.

HJELMSLEV, L. 1971, *Essais linguistiques*. Paris: Editions de Minuit.

HOUSE, J. 1977, *A Model for Translation Quality Assessment*. Tubingen: Narr.

HOWARD, R. 1988, *Madness and Civilisation*. New York: Random House.

HUDSON, K. 1978, *The Language of Modern Politics*. London: Macmillan.

— 1980, *The Dictionary of Diseased English*. London: MacMillan.

JOYCE, J. 1969, *Ulysses*. Harmondsworth: Pergamon.

— 1975, *Ulysses*. Translated by AUGUSTE MOREL. Paris: NRF Gallimard.

— 1976, *Ulysses* (Werke 3.1 and 3.2). Translated by HANS WOLLSCHLÄGER. Frankfurt am Main: Suhrkamp.

KADE, O. 1979, *Sprachliches und Aussersprachliches in der Kommunikation. Übersetzungswissenschaftliche Beiträge Bd. II*. Leipzig: VEB Enzyklopädie.

REFERENCES   177

KLEMPERER, V. 1969, *LTI: die unbewältigte Sprache.* Munich: DTV.
KOLLER, W. 1982, *Einführung in die Übersetzungswissenschaft* (2nd edn). Heidelberg: UTB Quelle und Meyer.
LAMBERT, JOSÉ 1985, Translated literature in France. In T. HERMANS (ed.) *The Manipulation of Literature.* London and Sydney: Croom Helm.
LEAVIS, F. R. 1953, *The Common Pursuit.* London: Chatto and Windus.
LEDERER, M. 1986, La traduction contrôle-t-elle encore ses moutons noirs? *Le français moderne,* 198–307.
LEECH, G. 1981, *Principles of Pragmatics.* London: Cambridge University Press.
LEVY, J. 1965, Will translation theory be of use to translators? In R. ITALIAANDER (ed.) *Ubersetzen.* Frankfurt/Bonn: Athenäum.
LEWIS, D. 1979, East German — a new language? GDR Monitor I Dundee.
MAGRIS, CLAUDIO 1986. *Danubio: una vera passione.* Milan: Garzanti.
MAILLOT, J. 1981, *La traduction scientifique et technique.* Paris: Edisem.
MAUSS, M. 1925, *Essai sur le Don.* Translated by Ian Cunnison (1966). London: Routledge and Kegan Paul.
McFARLANE, J. 1953, Modes of translation. *Durham University Journal* XLV.3, 77–93.
MEYER, MICHAEL 1974, On translating plays. *Twentieth Century Studies* 11, 44–51.
MONTPLAISIR, J. and DERNESS, L. 1983, *Union médicale du Canada,* 12 July 1983, pp. 619–20.
MOUNIN, G. 1963, *Les problèmes théoriques de la traduction.* Paris: Gallimard.
NABOKOV, V. (1964): see PUSHKIN (1964).
NEUBERT, A. 1985, *Text and Translation.* Leipzig: VEB Verlag Enzyklopädie.
— 1986, Translatorische Relativitat. In M. SNELL-HORNBY (ed.) *Ubersetzungswissenschaft — eine Neuorientierung.* Tübingen: Francke.
NEWMARK, P. P. 1980, Teaching specialized translation. In W. WILSS and S. O. POULSEN (eds). *Angewandte Übersetzungswissenschaft.* Århus: Århus Wirtschaftsuniversität.
— 1982a, Translation and the vocative function of language. *Incorporated Linguist* 21, 1.
— 1982b, The translation of authoritative statements: a discussion. In J. C. GEMAR (ed.) *Language du Droit et Traduction.* Quebec: Linguatec.
— 1985, *The Application of Case Grammar to Translation.* Trier: LAUT. B/128.
— 1986, Translation studies: Eight tentative directions for research and a few dead ducks. In L. WOLLIN and H. LINDQUIST (eds) *Translation Studies in Scandinavia* (pp. 37–50). Proceedings from the Scandinavian Symposium on Translation Theory (SSOTT) II, Lund 14th and 15th June, 1985. Lund.
— 1986, *Approaches to Translation.* New York: Prentice-Hall.
— 1988, A further note on communicative and semantic translation. In *A Textbook of Translation.* London: Prentice-Hill.
NIDA, E. A. 1964, *Towards a Science of Translation.* Leiden: E. J. Brill.
— 1975, In A. S. DIL (ed.) *Language, Structure and Translation.* Stanford: Stanford University Press.
NOVE, A. 1983, Article in *The Guardian* 20th October.
PAEPCKE, F. 1975, In CEBAL No. 3, Copenhagen.
— 1986, Im Übersetzen Leben. In K. BERGER and H. M. SPEIER (Hrsg.) *Übersetzen und Textvergleich* (pp. 158–75). Tübingen: Narr.
PUSHKIN, A. S. 1964, *Eugene Onegin.* Translated by V. NABOKOV 1964. New York: Bollinger.

REICH, H. H. 1969, *Sprache und Politik*. Munich: Hueber.

REISS, K. 1976, *Texttyp und übersetzungsmethode. Der operative text*. Kronberg T/s.

RIEU, E. V. 1953. Translation. In Cassell's *Encyclopaedia of Literature*. Vol. 1. London: Cassell.

RYCROFT, CHARLES 1956, *Imagination and Reality*. London: Hogarth.

SCHARF, B. 1971, *Engineering and its Language*. London: Muller.

SCHLEIERMACHER, 1798 Über die verschieden Methoden des Übersetzens. In H. STORIG (1969) *Das Problem des Übersetzens*. Stuttgart.

SCHMITT, PAUL 1986, In M. SNELL-HORNBY (ed.) *Ubersetzungswissenschaft — eine Neuorientierung*. Tübingen: Narr.

SEIDEL, G. 1975, Ambiguity in political discourse. In M. BLOCH (ed.) *Political Language and Oratory in Traditional Society*. London: Academic Press.

SINCLAIR, J. (ed.) 1987, Introduction, *Cobuild Dictionary*. London: Collins.

SORVALI, I. 1986, How to measure information content. *Babel,* 32/1, 58–63.

TOURY, 1980, *In Search of a Theory of Translation*. Tel Aviv: Porter Institute.

TRUDGILL, P. 1974, *Sociolinguistics: An Introduction*. Harmondsworth: Penguin.

TYTLER, A. F. 1907 (First edn 1790) *Essay on the Principles of Translation*. London: Dent, Everyman's Library.

VAN RAZZORI, G. 1985, *Memoirs of an Antisemite*. London: Picador.

VERMEER, H. J. and REISS, K. 1984, *Grundlegung einer allgemeinen Translationstheorie*. Tübingen: Niemeyer.

VINAY, J. P. and DARBELNET, J. 1965, *Stylistique comparée du français et de l'anglais*. Paris: Didier.

WAGNER, H. 1981, The public language of the GDR. *Bradford Occasional Papers*. Bradford: Bradford University.

WELDON, T. D. 1953, *The Vocabulary of Politics*. Harmondsworth: Pelican.

WIDDOWSON, H. 1979, *Explorations in Applied Linguistics*. Oxford: Oxford University Press.

WILSS, W. 1982, *Science of Translation*. Tübingen: Narr.

Index